The
GE
WORK-OUT

The
GE
WORK-OUT

How to Implement GE's Revolutionary Method for Busting Bureaucracy and Attacking Organizational Problems—Fast!

DAVE ULRICH
STEVE KERR
RON ASHKENAS

WITH DEBBIE BURKE AND PATRICE MURPHY

McGraw-Hill

New York   Chicago   San Francisco
Lisbon   London   Madrid   Mexico City   Milan
New Delhi   San Juan   Seoul   Singapore

McGraw-Hill

*A Division of The **McGraw·Hill** Companies*

1 2 3 4 5 6 7 8 9 0   AGM/AGM   0 9 8 7 6 5 4 3 2

ISBN 0-07-138416-2

The sponsoring editor for this book was Richard Narramore, the editing supervisor was Sally Glover, and the production supervisor was Maureen Harper. It was set in Janson by *North Market Street Graphics.*

Printed and bound by Quebecor Martinsburg.

McGraw-Hill books are available at special quantity discounts to use as premiums and sales promotions, or for use in corporate training programs. For more information, please write to the Director of Special Sales, McGraw-Hill, Professional Publishing, Two Penn Plaza, New York, 10121-2298. Or contact your local bookstore.

 This book is printed on recycled, acid-free paper containing a minimum of 50% recycled de-inked fiber.

Contents

Acknowledgments

WHILE THE WORDS in this book are ours, many of the ideas and experiences come from others to whom we acknowledge a tremendous debt of gratitude and appreciation. First and foremost among these is Jack Welch, former CEO of GE and the original initiator and driver of the Work-Out process. Much of this book, and indeed much of our collective thinking, has been influenced by Jack's leadership of GE and unwavering pursuit of higher performance through a belief that people can do extraordinary things. Jack gave all of us the opportunity to test and stretch our ideas about organizational change in the cauldron of GE. In particular, he gave Steve Kerr the chance to learn how *learning* could become a competitive advantage.

Although Jack Welch generated the initial energy behind Work-Out, the real learning occurred through the day-to-day trials and experiences of GE leaders, managers, and employees. During the formative years of Work-Out, and over the past decade, hundreds of GE leaders have opened themselves up to new ways of thinking and behaving. For many it was not easy. For others it was exhilarating. For all, it was a learning experience that has influenced the way we think about organizational change. This book would not have been possible without your efforts and your willingness to share your struggles and triumphs with us, and sometimes even let us walk with you through the experience.

Managers and leaders from other organizations also contributed to our thinking, and helped us understand how Work-Out principles could be applied to settings other than GE. We thank you for giving us the opportunity to learn along with you, and to share your stories.

Within GE, there were a number of other individuals who were crucial to the development of Work-Out. Jim Baughman, the former head of Crotonville, helped Jack Welch conceive of the idea of Work-Out and then spearheaded its translation into an organized program across GE. His wisdom about organizational change, and his personal support and counsel during the early years of Work-Out, made much of our learning possible. Several members of the Crotonville staff at that time also provided valuable support, including Dick DiPaola, Jon Biel, Deb Keller, Jacquie Vierling, and Amy Howard.

As you will read in Chapter 1, the development of Work-Out at GE was truly a team effort. And many colleagues stood side by side with us during the development and learning about Work-Out. In particular, we would like to mention former Harvard Business School professors Todd Jick and Len Schlessinger, who were part of the original management team. Consultant Deborah Shah, also part of that team, was instrumental in helping to organize the early efforts. Several other professors and consultants collaborated with the three of us and were instrumental in helping us navigate the tricky currents of GE, including Dick Beatty, Mary Anne Devanna, Jack Gabarro, Jeffrey Gandz, Bill Joyce, Rob Kazanjian, Rich Korn, Dale Lake, Ian MacMillan, Bob Miles, Craig Schneier, and Noel Tichy.

The original idea of this book came from our editor at McGraw-Hill, Richard Narramore. Throughout our struggles and missed deadlines, Richard continued to believe that we had a valuable book inside of us just waiting to come out. We appreciate his patience and belief, and hope that the final product justifies his resolve.

A number of people helped us turn Richard's idea into reality. Debbie Burke, a former Crotonville staff member and an early internal Work-Out consultant at GE, helped to get the ball rolling by interviewing each of us, pulling together reams of existing materials, and suggesting ways of structuring and organizing the book. Her efforts over many months are acknowledged through her listing as a contributing author. Also serving as a contributing author was Patrice Murphy, a senior consultant at Robert H. Schaffer & Associates. Patrice was instrumental in organizing and drafting a number of the how-to chapters, and in chasing down the figures and materials needed to make this a useful book.

Several other consultants at Robert H. Schaffer & Associates also contributed. Matthew McCreight and Elaine Mandrish provided case materials and examples. Katy Paul-Chowdhury developed several of the figures and reviewed material in the appendices. Emilieanne Koehnlein and Joanne Young provided vital administrative support, as did Ginger Bitter for Dave Ulrich and John Christopher for Debbie Burke. In addition, Alissa Ferro of the Berkshire Institute worked with Debbie Burke to turn fragments of source materials into sentences and paragraphs.

To pull this book together, we owe an immeasurable debt of gratitude to our developmental editor, Hilary Powers. Hilary provided the discipline, organization, and writing skills that we needed to turn 1000 pages of material into a finished book. The fact that she did this with an unwavering sense of humor and good cheer made the difficult last stages almost fun. Without her insights and persistence, the book might never have been completed.

And finally, we wish to thank our families for giving us the support, love, encouragement, and time to engage in the extracurricular effort of writing a book. All of us have day jobs that already take us away from home all too much—so supporting us in writing this book is in many ways above and beyond the call of duty.

> —Dave Ulrich, Ann Arbor, Michigan
> —Steve Kerr, New York
> —Ron Ashkenas, Stamford, Connecticut
> February, 2002

Introduction:
The Power of Work-Out

GE IS ONE of the most successful companies on earth. Yet every day, thousands of people at GE face the very same set of problems and challenges that confront every other organization in the world, regardless of size, shape, or mission. What's the best way to deliver products and services to our customers? How can we improve our margins and our efficiency? How do we get everyone onto the same page? How do we stay ahead of the competition? How do we attract, develop, and retain the best talent? How can we make the best use of technology? How do we move quickly to new opportunities?

Does GE have answers to all these questions while other organizations do not? Of course not. But what GE does have that most organizations lack is a deeply engrained and internalized process for addressing and solving its problems—quickly, simply, and with the involvement of people who will ultimately carry out the decision. That process is called *Work-Out*. This book will show you how to apply Work-Out in your own organization to solve your organizational problems.

No program—not even Work-Out—can transform your organization overnight. But in the short run, Work-Out will help you solve problems faster. And in the long run, it can help your organization develop the culture and the skills necessary to move more quickly, nimbly, and successfully in our complex, global world.

A Quick Look at Work-Out

At its core, Work-Out is a simple, straightforward methodology for cutting out bureaucracy and solving organizational problems—fast. Large groups of employees and managers—from different levels and functions of the organization—come together to address issues that they identify or that senior management has raised as concerns. In small teams, people challenge prevailing assumptions about "the way we've always done things" and come up with recommendations for dramatic improvements in organizational processes. The Work-Out teams present their recommendations to a senior manager in a "Town Meeting," where the manager engages the entire group in a dialogue about the recommendations and then makes yes-or-no decisions on the spot. Recommendations for changing the organization are assigned to "owners" who have volunteered to carry them out and follow through to get results. That's Work-Out in a nutshell.

Work-Out can be applied to almost any type of problem. It was first used at GE to harvest the low-hanging fruit of overgrown bureaucracies—to reduce meetings, reports, and approval levels. It can be used to cut in half process times in product development, order entry, employee communications, and more. Or Work-Out can be used to bring your people together with customers or suppliers to develop innovative ways of doing business together.

Work-Out also can be used by almost any type of organization—public or private, commercial or not-for-profit, large or small. While developed at GE, and now part of GE's DNA, Work-Out also has been successfully adapted in organizations ranging from General Motors to the State of West Virginia, to the World Bank, to Zurich Financial Services. But in all of these organizations, no matter what the issue, the process remains much the same. Bring together the people from the organization who know the issues best. Challenge them to develop creative solutions. Decide on the solutions immediately in a public forum, and empower people to carry them out.

Low-Hanging Fruit

Work-Out often starts with an attack on the low-hanging fruit of bureaucracy—getting unnecessary and unproductive work out of the organizational system. For example, one of the earliest Work-Outs at GE Capital, sponsored by the Chief Financial Officer, focused on identifying and eliminating unnecessary administrative procedures—things that "get in the way" of doing business and serving customers. After an initial introduction by the CFO and an external consultant, 40 people from various businesses and functions within GE Capital broke into small groups and started brainstorming. What procedures didn't make sense? Where were they wasting time? What activities seemed to add little value?

The CFO of GE Capital at that time didn't really expect very much to come out of this discussion. After all, he thought, GE Capital was one of the fastest-moving, least bureaucratic units within GE. It wasn't a tired old industrial business with 100 years of antiquated procedures. But, who knows, maybe a few good ideas would emerge.

Much to the CFO's amazement, with a minimum of prodding, a floodgate of comments seemed to pour out of the participants. Facilitators covered page after page with notes about bureaucratic procedures for expense reimbursements, making travel arrangements, obtaining office supplies, updating personnel data, taking education courses, upgrading software, and more. Some of the bolder participants talked about the bureaucracy associated with core business functions too—such as filling out forms for deals, preparing presentations for approval meetings, keeping track of customer data, overwhelming amounts of extra analysis to justify various investments or initiatives. After a couple of hours, the walls of a large meeting hall were covered with flip-chart pages. The facilitators then asked the CFO to leave and let the participants sort out the best ideas from this "raw material."

After a break, each small group shared its ideas and comments with the rest of the participants. Although there was lots of overlap, the sheer number of ideas was still impressive, far more than anyone had imagined. After a great deal of discussion, the group decided to divide the ideas into three "themes"—expense approvals and reimbursements, materials purchasing, and deal analysis and approvals. People then volunteered to be in one of the three groups to address these themes. They then spent the rest of the day inventorying the ideas that fell into their "category" and selecting which ones were really worth pursuing. For each one selected, the teams roughed out the estimated "impact" of the change—either in terms of dollars saved or time captured.

The next day, the three groups reconvened in a plenary session to "dry run" their recommendations and make sure everyone was on board. After lunch, the CFO returned, along with a number of other senior GE Capital managers to hear the recommendations. For several hours, all 40 participants, plus the senior managers, talked through the ideas one at a time in a "town meeting." After each idea was discussed, the CFO was asked to say "yes" or "no," right away, on the spot. Although feeling very uncomfortable about making these kinds of decisions at first, he eventually warmed up and got into it. Before too long, among other things, expense reports did not need multiple approvals, people could purchase approved software without going through the IT organization, and a predeal process was established to see if deals were worth pursuing *before* going through all the analytics. For a company that "didn't have any bureaucracy," a lot of streamlining was starting to occur—fast.

More Than Just Problem Solving

If Work-Out was only about solving problems or reducing bureaucracy, it would still be a powerful methodology that organizations could incorporate into their repertoire of business tools. But at GE, and at many other firms, Work-Out is more than that. It is also a catalyst for creating an empowered workforce that has the self-confidence to challenge the inevitable growth of organizational bureaucracy. It can help create a culture that is fast-moving, innovative, and without boundaries. Whether it is intended or not, Work-Out also becomes a vehicle for developing managers and leaders who make quick decisions in an energizing dialogue with employees—instead of hiding in their offices making decisions by fiat (or avoiding tough decisions). This is why Work-Out is at the core of what Jack Welch calls the "social architecture" of GE—the very way that the firm works. And having Work-Out in its DNA has given GE a powerful foundation for implementing other important initiatives, including Six Sigma and e-commerce.

You can read this book with an eye toward using Work-Out to solve problems and reduce bureaucracy in your organization. But if you keep reading—and if you organize or participate in a Work-Out and feel its energizing power—you will get a sense of how frequent Work-Outs can transform the social architecture of your own organization.

A Story 10 Years in the Making

Transforming the DNA of a firm does not happen overnight, nor does the writing of a book. This book has been more than a decade in the making, starting with the birth of Work-Out at GE in the late 1980s. As insiders to the process, we had a unique perspective on Work-Out's origins, its original intent, its early development, its evolution within GE, and its application to dozens of other organizations around the world. *The GE Work-Out* gives you access to these perspectives.

Dave Ulrich (then and still a professor at the University of Michigan), had taught in programs at Crotonville—GE's management development institute—in the 1980s and was perhaps the first consultant to discuss the Work-Out concept with CEO Jack Welch and Jim Baughman, then head of Crotonville. He helped form the management team that governed the rollout of Work-Out and remained a key counselor to GE for years thereafter. Steve Kerr, then a professor at the University of Southern California and now the Chief Learning Officer for Goldman Sachs, joined the effort in 1988 as a consultant for the GE Nuclear business. On the strength of his success there, he joined the inner circle of consultants and eventually became GE's first Chief Learning Officer, with responsibility for Crotonville. Starting in 1988, Ron Ashkenas, then and still a managing partner at Robert H. Schaffer & Associates, worked with the oldest and youngest GE businesses—Lighting and GE Capital—to craft their specific flavors of Work-Out. He eventually also helped adapt Work-Out to GE Aerospace, GE Electrical Distribution and Control, GE Supply, and dozens of companies outside of GE.

From the early days, when we were helping design and implement Work-Out at GE and then later when we were adapting it in our work with other companies, we have always wanted to combine our individual experiences and share lessons learned with others. This book is the result. Our purpose is not to glorify GE—or to position Work-Out as the next "flavor of the month"—but to share the GE transformation experience and methods in ways that might be useful for leaders facing change and trying to help their companies succeed. The fact that Work-Out was developed in the late 1980s and then reinstitutionalized in GE in 1999 reinforces the idea that it has staying power. But we believe that this power goes beyond just GE. From our point of view, the principles of Work-Out have application for leaders in all types of positions and in all types of firms.

Work-Out can help your organization change, fast. A decade ago, when the Work-Out ideas came together, its focus on rapid response helped firms like GE compete. In today's ever-changing business context of constant change, these principles apply even more. The late 1980s may seem like ancient history, but Work-Out has become more relevant, not less, since it first took shape.

A Multifaceted Account

Although we were all part of the same team in the development of Work-Out at GE, our experiences in implementing the process were varied as we tailored Work-Out to different businesses, clients, and starting points, both within GE and elsewhere. Therefore, the book injects elements of the Work-Out story and describes types of Work-Outs that may be unique to our individual perspectives. In other words, there is no "one way" or "right way" or "perfect way" to do Work-Out, and the multiplicity of Work-Out stories in this book will reflect that reality. A Work-Out can be either very simple or very complex. Sometimes we did Work-Out with very simple frameworks and tools, allowing enormous flexibility and creativity in the process. At other times, Work-Out was more structured and disciplined with prescribed tools and applications. By detailing our experiences in all of these different settings, we convey the richness of Work-Out and how you can apply it to whatever challenges that you and your organization face.

Work-Out did not emerge out of thin air. We believe that if you want to get the most out of it, you should understand its roots, which we describe in Chapter 1.

There was already plenty of change afoot in GE by the time Work-Out began in the late 1980s. The company had already achieved the distinction of being #1 or #2 in every industry in which it competed, and had acted on CEO Jack Welch's mandate to "fix, close, or sell" any business that did not meet the criteria. The more than 150 separate strategic business units had already been drawn together into 13 core businesses, and Welch had spent years downsizing and delayering. In other words, huge amounts of change, leading to tremendously positive results, had already been accomplished.

But GE in 1988 still faced an enormous challenge. The strategic shifts and the downsizing and delayering had reduced the workforce by 25 percent, but the workload that these remaining people had to do stayed the same. Employees and managers felt overloaded and overwhelmed trying to work in the same old ways. As Welch later explained, the "hardware" of the company had changed, but the "software" had not. Meeting this challenge provided the original impetus for Work-Out. But reducing unnecessary work also meant that all work, and work processes, became fair game. And that required the eventual creation of an entirely new culture and way of working across an organization with hundreds of thousands of people around the globe. Work-Out was the organizational "software" that made this change possible.

No Snake Oil

Despite its massive impact on GE and other firms, Work-Out is not a magic elixir. It is a simple set of concepts, tools, and experiences that have been effective at GE and many other organizations—businesses, universities, not-for-profit organizations, and state governments.

In its most robust form, Work-Out changes culture, develops new kinds of leaders, improves teamwork, develops analytical ability, creates new language, bridges organizational boundaries, supports succession planning, improves customer and supplier relationships, and gives everyone in the organization powerful new roles in achieving excellence.

But even in its simplest form, when stripped to its essence, Work-Out allows people to get some obstacles out of the way so they can do their work better. In many organizations, that alone would be a significant gain.

Work-Out for You

This book will help you understand and implement a GE-style Work-Out. It describes GE's Work-Out approach to busting bureaucracy and solving organizational problems. And, more importantly, it guides you through the decisions you need to make to plan for and implement your own Work-Out. Through case examples from GE and other organizations where Work-Out has been used, you will observe the big moves and the subtle shifts that can make Work-Out successful in a variety of settings. You will understand the planning meetings, leadership coaching sessions, and the famous Town Meetings that are the Work-Out hallmark. You will see the challenges, obstacles, and successes that Work-Out Leaders, participants, and consultants experience. And you will see what it feels like to be engaged in a Work-Out, and what it takes to make the effort successful.

As we said at the beginning, Work-Out sounds simple, and it is: Get a group of people together for a few days. Identify problems and solutions. Present them to key leaders. Get yes-or-no decisions. Applaud. Implement. Do it again.

Simple, yes; easy, not necessarily.

But it is powerful. And once you make the decision to try it, Work-Out can reward you and your organization many times over. This book is intended to be your guide to flying solo in Work-Out, using the resources your company already has. That may not be enough to get you to maximum impact, but it surely will start you thinking, help you get some other people engaged, and enable you to run a Work-Out event. Once you look at your organization's strengths realistically, you'll be able to pick the right starting point. As you move through Work-Out, you should be able to make Work-Out a "natural act in a natural place"—in other words, not an isolated event in a training workshop or hotel somewhere, but a way of doing business every day at work. That's what it became at GE.

It is important to tailor Work-Out to your organization's specific needs.

- Do you need to develop strong leaders who can mobilize people to do something outstanding?
- Is bureaucratic, nonvalue-added work taking up too much time for too many employees?
- Does it take forever to get things done that should be done quickly?
- Are you facing a huge problem that needs to be solved pronto?
- Do you have recurring problems that you've learned to live with because they never become quite painful enough to do something about?
- Are you being eaten alive by a zillion little problems that block progress and divert energy?
- Are your people complaining about how hard it is to do their jobs well?

Each of these conditions would suggest a different way to *start* Work-Out, to wire it for success. Once started, all Work-Out efforts follow approximately the same basic pattern. Then, enhancements are customized to fit conditions in each organization.

This book also helps you avoid the most-likely Work-Out pitfalls, the deadly and dangerous missteps that can undermine Work-Out efforts. Managers, employee participants, and consultants who have used Work-Out will—through our voice—share their experiences with you, serving as your guides as you embark on the Work-Out process. Based on their experiences, we provide you with conceptual frameworks, tools and activities, best practices, and hindsight interpretations. With their help, you can launch a Work-Out process that can take your organization to new levels of success.

Who Will Benefit from This Book?

Wherever you are in your organization, if you're in a position to influence the way things get done, this book can help you. For the senior leader or manager who wants to improve organizational performance quickly, it offers a tried-and-true method to make it happen. If you want to strengthen customer relationships, it offers a way to make real improvements that weld your customers' interests to your own—and the same principles apply up the value chain as well, bringing suppliers and producers into ever-more-profitable synch. And besides guiding Work-Out leaders and sponsors through the program, the book helps participants at all levels get the most mileage out of the time and thought they put into it.

If your role is to help managers improve performance quickly—either in a staff function such as HR or as an external consultant—this book offers a systematic way to address problems and opportunities of any size. It will help you help your clients get immediate action—concrete results they can take to the bank to measure the worth of your advice.

A Guided Tour

This book is organized into three parts. The first—"What Is Work-Out?"—gives you the background on how Work-Out evolved at GE, how it works, and how to assess your organization's ability to implement it. Chapter 1 presents the story of how GE developed and uses Work-Out. There you will see what GE leaders, employees, and consultants found to be most helpful, most important, and most problematic about Work-Out. You will also get a sense of the resources GE employed, the heritage on which it built, and the gains it generated with Work-Out.

Chapter 2 presents the basis for Work-Out in the latest thought on organizational behavior, culture, and change. It helps you understand why Work-Out works, both as a problem-solving tool and as a vehicle for longer-term transformation.

Chapter 3 helps you identify and prepare for the normal skepticism and resistance that Work-Out—like any change process—is sure to generate. The chapter then guides you through an assessment of your own company's strengths and deficits, and helps you determine how ready your organization is for Work-Out. It will point out how and where you could start a Work-Out effort, given your company's particular realities. If you can't find a strong enough starting place for a large-scale program, it shows you how you can take a more modest approach to get ready.

If you are ready to go, Chapter 4 will show you how to do the basics—how to lead a fast, simple Work-Out right away.

Part Two—"Making Work-Out Happen"—provides a hands-on guidebook to all the details of installing Work-Out in an organization. Chapter 5 gives an overview of the pieces, practices, and program elements of the Work-Out approach. Work-Out is not just an event, although the workshop and Town Meeting forum is central to the approach. It is a system of integrated activities that create specific decisions that can easily be implemented and later evaluated. You need to keep the whole process in mind—like an entire journey. The chapter's road map is intended to chart your route so you know where you are, where you have been, and what is yet to come.

Chapters 6, 7, and 8 are detailed maps of each part of the Work-Out trip through one cycle—the planning phase, conducting the Work-Out event (including the Town Meeting), and implementing Work-Out decisions during the first weeks after the Town Meeting. In each, you will read about what other companies did at this stage, how they did it, and what you need to know and do to travel this particular piece of the road. You will find stories, examples, charts, and tools that are most appropriate for the activities you are undertaking. They describe a way to do Work-Out, but you should feel free to customize Work-Out to the needs of your organization. These chapters coach you in creating the Town Meeting, where smart and courageous decisions can take place, and they describe the roles and responsibilities of all the participants at each stage of the Work-Out process.

Companies, people, and business problems all differ, so Chapter 9 describes variations that contain the essence of Work-Out, yet accommodate the idiosyncrasies of different organizations, businesses, employees, and leaders. It will show you how to customize the process for maximum impact on your organization's most critical concerns— whether they be busting bureaucracy, streamlining processes, or strengthening the customer-supplier value chain. Chapter 10 then provides an extended case study of how one organization—Zurich Financial Services UK—used Work-Out to transform its culture and its results.

Part Three, "Work-Out's Long-Term Payoff," is about how Work-Out can be a vehicle for transforming *your* organization. It explains the value of shifting Work-Out from a one-time experience, or even a sequence of experiences, to an embedded and essential part of your business. At its most powerful, Work-Out becomes *what you are* and *what you do naturally*. It *becomes* your organization's culture—a culture where "natural acts" of good communication and smart decision making can take place naturally, without the need for special meetings. When Work-Out takes hold, stuffy, rigid, bureaucratic, hierarchical, slow companies become smart, agile, spontaneous, energetic, and quick. And more successful. And better places to work.

Chapter 11 describes the leadership characteristics and behaviors necessary to support and sustain Work-Out in the longer-term, and how to accelerate the development of such leadership to build a fast and agile organization. Every firm needs to have its own "leadership brand" that sets it apart from others, and Work-Out can be a powerful way of creating, developing, and reinforcing that brand, both with today's leaders and with the facilitators who will become leaders of the future.

Most leaders begin Work-Out as a pilot or experiment. Chapter 12 explains how to move Work-Out from a one-time event to an ongoing process within the company. This chapter catalogues decisions about picking the pilot area, using facilitators, investing in a governing body, measuring results, and other actions designed to ensure success.

Chapter 13 examines how Work-Out changes culture. At its most robust, this is the ultimate agenda of Work-Out. We define culture as the identity of the firm as seen by its best customers, made real to employees. Culture change comes when a firm develops a strong agenda of principles and characteristics it wants to be known for, then makes this agenda real to both employees and customers. Work-Out tools are a way of making a new identity come to life in employee behavior and customer experience.

Finally, Chapter 14 is designed to inspire you and spur you on to make Work-Out your own, no matter what your position within the firm. Although Work-Out is about improving company performance, it is also about empowerment and engagement—not for others, but for every one of us. Whether you are the CEO or a frontline manager, you can use Work-Out to drive your organization forward. We guarantee you will find it exhilarating and exciting. It can give you a new approach to your professional life, and a new leap in your own personal development. This chapter will help you see that you do not need to wait for someone else to get Work-Out started. You can do it yourself.

In the appendix we have referenced all of the book's Work-Out materials in one place. This "Work-Out Leader's Tool Kit" will make it easier for you to access the many tools that are provided throughout the book. We also have included a simulation case for training Work-Out facilitators, and we share a talk given by Dave Ulrich to GE officers in 1990, when Work-Out was about a year old. It captures some of the early concepts and experiences of the effort and may help with your own first steps.

If this all sounds enticing, get ready, and go do Work-Out! Let this book guide you, and have a good trip!

PART I

What Is Work-Out?

Work-Out, GE, and the Largest Corporate Transformation in History

"One of the ways we'll know that Work-Out has been successful is that my style of leadership will no longer be tolerated in this company."

—Jack Welch

IN MOST ORGANIZATIONS, change efforts come and go—and somehow rarely make a difference. But at GE, a company with hundreds of thousands of people spread across the globe and businesses ranging from jet engines to light bulbs to credit cards, one particular change process helped spark a complete transformation—Work-Out. The transformation that it launched in the late 1980s continues today to help GE reduce bureaucracy, empower people, and continually reinvent ever-more-effective ways of doing business. Without it, GE might be just another company. With Work-Out as part of its DNA, GE has become one of the most admired, profitable, and innovative companies on earth.

At its core, Work-Out is a very simple concept. It is based on the premise that those closest to the work know it best. And when the ideas of those people, irrespective of their functions and places in the hierarchy, are solicited and turned into action—on the spot—an unstoppable wave of energy, creativity, and productivity is unleashed throughout the organization. At GE, there have been literally hundreds of thousands of Work-Out "Town Meetings," where ideas have flown in torrents—giving GE access to the only unlimited resource on the planet, the imagination and energy of talented people.

Work-Out did not appear fully formed like Venus from the sea. Starting with Jack Welch's vision of what GE could become, Work-Out evolved from the efforts of thousands of people struggling, learning, and grappling together to translate vision into reality. This chapter tells the story of that evolution.

Birth of an Idea

In the middle of 1988, Jack Welch and Jim Baughman—head of the GE management-development center at Crotonville, New York—were flying home from a visit to GE's Appliance Park in Louisville, Kentucky. Concerned about poor quality and low productivity in the Major Appliances business, Welch had met with groups of frontline workers, usually without their managers, and asked them what it would take to improve performance. Over and over again, he heard the same refrain, "We have lots of ideas. We know what needs to be done. But nobody listens. Nobody lets us do it." And when he asked managers why they weren't letting their people act on ideas, he heard the other side of the story, "We don't have time. We have half as many managers here now as two years ago, but just as much work to get through. We have just as many bureaucratic requests to answer, forms to fill out, and meetings to go to. And anyway, whenever we do want to try an idea, we have to go through so many people to get approvals and money that it'd be out of date before we started. Why bother?"

This began to sound like a broken record. Everywhere Welch went, he heard the same thing. Workers had ideas, but no authority to act. Managers had authority, but no time to evaluate and approve. Organizational gridlock. Bureaucratic standstills. The GE machine wasn't in danger of grinding to a halt, but it was far from working at its best.

Welch's GE: The Neutron Jack Era

Obviously, this was not what Jack Welch had in mind back when he began the restructuring of GE in 1981. From Reginald Jones—a storied figure in corporate America—Welch had inherited one of the oldest and most successful companies in the world. GE innovations ranged from light bulbs to turbine engine technology to Lexan plastics and industrial diamonds—and as far afield as consumer financing. Its organizational processes and approaches—decentralized management, financial analysis and control, strategic planning, and management education—were being taught at leading business schools and modeled throughout the corporate world.

But despite the record of success, the GE of 1981 faced severe problems. Decentralization had led to a proliferation of "strategic business units"—numbering more than 150 when Welch took over. The emphasis on financial analysis and control had led to multiple management layers, large staff organizations, and a choking tangle of bureaucratic machinery. With so much internal "process" to deal with, GE's businesses were more often than not turned inward, virtually ignoring changes in the marketplace. Decision-making processes were slow and painful, often leading to white papers and reports rather than action. And financial performance, while steady, was unspectacular, rising with the U.S. Gross National Product but never exceeding it.

Welch believed that GE's clogged organizational arteries posed a threat to its survival, so he set out to remake one of the most successful companies in the world. He began by requiring each business unit to be either first or second in its market. If it was not, the business manager had to "fix, sell, or close" the unit. This led to major consolidations, combinations, reconfigurations, and jettisoning of business units that, as Welch later noted, "even God couldn't fix." Long-standing GE namesake businesses like Small Appliances and Televisions were sold off. Other, higher-performing businesses, such as RCA (including NBC Television) and Borg-Warner Plastics, were acquired. When the smoke cleared in the late 1980s, GE had gone from dozens of business units to thirteen major businesses, each of which was number one or number two in its market.

At the same time, Welch was determined to dismantle the costly bureaucracy that had been built up in the endless effort to control the sprawl that was GE. He quickly removed organizational layers, including the powerful corporate sectors and their staffs. The corporate strategic planning staff was gone, as well. Strategic decisions were now made by the people who ran each business, and by Welch himself. Within the businesses, spans of control were increased and staffs were reduced. General managers were given more and more accountability to run their businesses. Each change focused work on the strategic necessity of taking and holding first or second place in the market. People and jobs outside that strategy disappeared. In all, nearly two hundred thousand people left GE when their businesses were sold or their jobs in surviving businesses disappeared and they couldn't or wouldn't learn what they needed for new ones in the company. Jack Welch became known as "Neutron Jack"—the human bomb that left the buildings intact while getting rid of the people.

Rebuilding the System

Although GE led the way, many U.S. companies downsized during the 1980s. Most saw short-term improvement in their financial performance as a result of the reductions. But far fewer knew what to do after the cuts to refocus or revitalize their companies. As a result, some disappeared. Some, like IBM, went through real crisis before they were turned around. But GE was a notable exception largely because Jack Welch initiated a second act after the downsizing, establishing new structures to replace the old ones. Replacing the old layers and corporate-staff functions were a number of new or revitalized management processes—yearly strategic planning and budgeting mechanisms, organizational and human-resource reviews, regular operational reviews, and periodic internal audits. The centerpiece, a simple structure that held the others together, was the Corporate Executive Council, or CEC. Members of the CEC were the heads of GE's 13 business units, a few key corporate staff leaders (finance, legal, HR), Welch himself, and his vice-chairmen, Larry Bossidy and Ed Hood. Meeting quarterly, the CEC became the vehicle for running GE.

Previously, each business head would "come to Fairfield" for a private report on that line of business. Now, the leaders of all the businesses heard the same information at the same time, from one another and from the chairman. They got to know one another better. They began to share resources and ideas. They committed to making up the shortfalls when a business stumbled. They also shared operational and organizational best practices that let them reduce the impact of problems and avoid further errors. Running through all of these changes was the need for GE's business leaders and managers to be more accountable for results, to manage both strategy and people, and to remain focused on the customer. But this represented a major intellectual and behavioral shift. Most GE managers had grown up in a company that valued thorough analysis and justification before action, divided accountability between staff and line, told employees what to do and expected them to do it, and gave customer views short shrift.

To help create a new management culture after the period of intense downsizing, Welch revitalized and reinforced the leadership and management-development function of Crotonville, which had been founded as GE's management-development center in 1956. To refocus Crotonville on the company's strategic needs and make it a powerful vehicle for transforming the company's management, in 1983 Welch asked Noel Tichy, a professor from the University of Michigan, to run Crotonville for two years. With Welch's unwavering support, Tichy developed a series of programs for managers at different levels.

By the mid-1980s, Welch began to use Crotonville as his private listening post and transmitter. Once a month, Welch helicoptered into Crotonville and engaged in dialogue with the various classes that were meeting. Standing in the "pit" (the center of the amphitheater-style classroom in Crotonville's education building), Welch talked with managers about what was happening in their businesses, and how they and their people were reacting to the transformation of the company. Challenging, provoking, and listening, Welch used Crotonville both to convey his philosophy of leadership and to take the company's pulse. However, the things Welch was hearing at Crotonville and places like Appliance Park by the middle of 1988 were very similar. Financial performance was improving, and the restructuring of the company was in place. But the underlying management culture of GE was still slow, bureaucratic, and analytical. Managers relied on command and control rather than engagement and empowerment. Employees at all levels lacked the confidence to challenge old ways of doing business. And few managers other than Welch himself had the courage to stand in front of employees and engage in the back-and-forth of a Crotonville-style pit dialogue. Too many managers hid behind their staff, not dealing directly with their employees. If GE was to survive in the rough-and-tumble, globally competitive world that Welch foresaw for the 1990s and beyond, its management culture—what he called the "software of the company"—would have to change.

There's Too Much Work

Exacerbating this situation was the constant pressure, repeatedly pointed out by class participants, Crotonville staff, and some consultants, of "too much work and too few people." Similar concerns were reflected in the corporate employee-attitude surveys and communication surveys conducted regularly throughout the company. Hearing this again and again made Welch realize that the wrenching transformation of the past several years had changed the strategy, structure, and cost-base of GE, but not the way day-to-day work got done. People were still filling out the same forms, requesting the same approvals, attending the same meetings, writing the same reports. Except now there were far fewer hands to do these tasks. The people were gone, but the work lingered on. And the bureaucratic thickets made fast-paced, customer-focused innovation next to impossible.

Beyond this, morale was low throughout the company. In Schenectady and other long-standing GE locations, fewer and fewer employees wandered through the miles of factory aisles and office corridors. The informal organization—the ties of friendship that get things done around and across a bureaucracy—was in complete disarray. No one knew who to go to for an answer, or even what to do with an answer to a problem they recognized. One business did not publish an internal phone book for three years; so many people were leaving so fast that it was hard to know whose name to include, and at what number. In one business whose roster had been cut in half, an engineer with 30 years on the job expressed his fear that no one would find him for days if he died at his desk, and the person who would eventually see his body would have no idea who he was.

Sad as they were, these stories were understandable from old-line businesses that had shrunk so traumatically. But similar stories were emerging from the "good" businesses, the ones where GE really was number one or number two in the market and where the staff was full of bright new people hired off the best college campuses. Crotonville participants—selected because they were new or successful or high potential—were eager to realize Welch's vision of the new GE, but they all experienced the old GE back at their desks.

One long June evening in 1988, a group of them expressed their frustration, in no uncertain terms, to Jim Baughman (who had taken over at Crotonville after the end of Tichy's two-year tenure). These high-potentials—all with three to five years' experience at GE and all earmarked as prospects for its top ranks—were thoroughly unhappy. When they finally finished telling Baughman what was wrong in their businesses, he made a graceful escape from the meeting room—rubbing his aching head and saying he had never had an experience quite as powerful as that one in GE. He had become accustomed to these kinds of complaints from old, limping, or "bad" businesses. But the participants in this session had been from Medical Systems, Plastics, and Capital—the "good" businesses on which the future of GE was riding.

With all of this churning in the background, on the plane ride home from the Appliances visit, Baughman encouraged Welch to act on his insights about the culture of GE. "Let's find a way to get work out of the system," they said to each other. "And let's call the process 'Work-Out'!"

From Idea to Action

To translate the idea of Work-Out into reality, Baughman called a meeting of the Crotonville faculty, many of whom were professors or consultants, in September 1988. With 30 management thinkers in the room, Welch presented his view of what he called the "GE Engine"—a corporation fueled by financial, strategic, and organizational success. He maintained that the company had made good progress in the financial and strategic areas, but had a long way to go in the organizational area. He talked about the importance of creating a "liberated" organization, where people were engaged and freed up to innovate and serve customers. Following this presentation, the faculty debated with Welch how to make his ideas happen. Many cynics doubted that the same "Neutron Jack" who had laid off so many thousands of people could be serious about creating a "liberated" organization.

Following the Crotonville meeting, Welch and Baughman continued to talk about the idea of Work-Out. Eventually, the rough sketch of a process began to emerge. Large groups of employees from different levels and functions would participate. Small groups would brainstorm ideas for getting rid of work. Senior managers would accept or reject these ideas in "Town Meetings"—forcing them to engage in discussions that would simulate the experience of Crotonville's "pit."

The more they talked, the more Welch realized that, if done right, such a process would not only get rid of unnecessary work, but also would help to create the management culture—the organizational success—that he was looking for. And it would be a positive initiative, building something new in contrast to all of the downsizing and restructuring of the previous years. To make this happen, Welch asked Baughman to take the lead—to pull together a group of experts in the field of leadership development and change management who could drive this process throughout GE. Baughman then asked Dick DiPaola, a long-time Crotonville program manager, and Jon Biel, a new one, to meet with Dave Ulrich, who was one of the external Crotonville faculty members, and brainstorm how to create this new organization that Welch was looking for. Ulrich, realizing that this would be a potentially massive project, asked Len Schlessinger and Todd Jick, both Harvard Business School professors, and Deborah Shah, an external consultant, to join him and the Crotonville managers as a "management team" for the effort.

And so it was that in late 1988, this group of business-school professors, consultants, and Crotonville staff gathered several times to sketch out the basics of the Work-Out process and how it might be employed throughout GE.

Corporate Cultural Revolution on a Grand Scale

In the days and weeks that followed, the Work-Out management team, with internal GE coordinators Jon Biel and Dick DiPaola, grappled with the reality that creating a new management culture for a company the size of GE was no easy task. For one, each of the 13 major GE businesses was the size of a Fortune 50 company, and most had units scattered around the globe. And each one was run by a hard-nosed, ambitious executive who had been well schooled in the old way of running a business—and who might not want (or be able) to change. Yet without changing the behaviors of the 13 business leaders—not to mention the heads of the corporate staff groups—the underlying management culture of GE would remain unchanged. In other words, Work-Out was not simply about reducing work—it was about changing the management culture of 13 huge businesses and a still-massive corporate staff—simultaneously. As such, it was perhaps the largest corporate-change attempt in the history of the world. And there was no crisis or burning platform to spur the participants to action.

Given the scope of this effort, the management team quickly recruited more leadership development and change-management experts to help out, including Steve Kerr and Ron Ashkenas. The management team felt strongly that such expertise should not come from one large consulting firm, but rather should be a hand-picked consortium of professors and consultants who would have credibility with GE's senior business leaders, and who could work together to make Work-Out a reality. This followed the GE tradition of selecting individual experts to collaboratively develop Crotonville programs and teach them, rather than hiring a consulting firm that would simply deliver its own program. The management team's goal was to appoint one "lead consultant" for each GE business, as well as one for each of the major corporate-staff units. The lead consultants would then each recruit others, as needed, to work with their assigned GE business or functional units.

Moving quickly, the initial "core team" of lead consultants met for the first time at an airport hotel in New York on January 3, 1989. After an initial briefing by Jim Baughman on the company and the goals for Work-Out, the core team held a series of working sessions to help flesh out the initial thinking about Work-Out and how it might be applied in the businesses. And with that, Work-Out was off and running.

Learning from Experience

Following the January kick-off meeting, each lead consultant worked with Baughman and his Crotonville staff to arrange visits to the GE businesses or functional units. Not surprisingly, most of the lead consultants discovered that the GE business and functional leaders were far from welcoming the idea with open arms. Although Jack Welch had introduced the idea of Work-Out at the most recent Corporate Executive Council meeting and at the January officers' meeting in Boca Raton, Florida—and had stressed that everyone would participate (whether they liked it or not)—the business leaders had very different views of what this meant, how serious Welch was about it, and how much freedom they would have to tailor it.

GE Lighting, for example, was already about to launch a series of workshops on business strategy—so maybe they would just call them Work-Outs and be done with it. Aircraft Engines was deeply committed to the Deming continuous improvement approach, and Work-Out struck its management as just a small subset of what its people were already doing. And GE Capital, in its own opinion, wasn't really like those "industrial" businesses, and didn't really have any bureaucracy, so Work-Out didn't really apply there. In fact, none of the business or functional units were keen to start Work-Out right away. They all had their unique situations, their reasons why the process wasn't quite appropriate for them, their ongoing programs that met the objectives of Work-Out anyway. So almost all of them went through the motions of compliance and met with the consultants—and waited to see whether Welch would really follow through.

Only the Corporate Audit staff, eager to be first at any Welch initiative, jumped at the chance to pilot test Work-Out. But it was a rocky launch; most auditors wanted to "take work out" of the client organizations they were reviewing, rather than look at their own processes. The consultants were ill-prepared to deal with these highly energized, "can-do," future corporate officers. So even the Audit executives, though intrigued by the potential of Work-Out, were uncertain about how to apply it in their own organization.

Jack Welch, of course, was never one to start a process and not follow through. In those early days, both he and Larry Bossidy talked constantly about Work-Out, asked business leaders what they were doing to get it started, kept it on the CEC agendas, and tried to take away any excuses that managers had for not starting. Thus, Welch agreed to fund the first year completely so that budget would not be an excuse. And business leaders who felt they lacked the right chemistry with their assigned lead consultant could request a replacement (although after the second request, Welch would raise the question of the business leader's commitment). Each business and functional leader also could choose the issues to focus on and the number of sessions to do—although Welch let it be known that he expected every GE employee to "have a taste of Work-Out by the end of 1989."

But for some things, business leaders had no choice. Work-Outs had to be started. The sessions had to be cross-level and cross-functional, with relatively large numbers of people (40 or more). And the business or functional leader had to run the concluding Town Meeting in person—and make yes-or-no decisions before leaving the room. And with Welch relentlessly asking business leaders what was happening, movement started to occur.

In addition to the demands from above, most of the lead consultants also discovered that there were indeed people within the businesses who embraced and welcomed the idea of Work-Out. Welch's instinct was right on target; many GE employees really were feeling overwhelmed with nonvalue-added work and did welcome an opportunity to remove bureaucracy and to make greater contributions. Thus, although business leaders and many of their direct reports were often reluctant to take part or even felt threatened by Work-Out, many of their subordinates were eager to get started.

But nowhere was it easy. At GE Nuclear Energy, for example, senior managers pointed out that, in the wake of their recent brutal downsizing (from more than 6000 employees to less than 3000), much of the bureaucracy in their business had already been eradicated. They were also happy to point out that they were the most regulated business in GE, and whatever bureaucracy remained was required by the NRC, the state utility commissions, and various other regulatory bodies. (Incidentally, data collected during the first year revealed that, of all the bureaucratic policies and processes identified, only *seven percent* were inflicted upon General Electric by some regulatory authority.)

As evidence of the cynicism and suspicion within GE Nuclear that Work-Out was merely a disguise for another round of downsizing, within days of its inception the initiative was dubbed "Heads-Out." In this climate, the decision was made to do almost no preparation in advance of the initial session. Invitees to the first Work-Out were told to "bring only your intelligence and your imagination." The Work-Out agenda, topics, and partitioning into subgroups was all done during the session, by and in full view of all participants.

The Nuclear experience was typical of the dilemmas that consultants and managers faced in the initial implementation of Work-Out. On the one hand, Work-Out was an "empowerment initiative" and meant to "liberate" employees. Yet at the same time, Work-Out was a corporate initiative that everyone was forced to do, whether they wanted to or not. It was a double message that many people had trouble reconciling. Some of the consultants rationalized it by saying that it was necessary to "use the culture to change the culture." And even Welch recognized it when he responded to a Crotonville student's question about how he could square Work-Out's objectives with his own style, by saying, "One of the ways we'll know that Work-Out has been successful is that my style of leadership will no longer be tolerated in this company."

Despite these dilemmas, and continued resistance and skepticism, the lead consultants fanned out and began to design initial Work-Outs in all of GE's businesses and functions, mostly focusing on "low-hanging fruit"—that is, bureaucratic mechanisms that could be quickly and easily eliminated or changed. At NBC, for example, the consultants held initial Work-Out meetings on streamlining the expense-reimbursement process. At GE Capital, the initial Work-Out in the finance function targeted reports that could be eliminated, streamlined, produced less frequently, or distributed differently. And at GE Nuclear, the initial Work-Out dealt with such topics as desk calendars, gate passes, and credit-card-reimbursement practices. In GE Nuclear, probably the most important outcome from the initial Work-Out was that people began to trust the process. The obvious unimportance of the problems being tackled served to convince even the most suspicious employees that, whatever Work-Out was, it wasn't just another attempt to downsize the business.

The Light Bulb Goes on at GE Lighting

The first Work-Out at GE Lighting was typical of these early sessions. To prepare for the Work-Out, Ron Ashkenas, who was assigned as the "lead" external consultant, met with the business leader, John Opie, in late January, 1989. Opie, a long-time veteran of GE and a superb operational manager, gave Ron a personal tutorial about the Lighting business, complete with over 40 overhead transparencies, saying, "If you're going to help us, you better understand our business." Out of this session, Opie identified a number of business topics that might benefit from a Work-Out approach, including product development, the distribution process, production attainment, customer service, and more. Product development was selected as the topic for the first Work-Out, which Opie wanted to hold before the end of March so that he could report that he had "done one" at the April CEC meeting in Fairfield.

Like most of the other GE business leaders, Opie was willing to give the process a try—and was not about to countermand Jack Welch's initiative. But he was clearly skeptical.

Following the meeting with Opie, Ashkenas made a presentation about Work-Out to the Group Staff, the leaders of the various units of GE Lighting. Although there was a spirited discussion about bureaucracy reduction and the value of the Work-Out process, the majority of the team was far from supportive. But they also were good GE "soldiers" and agreed to go along.

Given the lukewarm reception to Work-Out, it was critical that the first one in Lighting demonstrate some degree of success. To that end, Ron worked with a small design team to organize the first session. It included the Vice President of Engineering (who was responsible for product development); the Vice President of Human Resources; and the head of Human Resource Development, Carol Pasmore, who was assigned as the internal "program manager" for Work-Out. Together, this group decided that the participants in the first Work-Out would be members of five key product-development teams, each of which was already cross-functional (including people from engineering, manufacturing, marketing, finance, product management, purchasing, international, forecasting, quality, and more). The focus of the Work-Out would be how each of these teams could accelerate their progress by reducing unnecessary bureaucracy.

At the beginning of March, all of the participants were invited to the session through a formal letter from John Opie. They also were sent a package of prereading material, which included several articles, background on Work-Out, and product-development summary sheets for each of the five teams. In addition, several other facilitators (internal and external) were recruited and briefed, and logistical arrangements were made with a nearby hotel. In a matter of weeks, everything was in place, and people in Lighting were starting to wonder what this was really all about.

The Work-Out itself began on a Tuesday evening with an informal cocktail reception and dinner. After dinner, Ron Ashkenas and Carol Pasmore presented an introduction to the Work-Out process, followed by some lighthearted team-building activities to give people a chance to get to know each other, and to break the tension. John Opie and some of his direct reports participated in the cocktails and dinner, and many of the participants had a chance to meet them informally, often for the first time.

The next morning, the Work-Out began in earnest. John Opie opened the morning by presenting an overview of GE Company's business strategy and Lighting's place in it. He then focused on the Lighting business, sharing the financial and strategic picture, and giving his view of the major challenges and opportunities that the company faced. After a break, the three vice presidents of Manufacturing, Marketing, and Engineering each presented the plans for their divisions and how they fit together with Lighting's overall business strategy. For most participants, this was the first time that they had ever had this kind of overview of the Lighting business, from senior executives who were often perceived as powerful, distant, and sometimes intimidating. To stimulate discussion with them about the company strategy, questions were developed by "table groups" so that no one person had to break the ice. This generated another hour of spirited dialogue. The process had begun.

After lunch, the senior executives all left and the product-development teams met on their own. Working with their facilitators, each team was asked to do a brief "situation analysis" of what was currently working in their product-development efforts, and what was not. Then they brainstormed about things that were getting in the way of progress—and what it would take to speed development on their products by 30 percent to 50 percent. The brainstorming items were then categorized using what they called the RRAMMPO matrix (reports, reviews, approvals, meetings, measures, policies, other.) These long lists were then prioritized according to "realistic ability to make it happen" and "impact on new-product development and quality of work life." By the end of the day, each product-development team had a series of recommendations that were shared over dinner and during a sports tournament in the evening.

On Thursday morning, a few members of each product-development team prepared presentations on their highest-priority ideas. At the same time, everyone else met in "functional" groups (marketing and sales, manufacturing, engineering, international, and finance) to identify the implications of the various team recommendations on functional processes. This led to some consolidation of recommendations as people saw that many of the same bureaucratic barriers were getting in the way of all the teams. All 60 participants then worked together during the rest of the morning to dry-run the recommendations, sort out the most important ones, and make sure that everyone in the Work-Out was "on board."

Following lunch, John Opie and his senior managers returned, and the Town Meeting to present and discuss the recommendations began. Ron Ashkenas introduced the session by reviewing the ground rules— mainly that each recommendation could be commented on by anyone, but that at the end of each discussion, John Opie would have to make a "yes-no" decision, and a volunteer from the group would then have the authority to make the recommendation a reality. For most participants, this was an astounding ground rule, and one which most did not believe would be possible. Then tension and excitement was palpable.

In the following three hours, Opie and his managers heard literally dozens of ideas, some small and some quite significant. For example, during the Town Meeting Opie discovered that the product-development teams were spending half of each month preparing for or conducting review meetings with different functions, instead of working on new products. In other words, separate reviews were being held for each new-product team, with manufacturing, marketing, product management, engineering, and more. And each one required separate preparation and follow-up. When the Work-Out team recommended that the reviews be combined, Opie readily agreed—and began to see that Welch's crazy idea might indeed have real value. Other ideas were less dramatic. For example, engineers recommended that they no longer fill out "engineering time sheets," which were meant to allocate their time, and cost, to specific projects. The rationale was that such bookkeeping was only really needed in government projects (which Lighting did not have), the numbers were inaccurate (the system did not allow for more than eight hours per day), nobody really used the numbers, and the product-team leaders knew who was working on projects anyway. Again, Opie agreed. When another team recommended that the Manufacturing and Engineering functions be combined into one organization, Opie said "no," but through the discussion, he uncovered a deep-seated communications problem between the functions, which started with his own vice presidents.

When the Town Meeting ended, over 60 people felt both exhausted and exhilarated. John Opie and many members of his team had experienced the power of unleashing their people. Welch's notion of a "liberated" organization all of a sudden began to make more sense. In other words, the genie was now out of the bottle. And there was no way to put it back in.

Ramping Up

On April 7, 1989, the lead consultants and Crotonville staff met again at a New York airport hotel, this time joined by Jack Welch. The newer consultants heard Welch's expectations directly for the first time. And Welch heard progress reports from each of the consultants—initial reactions in the businesses, what seemed to work, what were the next steps. At the end of the day, Welch challenged the team to accelerate the process, to ramp up and make a difference.

Bolstered by Welch's support, the lead consultants and the Crotonville staff picked up the pace. During the next several months, every business and corporate function launched the Work-Out process in some way. In many businesses, one or more full-time internal consultants were assigned to partner with the lead consultants and coordinate the process across product units, geographies, and functions. This coordination involved a lot of education, cajoling, encouraging, and coaching to help the executives who were expected to lead Work-Out play their roles effectively. Lead consultants recruited dozens of other external consultants to support sub-business units. The development of this large cadre of external consultants was not without its own problems. Not every consulting-team member fully understood or bought into the Work-Out model. Some tried to interest their internal partners in other approaches to change—some that would enhance Work-Out and some that could derail it. Nonetheless, consultants and internal GE people began to work together so that more and more people were trained to facilitate Work-Out sessions. Soon, a critical mass of expertise was built.

Throughout GE, the process of implementing Work-Out was idiosyncratic to each business and the people in it. It was built person by person, partnership by partnership, dialogue by dialogue, argument by argument, negotiation by negotiation. Some executives took to the challenge easily, while others were baffled by the need to engage in public displays of decision making. Among consultants and clients, there were conversations late into the evening, conference calls, questions, and experiments. Chaos reigned despite the financial and human resources devoted to the effort, and despite Welch's powerful, focused energy. Yet eventually, everywhere in GE, people gave it a decent try. And soon, skepticism began to turn into curiosity, curiosity grew into willingness, and willingness to try brought initial success.

During the rest of 1989 and into 1990, this pattern continued throughout GE. Business units and functions held Work-Out sessions and the process evolved. Welch quizzed business leaders about Work-Out results at CEC meetings and continually talked about Work-Out at Crotonville and every other forum. And the Work-Out "faculty" (as the lead consultants were now called) met every few months with the Crotonville staff, and often with Welch, to share progress and learnings. At the Boca Raton meeting of GE officers in January 1990, Dave Ulrich addressed the group and reported that over 100 Work-Out sessions had been run throughout the company. Clearly, Work-Out was not going away, as many line managers had hoped (see appendix for this talk).

Evolving Beyond Bureaucracy

As the Work-Out process ramped up, it also began to evolve beyond its initial focus on the "low-hanging fruit" of reducing bureaucracy. For example, in mid-1989, at one of the Crotonville-sponsored faculty meetings, Jack Welch viewed a mock documentary produced by NBC about using Work-Out to reduce bureaucratic processes. At the end of it, he chided the faculty about focusing on bureaucracy alone and challenged everyone to use Work-Out to address more fundamental business processes, such as order entry, product development, customer service, and collections. Throughout the company, this business-process focus then began to emerge.

At the same time, Work-Out also became more explicit about changing the company's management culture. Although that had always been a goal, it had been somewhat downplayed against the backdrop of cutting through bureaucracy. By the end of 1989, however, Welch, Bossidy, and the Crotonville leadership began to promulgate the mantra of "speed, simplicity, and self-confidence" as the key by-product of Work-Out. In some businesses, questionnaires and other tools were used to assess progress against these ideals. With external faculty collaborating with internal coordinators from Crotonville, led by Jon Biel, the Work-Out agenda evolved.

Early in 1990, the focus on business processes became more formalized. Crotonville and Fairfield staff, by looking at best-practice companies throughout the world, developed a set of tools by which people in Work-Out sessions could quickly develop "process maps" and use them to identify process improvements. These tools then began to be incorporated into Work-Out. By 1992, process mapping was standard practice in GE, and was being applied to processes throughout the company. For example, in February of that year, a team of people from every business in GE participated in a large-scale "order-to-remittance" Work-Out at Crotonville, sponsored by GE's CFO, Dennis Dammerman. The aim was to use process mapping and technology tools to dramatically improve cash flow across GE—a goal that eventually led to hundreds of millions of dollars in cash improvement.

By 1991, Work-Out also was being applied in GE locations throughout the world, particularly as the GE businesses themselves became more globally focused. For example, GE Lighting used the Work-Out process as a prime vehicle for incorporating Tungsram, the previously state-owned Hungarian lighting company, into the GE family. Work-Out there became the forum to teach Hungarian managers and staff some of the basic concepts of Western management—unit costs, product profitability, expense management, and the rest. Shortly thereafter, Work-Out was used to integrate Tungsram and the UK-based Thorn Lighting to form the new GE Lighting Europe—greatly accelerating GE Lighting's shift from a domestic to a global company.

By 1992, Work-Out also was being used in a variety of creative ways to deal with cross-functional and interdivisional frictions and rivalries. In one of these, GE Power Systems ran a Work-Out in which half the attendees were from finance and half from manufacturing. The finance managers presented first, explaining what the financial measures they were inflicting on the factories were intended to accomplish. Then the manufacturing attendees described to the finance people the "gaming" and generally dysfunctional behaviors that the financial measures were stimulating. This led all of the participants to spend the remainder of the time revising and devising measures that would achieve effective financial control and accountability—without producing the unintended consequences that had been identified.

As GE businesses became more comfortable with Work-Out and with the use of process mapping, the natural next extension was to customers and suppliers. The first pilot customer Work-Out was held in 1990 between GE Appliances and Sears, former competitors who were now developing an alliance because of the new Sears "Brand Central" retailing strategy. At this Work-Out, the two companies developed new ways of positioning GE products, getting them into the Sears stores, and providing seamless customer service. Within two years, all the GE businesses were doing Work-Outs with customers and suppliers, sometimes across multiple supply-chain boundaries. For example, one Work-Out, called "The Meeting of the Generals," was a session between General Motors and several GE businesses that supplied products for GM factories (such as lights, motors, and electrical equipment). As a result of this Work-Out, GE engineers helped one General Motors factory reduce its overall energy costs by 15 percent—thus leading to a "preferred supplier" arrangement between GE and GM.

Developing Internal Capability

By the end of 1992, the Work-Out process was well entrenched throughout GE, shifting, in Steve Kerr's words, from an "unnatural act in unnatural places to natural acts in natural places." More than a hundred thousand people had experienced the process, productivity was on the rise throughout the company, and many millions of dollars had been saved or generated. The challenge now was to institutionalize the process and make sure that there was sufficient internal capacity for it to continue and thrive.

The initial approach for making this happen was to develop facilitator and internal-consultant training and apply it across the company. Dozens of variations on such training were developed, and thousands of people were trained. At the same time, many of the businesses focused on training senior managers on how to be Work-Out sponsors and leaders.

Eventually, these efforts led to the realization that middle and senior managers at GE needed to learn not only how to sponsor Work-Out but also how to be "change agents and leaders." Thus in 1992 and 1993, some of the external faculty, in collaboration with Crotonville staff, developed and implemented the Change Acceleration Process (CAP) as a follow-up to Work-Out. In this process, drawn from experiences with other companies, teams of managers from a business took on major change projects and learned how to orchestrate an entire change effort, including communications, mobilization of political support, and creation of measures and rewards. Each team attended an initial workshop where they learned about the elements of effective change and developed their plans. Then they spent the next two months actually implementing the plans—some of which called for the sponsorship of Work-Outs. Afterwards, the teams reassembled for a follow-up workshop for additional training and to reflect on what they had learned.

A Process That Never Ends

Though Work-Out began over a decade ago, it continues to be a vibrant part of how GE operates even today. And it has continued to grow and develop—from a focus on eliminating bureaucracy to one on business processes, then on customers, then on change acceleration and beyond. In the later 1990s, Work-Out became the basis for GE's companywide push into Six Sigma Quality. And in the twenty-first century, it has become a basis for work on digitization and e-business. But throughout, the idea behind Work-Out has always been the same: Bring people together. Give them a business challenge. Trust them to come up with new ideas for how to get better every day. Decide what to do quickly and learn as you go.

"Speed. Simplicity. Self-confidence." This often-quoted phrase from Jack Welch explains his idea of "organizational success," which, combined with financial and strategic excellence, has made GE one of the most successful companies in the world. But the recipe for "Speed, Simplicity, Self-confidence" isn't secret—it's right here, and you can adapt it for your organization.

out such boundaries, the organization would be "dis-organized" and chaotic.[1]

Like a two-edged sword, however, these boundaries also become dangerous. People's scope becomes limited by job level, and they become more narrowly focused on their own functional expertise. They gradually lose perspective on each other's jobs. More importantly, they lose the big picture. They can no longer see how the various tasks, activities, and functions fit together to achieve the organization's over-all purpose. The boundaries, in essence, become more rigid and fixed. Employees start to identify more with their own unit or work group than with the company as a whole. They tend to spend more time looking inward at what they do and how it is measured and rewarded, rather than outward at what the customer might need or what the competition is doing.

As boundaries become more rigid, organizations lose their elasticity—their ability to change quickly and creatively in response to (or anticipation of) changes in the external environment. Senior managers get less and less input from people at lower levels—who often have access to better data about what is really happening with customers or within the organization. Frontline workers become skeptical about decisions made in the "ivory tower" of headquarters. Functions and divisions blame each other for performance problems and compete for scarce resources. And everyone tends to hunker down and defend what they think is "right" without an overall perspective on what might be most beneficial for the organization as a whole.

It is in this setting that Work-Out really shows its power. In an organization where boundaries have become somewhat rigid and fixed, and communication across them has become constrained, Work-Out creates the spirit of the start-up firm in a large, complex one. People from different levels and functions work together without regard to rank or title. Issues are debated in the spirit of what will be best for the overall organization, not just the individual units or functions. Decisions are made quickly, in an interactive forum where everyone can participate and have a voice. And people are empowered to implement—to "just do it"—without any further red tape, approvals, or bureaucracy. In short, for most organizations with traditional boundaries, Work-Out is an "unnatural act" of devolution that forces the firm back to an earlier stage of existence.

Growing into a New Type of Organization

Work-Out does not, however, take an organization backwards. Instead, it helps to transform an organization's boundaries so that they become more permeable. When this happens, information, ideas, decisions, feedback, and even resources start to move more quickly through the organizational bloodstream. The boundaries still exist—but they are no longer rigid barriers to action. Instead, they are elastic, flexible, and sometimes facilitating structures for getting things done faster and more effectively.

Consider the following example: SmithKline Beecham Pharmaceuticals (now GlaxoSmithKline) wanted to speed up the "back end" of the drug-development cycle, where data from clinical trials is analyzed and then prepared for submission to the Food and Drug Administration or other regulators. Traditional ideas such as adding more data analysts, increasing computing power, using outsourced analysis firms, and giving staff more training had already been tried, resulting in only modest gains. So a Work-Out was organized to see if a fresh approach could be developed and implemented quickly.

Participants in this Work-Out included professionals from a number of phases in the drug-development process—beyond just data analysis. These multiple perspectives immediately helped to make some of the previously rigid boundaries in the process more permeable. For instance, clinical researchers, biometric statisticians, data analysts, and experts in FDA requirements had never actually worked together—at the same time—to agree on a clinical-trial protocol. Instead, each of them worked on a number of drug candidates simultaneously, and tended to hand their work on to the next function sequentially, with lots of documents being passed back and forth "over the transom." By talking together, they came up with the idea of "reverse engineering" the process, starting with FDA requirements and then working backward. When they implemented this approach—starting with one drug—they were able to reduce the amount of data that was collected by almost 30 percent, which of course reduced the analysis time. Two other Work-Outs developed a series of ideas for improving the quality of data submissions from the trial sites so as to reduce the time needed to scrub and recheck the data.

Through this and a series of other Work-Outs, the company was able to take several months out of the overall clinical-submission process while substantially reducing the costs of data analysis. More importantly, it accelerated its evolution into a more flexible, fast-moving and high-performing firm. As discussed in Chapter 12, it effectively reshaped its culture while enhancing its business operations.

Work-Out as a Force for Growth

The pharmaceutical company's gains were possible because while each Work-Out event addresses specific business issues, Work-Out also explicitly aims to help an organization grow along five key dimensions:

- Focus on "stretch"
- Development of "systems thinking"
- Encouragement of lateral thinking
- Creation of true empowerment and accountability
- Injection of rapid-cycle change and fast decision making

1. Focus on "Stretch"

Part of Work-Out's power is its ability to force an organization to rethink what it is doing. The impetus for that rethinking is the establishment of what GE eventually called "stretch"—a goal or challenge that is significantly beyond the organization's current performance level.[2] The idea is that if a goal is modest or incremental (say, a five-percent improvement), then people will just work harder or make a few minor changes in what they are doing. But if management lays down the gauntlet and challenges a group to achieve a 30-percent or 50-percent improvement, then they will need to step back and fundamentally rethink how they are working.

With this principle in mind, Work-Out almost always encourages stretch of some sort. Sometimes, stretch is built into the goals, as with these examples:

- Reduce breakage in key products by 50 percent in four months.
- Accelerate the product-development cycle by bringing out the next new product in half the usual time.
- Reduce the number of customer claims by 30 percent in the next year—which means putting new processes in place within 100 days.

- Improve the accuracy of data entered into the system by 50 percent within three months.
- Reduce overhead costs by $10 million in six months.

And sometimes stretch is built into the dialogue about recommendations. For example, when a plant team at GE Lighting proposed that overtime approvals be reduced to just one supervisor instead of two, the business leader asked the group why approvals were needed at all. And that led to a discussion of why time cards were needed at all.

Note that for stretch to be effective it should first be tied to the overall business strategy so that it turns that strategy into a specific issue that employees can accomplish. It should also have a relatively short time frame and a specific way to measure results. The time frames need to be short to help create the sense of urgency that is part of Work-Out's energy and excitement. If people know that they have a year to work on something, then they probably won't put it high on the priority list until the deadline is in sight. If results have to be achieved right away, then action starts tomorrow.

The results measure ensures that the stretch goal is not just focused on a "nice-to-do" activity—it addresses something that will truly make a difference in the business. People in organizations are always choosing different ways to spend their time, and, faced with more choices than time allows, will tend to do things that they are used to. To force change, people need to see that their actions will indeed lead to better results. Work-Out allows you to set things up so high-value activities drive out low-value "busyness."[3]

2. Development of "Systems Thinking"

The concept of *stretch* disrupts the organization; it breaks up old patterns and makes people realize that they cannot continue to work in the same ways as before. To give them a different view of how the stretch goal might be accomplished, Work-Out encourages and even forces people to take a systems perspective. That is, the Work-Out goal can only be achieved if people see it as the endpoint of a set of processes that cut across functions within the organization—and perhaps even includes groups outside of the firm, such as suppliers and customers. No one department or business unit can get there on its own. Changing one program may affect others and hurt overall performance. "Systems thinking" looks at how parts fit together. For example, if someone in a Work-Out recommends abolishing a report to save one unit time, others will speak up if that report is critical to another unit's decision making. In that case, it would not make sense to abolish the report, but to prepare it more effectively.

This novel systems perspective is introduced in the initial design phase of Work-Out, as part of organizing the Work-Out event. At this point, the design team creates a high-level map that describes the various steps, processes, and subprocesses that are involved in producing the current results the business is getting. For example, in the pharmaceutical data-analysis Work-Out described earlier in this chapter, the initial, high-level process map looked like the one shown in Figure 2-1.

Based on this map, the design team was able to identify multiple points of focus for Work-Out, along with the key constituent groups who would need to participate in each one. Figure 2-2 shows the sequence of Work-Outs and mini-Work-Outs that came out of the Clinical Data Management area during just one year. By understanding the overarching process, the design team was able to ensure that representatives from different groups were present to help participants see the Work-Out issue through each other's eyes. Individually, all the participants understood their own tasks. But they did not fully understand or appreciate the impact of these tasks on each other, and on the process as a whole.

In many Work-Out sessions, facilitators also help the participants create more-detailed process maps that teach and reinforce the systems perspective. For example, detailed process maps were developed by various teams in the SmithKline Beecham Work-Out described earlier. Through the joint creation of such maps, participants from different functions not only begin to understand the areas outside of their own, but also they begin to identify psychologically with the whole system instead of just with their own part. As this shift in allegiance starts to occur, participants are more willing and able to see possible changes in the overall process, and they feel less defensive about ideas for change that may affect their own function. In other words, they begin to realize that they are all in it together and that achieving the stretch goal can only be done through collective effort.

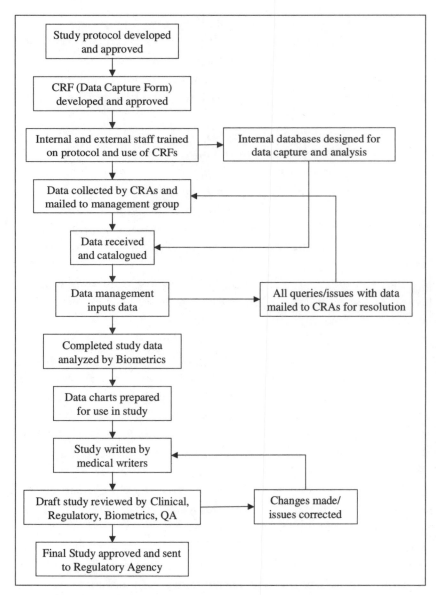

Figure 2-1 Pharmaceutical Data-Analysis Process.

This does not mean that taking on a systems perspective by itself eliminates resistance to change. Claiming that would be naive. However, encouraging the systems perspective is one key factor that helps soften up the boundaries—to make participants more open to looking at alternatives to how things have always been done.

Work-Out—September 1993 (Sponsor: CDM U.S.)

Result: CRF backlog reduced from 80,000 pages to 10,000 pages in three months.

    Mini-Work-Out—January 1994

    Result: CRF backlog maintained at 10,000 pages despite doubling of work volume.

Work-Out—January 1994 (Sponsor: CDM U.S.–Clinical U.S.)

Result: Queries reduced by 50 percent and cycle time by 75 percent in three months.

    Mini-Work-Out—May 1994

    Result: Develop SOP's; Target Additional Improvement Areas.

Work-Out—September 1993 (Sponsor: CDM U.K.–Clinical U.K.)

Result: Queries reduced by 50 percent and cycle time reduced by 33 percent in three months.

    Worldwide Best Practices—July 1994

    (Sponsor: CDM U.S./U.K.–Clinical U.S./U.K.)

    Result: Joint working group developed uniform tracking and standards world-wide regarding DRQ's/queries.

Work-Out—September 1994 (Sponsor: Clinical U.S.–CDM U.S.)

Goal: Remove as much data as possible from five protocols and develop process for minimizing unnecessary data collection across all protocols.

Figure 2-2 Work-Out Successes at SmithKline Beecham Pharmaceuticals: Clinical Data Management.

3. Encouragement of Lateral Thinking

Once participants feel the urgency to change and begin to see the whole picture of the current situation, they are then ready to focus on new ideas. How can the process be improved? What can be done differently to achieve the stretch goal?

Using the process map as a starting point, Work-Out asks participants to brainstorm ways of achieving the goal, and then provides a structure for quickly sorting through the ideas, selecting the best ones, and developing them into recommendations for change. As with any brainstorming process, Work-Out encourages people to toss out any idea, no matter how minor, how crazy, how seemingly impossible. And the process helps people learn how to build on each other's ideas, combine ideas, and think "out of the box." In fact, when the old Aetna Insurance Company implemented its version of Work-Out, the program's sponsors called it "Out of the Box."

Low-Hanging Fruit

While many change processes include brainstorming of some sort, Work-Out is unique in several ways. First, Work-Out begins by focusing on the "low-hanging fruit"—the easy, no-brainer fixes that can be made to virtually any process. Almost all operations, as they evolve over time, develop some amount of clutter or inefficiency—reports with unnecessary data that go to people who do not need them; requests for signoffs or approvals from people who may not be in the best position to decide; extra steps that take time but don't add value. Work-Out calls these inefficiencies "RAMMPP" activities, an acronym for reports, approvals, meetings, measures, policies, and practices. Work-Out acknowledges that these inefficiencies exist, and encourages participants to root them out right away, using the RAMMPP matrix in Figure 2-3 as a framework for assessing and analyzing them. Going through this process gives people an immediate sense of accomplishment and quickly serves to clean

	CONTROL					Could it be:
	Self	Department	Group	Company	External	1. Eliminated?
Reports						2. Partially eliminated?
						3. Delegated downward?
Approvals						4. Done less often?
Meetings						5. Done in a less complicated/time-consuming manner?
Measures						6. Done with fewer people involved?
Policies						7. Done using a more productive technology?
Practices						8. Other?

Figure 2-3 The RAMMPP Matrix.

up—and speed up—the process being addressed. When employees remove work that they don't find valuable, they feel empowered and in control of their work setting. As managers at an early Work-Out session at Wal-Mart said, this part of Work-Out is aimed at "getting the dumb" out of the system.

Reducing wasted motion and bureaucracy, however, is just a good start and is not sufficient to truly achieve stretch performance. After viewing the documentary "spoof" of the NBC expense-reimbursement process mentioned in Chapter 1, Jack Welch forcefully pointed out that streamlining bureaucratic activities such as expense reimbursement was only the beginning. If the process stopped there, he warned grimly, then the whole team should be fired.

A Clean Sheet

The idea-development process for Work-Out, then, can go far beyond just process streamlining. Participants also are asked to do "clean-sheet" process thinking—to consider how they might redo the process from scratch so as to achieve the stretch goals. In this context, the Work-Out facilitators encourage the group to challenge assumptions and explore why things need to be done in certain ways, or at all. What might competitors do? What would someone else do to put you out of business by doing this differently?

For example, in a Work-Out to reduce costs and increase speed of product distribution in GE's Lighting business, a team redesigned part of the process by starting from the customer's perspective. A major customer, they said, constantly receives shipments of many products at its loading dock. If a GE Lighting truck arrives at a time when other suppliers were also delivering, the driver might need to wait for space, causing delays both there and for the rest of the delivery route. Or if the truck arrives at a time when the customer warehouse doesn't have enough of the right space available, or personnel available, or the paperwork ready, more delays ensue. Thus, they reasoned, the best thing to do would be for the GE Lighting shipment to arrive at a preestablished, fixed, and regular time so that the customer could be prepared to receive it as efficiently as possible. And even better, if the timing was also concurrent with monthly billing and payment cycles, then the paperwork—or electronic invoicing and payment processing—could be prepared in advance so that the cash-flow process could also be more efficient.

Starting from this point, the GE Lighting team worked out a series of ideas for scheduled, regular deliveries to major customers, starting with one customer as an experiment. Working backward, the team then realized that this could also lead to a regular order of products for the customer, and a regular manufacturing schedule. While leaving room for a small percentage of exceptions in the regular order, they discovered that this kind of planning process for major customers took large chunks of time and money out of the entire order-make-ship-bill cycle. Over the next year, the process was expanded to dozens of customers, leading to significant productivity and customer-service gains.

Analysis

In addition to generating ideas, Work-Out also forces a quick but crucial analysis of the ideas so as to select those that are worth moving forward. In the process, it teaches participants not only how to generate ideas but also how to move quickly from ideas to action. Thus, following each brainstorming session in Work-Out, participants quickly sort the ideas that were developed into categories using a "Payoff Matrix" (see Figure 2-4). This tool forces people to think through both impact and achievability. The point is that an idea that might save millions of dollars is worth nothing if it cannot be implemented; often a more modest idea that can be put into play quickly can have more impact. The Work-Out culture, then, encourages a bias toward action—the notion first articulated by Kurt Lewin that the best way to change an organization is not to talk about it but to start to change it right now.

4. Creation of True Empowerment and Accountability

Work-Out is not just about generating ideas and recommendations. Part of its value is its ability to create a culture where ideas are translated into action and results. All too often people in organizations have great ideas about how to do things differently, but the ideas never go anywhere. The person with the idea can't get the time, permission, or resources to act, or faces outright resistance and gives up—or, more often, nobody picks up the ball on the idea. It is, in essence, a "disembodied idea," an idea without an owner.

	Easy to Implement	Tough to Implement
Small Pay-Off	Quick Win! (QW)	Time-Wasters (TW)
Big Pay-Off	Business Opportunities (BO)	Special Effort (SE)

Figure 2-4 Payoff Matrix.

One of the ground rules of most Work-outs is "no complaining, no blaming." Often employees want to turn empowerment forums into gripe sessions. When Work-Out participants had complaints, they were pushed to turn them into suggestions . . . of a report, approval, meeting, measure, or policy to change. Chronic complainers were not helpful unless they could turn their concerns into recommendations. Blaming often occurs when employees seek a cause of their disenfranchisement—"management won't let me do this." Employees are encouraged not to blame others but to focus on what they could do to make a difference.

Create Ownership

One of the keys to creating an action-oriented culture is to make sure that every recommendation that comes out of a Work-Out session has someone who is accountable for making it happen, and has the power to drive it forward. The Work-Out ground rules state that each team can present a recommendation at the Town Meeting only if one team member is willing to be the "owner" of the idea—to take accountability for driving it through to a result—if it's approved. Accountability for a Work-Out idea, however, does not mean that the owner personally implements the idea. Instead, it means that the owner mobilizes the resources needed, puts together a plan that everyone agrees to, ensures that everyone does their part, and has public accountability to the senior management.

Do Whatever It Takes

When an idea is approved at the Town Meeting, the business leader tells the owner to do whatever is necessary to make it happen. Part of Work-Out's power is that this delegation of authority is genuine, not just lip service. If an idea is approved at a Town Meeting, then the owner has the authority to make sure it is implemented—even if that means going across functional lines or pushing people at higher levels to do something. For many participants in Work-Out, this is a very difficult concept to accept. Most people do not like to buck hierarchical or functional authority—to challenge organizational superiors. They are most comfortable within their own organizational boundaries, and usually only make demands on people who work for them directly. Yet one of the ground rules of a Work-Out is that someone who is given the authority to implement a recommendation becomes a "virtual boss" with all the power and authority of the business leader in regard to that recommendation.

Review and Catch-Up

This empowerment and accountability is reinforced at the periodic reviews that occur 30, 60, and 90 days after the Work-Out event. At these sessions, each owner reports on progress in implementing the assigned Work-Out ideas, including whether there has been any resistance or difficulty. If the owner has encountered resistance—or people who have not done their part—the business leader is encouraged not to jump in, which would be the traditional (and easy) reaction, but to coach the idea owner about how to handle the resistance, what else to try, what to say. The business leader can of course step in as a final resort—but it is more powerful if the owner can learn how to influence people across functional and hierarchical lines. When an organization is open to this kind of influence, it is a sign that its boundaries are becoming more permeable and it is more capable of translating ideas into action.

5. Injection of Rapid-Cycle Change and Fast Decision Making

Like a chemical formula that needs a catalyst to create a reaction, the first four ingredients described in this section only become active when the last ingredient—speed—is added to the mix. Speed counts. Speed means decisions are made quickly. Speed means that action occurs. Speed engages people because they see progress. Thus, the fifth but perhaps most pervasive aspect of Work-Out is the constant drive for speed.

Most organizations talk a good game when it comes to speed in decision making, customer responsiveness, and other key processes. Yet the reality is that most organizations operate slowly. Processes tend to be sequential rather than simultaneous. Most people are not willing to make decisions right away. They would rather check with their boss, their colleagues, their subordinates. In this way, if the decision turns out to be wrong or to lead to undesired consequences, someone else can take the blame.

Senior managers who are supposed to be decision makers are often notorious for not making speedy decisions. To insulate themselves against failure, they tend to rely on staff experts and analysts to study issues for them and advise them. They also rely on hierarchy to help with decisions—making sure that all managers below them have signed off on something before they will make something official. For example, a number of years ago in the old AlliedSignal Automotive Sector, before Larry Bossidy became chairman, 26 signatures were required for capital expenditures above $100,000. We found that, on average, every approval took 4 days, so the 26 signatures meant over 100 days (21 weeks) before the decision was made. When the so-called decision finally arrived on the sector head's desk, so much time had elapsed that the business reason for the request was at least partially out of date, and so many people had looked at it that there really was no decision to make. The only real question for the sector head at that point was where to find room on the document for one more signature! It was no wonder that the business was in trouble.

One of the original aims of Work-Out at GE was to force a pattern of faster decision making and a rapid-cycle change process. In the decades preceding Work-Out, GE had developed an analytical, control-oriented culture. Nobody made decisions without a thorough justification, often prepared by or with the help of the Audit staff or Finance function. Long papers and detailed presentations were common. Fast decisions—and decisions made "close to the action"—were rare. Jack Welch, realizing that the survival of the company in the 1990s and beyond would depend on being faster than the competition, wanted to foster the idea of "speed." And Work-Out was the vehicle to make that happen. As he said, "Faster, in almost every case, is better."

Although the injection of speed is apparent throughout the Work-Out process, it is most visible in the context of the Town Meeting. It is here that senior business leaders are challenged to make decisions on the spot, right away, without all the usual crutches of time, analysis, staff opinions, and deep consideration. Instead, the business leader needs to listen carefully to truly grasp the idea, ask questions to get a good understanding of the implications, solicit views from other people attending the Town Meeting, and then make a decision—either yes or no. And for each Work-Out recommendation, this decision cycle needs to be a matter of minutes, rather than days, weeks, or months. But the idea of speed is not just a one-time phenomenon aimed at Town Meeting decisions. It is a pervasive concept that begins to shape the entire cycle of action, experimentation, and change in an organization, and as such, it shows up before, during, and after the Town Meeting.

Before

For most senior business leaders, the Town Meeting decision process is the single most challenging aspect of Work-Out. We have seen otherwise powerful, intimidating managers stutter and sweat when forced to make a decision in the moment, while subordinates and direct reports are watching. As we coach, counsel, and debrief them, we often hear anxious questions: "What if I don't fully understand the issue? What if I make the wrong decision? What if I don't agree, but everyone else wants to do it? How can I say 'no' without offending people? If I say 'yes' to everything will I appear weak?" These are, of course, natural human reactions, and Work-Out forces them to the surface. But it does so with an intentional bias—that making decisions faster, even if some are wrong, will balance out to be much better for the organization than taking the time to get each one exactly right.

During

Making decisions faster at the Town Meeting sets up a whole pattern of speed that continues throughout Work-Out. For one, the business leader is encouraged not only to make decisions quickly, but to model decision logic so that participants in Work-Out sessions learn how to make faster decisions in their own spheres. That is why the Town Meeting is not just a session for presentations and decisions, but one of debate and discussion. It is there that the business leader can frame not just the decision but the way to think about decisions in general. For example, at a Town Meeting in GE Lighting's Hungarian acquisition, Tungsram, the business leader, George Varga, had to constantly remind the participants that many of the decisions they were bringing to him could be made by them independently, without consulting him. Facing a group that was just learning to set aside a state-owned, centralized decision-making culture, Varga used the Town Meeting as an opportunity to teach which decisions could be made at lower levels, and which required more senior consideration.

After

After the Town Meeting, speed continues to propel the Work-Out process. In many designs, an action-planning meeting for team leaders and idea owners is held immediately after the Town Meeting, or the next day. This meeting makes sure that people do not just walk out with good intentions. They go home with action plans, timelines, and specific responsibilities for implementation. In some cases, idea owners meet with the overall sponsor weekly to review progress—and hold more formal reviews at 30-, 60-, and 90-day intervals. This keeps the heat on the participants to move forward, to try things, to learn through action. It also allows wrong decisions to be caught early and modified or abandoned, and new learnings or ideas to emerge as action evolves.

Not Just an Antidote to Big Bureaucracy

Although Work-Out is ideally suited to large organizations whose boundaries have become calcified and inflexible, it is also applicable to small organizations. While small firms generally do not suffer from functional stovepipes, overbearing hierarchies, and large, unwieldy structures, they often struggle with issues on the other end of the continuum: lack of clear process, insufficient focus and prioritization, and overemphasis on a single leader for all decisions. These kinds of problems often cause small firms to waste resources, operate with an inefficient frenzy, and neglect chances to develop people for broader responsibilities.

Work-Out can counter these problems in small firms by helping the business leader (often the founder) quickly shape the level of structure and process needed to run most effectively at a given stage, focus on key issues rather than try to do everything, and develop other people to move smoothly into responsible positions as things grow beyond the reach of the central leader.

GE Capital's Equity business, which invests in and manages a portfolio of hundreds of small companies, encourages its portfolio companies to use Work-Out to solve problems and to manage the inevitable strains associated with growth. One of its companies, MediaVehicles, a firm that sells advertising on the sides of trucks, is a good example of this approach. Encouraged by the GE Equity portfolio manager who chaired the board, the founder and head of MediaVehicles brought together his entire organization (10 people) for a first Work-Out session a year after the company was started. At this session, the entire team worked on ways of improving the sales process (by agreeing on a few key markets and types of offerings) and more rapidly growing the sales pipeline. The outcomes of this session helped the company to grow its top line more rapidly in the next year, and also gave the founder greater insights into the skills and interests of his team. (For example, a secretary who demonstrated creativity and promise during the Work-Out sessions began to take on some major marketing activities—and eventually became a marketing manager.) A year later, a second Work-Out, again with the whole company (now 25 people), focused on improving operational processes so that the now-larger base of customers could get their advertisements on the sides of the trucks more quickly and at less cost. Subsequent sessions helped the manager build financial and other operational processes, while creating a management team that was not dependent on him for moving forward.

Work-Out Forces a New Kind of Dialogue

Whether Work-Out is applied in a large firm or a start-up, an underlying reason for its success is its ability to create dialogue. Most organizations, no matter their size, constrain dialogue from occurring between people at different levels, different functions, different locations, or different partner organizations. Some of these constraints are conscious and intentional. For example, many firms do not discuss financial data with all employees, and certainly not with customers and suppliers. Other constraints are practical. Managers do not have the time to interact with everyone in their organization, let alone with people in other units and with customers and suppliers.

Many of the constraints on dialogue, however, are psychological and cultural—and often dysfunctional. For example, people at lower levels of an organization tend not to interact often or easily with senior executives for many reasons, few of which are practical or intentional. Some may avoid contact because of learned patterns of deference; others may fear people they see as having power over them; still others may presume that senior leaders do not want to hear their views. Some of these behaviors are rooted in reality while others are not, but the anxiety behind them all is so powerful that the assumptions are never tested, and the behaviors never change. Thus, many senior executives rarely have a chance to hear the unadulterated perspectives and ideas of their frontline troops. What they get is usually filtered through multiple layers and then colored to be acceptable. And by the same token, most people on the front lines do not have the chance to hear senior executives think out loud, explain strategies and contingencies, and shade in the gray zones of most corporate pronouncements and decisions. On both sides, it is a dysfunctional constraint on dialogue that serves neither the organization nor the individuals well.

Even before the advent of Work-Out at GE, Jack Welch used to counter this constraint by holding Town-Meeting-type dialogues at Crotonville or on visits to business sites. Through the direct give-and-take with people at lower levels, without the filter of their managers, Welch felt that he could get a better sense of what was happening in his businesses than he could get from any number of reports and meetings with managers. And he felt that in these sessions, he could get across his message about key strategic and cultural themes of GE. Crotonville was his opportunity for dialogue. For Welch, Work-Out was a way of forcing all his managers to engage in this kind of process—to open up the channels of dialogue throughout the company.

Constraints on dialogue, however, are not just between senior and junior levels of an organization. Other constraints block communication across functions, between product groups, and across geographic and cultural lines. Work-Out opens up these channels too and encourages people who would not ordinarily interact with each other—and in fact who often blame each other for their problems—to learn how to talk, solve problems together, and interact constructively. For example, in a consumer-products manufacturing company that had recently implemented an SAP information-management system, human-resources specialists blamed the corporate-systems staff for unwieldy administrative processes and inaccuracies in employee data. And the systems professionals accused the HR people of making things worse by trying to load the system up with unnecessary functionality. When they spent two days together in a Work-Out session, both functions realized that there were no villains and that the problems could be resolved through jointly designing processes that took advantage of the capabilities of the system.

Most organizations also constrain the dialogue between themselves and their customers and suppliers. Instead of operating as part of a value chain, many organizations treat their customers or suppliers as adversaries, haggling with them over prices, terms, and conditions. For managers who want to change this dynamic and create a different kind of relationship with business partners, Work-Out is a vehicle for encouraging extra-organizational dialogue.

Whether the dialogue is across levels, functions, geographies, or organizational boundaries, Work-Out teaches participants the basics of how to truly talk with each other. First is the learning about how to understand each other's language. One of the reasons why dialogue is constrained in organizations is that people often do not take the time to understand each other and to realize that the same words can carry different meanings. For example, in the HR-Systems Work-Out mentioned earlier, people from both functions used the phrase "work flow" to describe certain issues and problems. Only after considerable discussion did everyone come to realize that the HR people were referring to the process of work activities (as pictured on a work-flow chart) while the systems people were referring to electronic transmission of data. This kind of listening and understanding is essential for people to work together. It is thus the first phase of dialogue that is encouraged in Work-Out—what we call learning how to "talk the talk" of each other.

Once people have more of a common framework for talking about their worlds, they can begin the process of joint problem solving. To do this, however, requires a next level of dialogue—what we call learning how to "translate talk into walk." Participants in a Work-Out need to learn how to go beyond understanding the as-is state and begin to envision a different future, without being defensive or self-limiting. In many cases, this is not easy. People naturally want to stay in their own comfort zones and defend the way they do things. After all, they are not intentionally trying to do a bad job. Just the opposite. Thus, well-meaning people in Work-Outs often find themselves using phrases such as "we tried this several years ago," or "that's a good idea, but—" or "our customers (or suppliers, bosses, regulators, or investors) will never go along with this."

Part of the learning in Work-Out is how to overcome and deal with these kinds of natural, human behaviors that constrain the problem-solving phase of organizational dialogue. To do this, facilitators and team leaders (and team participants) challenge these action-limiting assumptions; they continually ask "why not?" and encourage people to generate large numbers of ideas before doing any evaluation or analysis. In addition, Work-Out teaches people how to select action ideas that might have the best chance of success, and carve out projects that can be tested in 90 days or less. This focus on short-term "experimental" actions helps people become more comfortable with change, knowing that the short-term focus reduces the risks and increases the chance of keeping things under psychological control.

Identifying action ideas is of course not enough. Thus, the third stage of dialogue that Work-Out teaches is how to implement ideas, or how to "walk the talk." With each Work-Out—sometimes during the session and sometimes immediately afterwards, recommendation owners and other team members learn how to construct action plans that lay out the key steps for implementing their approved ideas—including responsibilities, measures, and deadlines. These plans are reviewed with the Work-Out sponsor and with other teams and continually strengthened and updated as people move into action. For many people in organizations, implementing a change program, no matter the scope, is a significant learning process. Thus, the disciplines of action planning and measurement, and the associated review processes at regular intervals, are critical parts of the "walk the talk" process.

These three phases, taken together as shown in Figure 2-5, help an organization create a new and more sophisticated kind of dialogue—a dialogue that, over time, helps to make all the organizational bound-

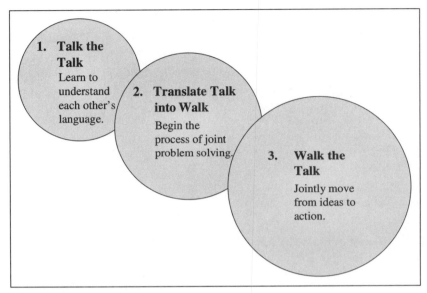

Figure 2-5 Three Phases of Work-Out Dialogue.

aries more flexible, elastic, and open to change.[4] This development of "Work-Out dialogue" is a major reason why Work-Out has such power and impact—and can affect the results and culture of all kinds of organizations.

Taking Work-Out to the Next Level

Once an organization has engaged in the Work-Out process and has made its boundaries more permeable, where does it go from there?

The first answer to this question is that, in reality, the Work-Out process never really ends. Organizations, no matter their size or scope, always have the human tendency to accumulate plaque in their arteries and clutter in their closets. Policies, procedures, reports, and "fixes" are always being created in response to new conditions—so that there is always a need to revisit them and weed out those that have outlived their usefulness. By the same token, organizations are constantly reorganizing, finding new customers and suppliers, and changing processes and procedures. So these too need constant reworking. That is why, almost 10 years after Work-Out was first created at GE, Jack Welch asked every business to conduct a six-month "Work-Out blitz" to drive out newly accumulated bureaucracy. It is also why this book can be written many years after Work-Out was conceived and still have application to managers who want to empower employees and act more quickly right now.

A second and deeper answer to the question, however, is that Work-Out creates the foundation for organizations to engage in other change processes more effectively. In essence, Work-Out creates an organization that is more capable of change—more open to new ideas, less rooted in the past and more attuned to the future.

The best example of how Work-Out can be the foundation for constant change, of course, is GE. Once the change-oriented Work-Out culture was embedded in GE, the company was then able to successfully orchestrate a series of extensive change initiatives, most notably Six Sigma Quality[5] and Digitization (e-commerce and Web-based processes). It is unlikely that these kinds of initiatives could have been introduced, disseminated, and internalized so quickly in a company the size of GE without the Work-Out culture as a base. In fact, in the late 1980s, when Work-Out was first introduced, a number of the GE business leaders, particularly in the Aircraft Engine business, lobbied vigorously for a Six Sigma approach instead of Work-Out. At the time, Motorola was trumpeting its success with Six Sigma, and the Total-Quality movement was just gaining momentum. Jack Welch, however, felt strongly that a highly analytical approach such as Six Sigma would have reinforced GE's already exaggerated tendency to analyze and audit rather than act. And it would not have changed the underlying culture of hierarchy and constrained dialogue.

In retrospect, it's clear that Welch was correct. GE became a more flexible and change-oriented culture through the first half of the 1990s, and was thus much more capable of implementing Six Sigma in the second half of the decade. Through Six Sigma, GE was able to accelerate process improvement and customer focus and realize hundreds of millions of dollars in cost reductions and productivity enhancements, in addition to what had already been gained through Work-Out. In contrast, Motorola, which pioneered Six Sigma in the 1980s, did not develop a sufficiently fast and flexible culture to underpin its focus on quality. The result was a series of strategic missteps, delays in shifting to digital technology, and struggles to integrate acquisitions—all of which dragged down the company's performance.

From Theory to Practice

In this chapter, we have described the underlying theory that makes Work-Out such a powerful tool for both performance improvement and cultural change. By giving people new ways to conduct dialogue, Work-Out creates an organization with more flexible, permeable boundaries— which is thus more capable of rapid innovation and change.

But Work-Out does not come into being just because someone calls its name. Even though it is an empowering, involving process that can capture the hearts and souls of people at all levels, it is still as prone as any mandated change effort to evoke resistance both direct and subtle. In the next chapter, we turn to the knotty question of organizational readiness—how to predict the initial course of Work-Out in an organization, and how to recognize resistance and turn it into support.

Is Your Organization Ready for Work-Out?

When and Where to Start

IN OUR VIEW, every organization of more than a dozen or so people can benefit from Work-Out in some way. That means there's probably something Work-Out can do for you right now. But where do you start? How do you get moving?

As we have described elsewhere, even GE, after 10 years of Work-Out experience and several years of intense focus on the Six Sigma process, reinstituted a Work-Out blitz across the entire company in the year 2000. The reason? Bureaucracy keeps coming back, like weeds in the garden. Walls between functions and levels are always hardening, like drying cement. Focus on customers is hard to maintain. And business processes can always be streamlined. So every company always faces challenges where Work-Out can make a difference—either in reducing costs, reducing cycle times, accelerating innovation, or solving problems that cut across boundaries. And this applies to megafirms like GE as well as small businesses and start-ups.

But readiness is a different matter. A company can have a use for Work-Out—even a compelling need for Work-Out—when many of its key people are far from ready and willing to start the process. *Readiness*, then, is more of a psychological issue, a matter of motivation. And it is not necessarily logical or rational. People have an infinite capacity to avoid painful realities. Given how easy it is to deny that smoking is harmful to your health or to maintain that driving without a seatbelt is OK for you, it's hardly surprising how tempting it is to continue to do things on the job that are irrational but comfortable.

Here's a classic example: Several years ago, a prominent organization with strong business ties to GE came to Crotonville to learn how to "do Work-Out." At the time, this organization was struggling with cost, quality, and distribution issues, and many of its dominant market positions were eroding. So there was plenty to work on. But the company was highly balkanized, with many fiefdoms competing for power and influence. These dysfunctional behaviors were so deeply rooted that in the course of two days, the company's team could only come up with one recommendation in their Work-Out session—and then the business leader could not make a definitive decision on it. Everyone involved found it too uncomfortable to challenge the status quo or deal with conflict. Even the one recommendation was tabled for further discussion. And as a result of this experience, the company's management dropped the idea of using Work-Out as a tool for addressing the urgent problems they faced.

In this case, there certainly were business needs. But the motivation and ability to use Work-Out as a vehicle for addressing these needs was very low. What might prevent you and your organization from engaging in Work-Out—and how might you deal with these very real push-backs?

Get Ready for Resistance

As we have described, Work-Out is a relatively simple, straightforward process for attacking business problems, making rapid decisions, and creating an action-learning cycle. And almost every organization could use it. Yet despite its simplicity and proven track record, it's sure to run into resistance, just like any other approach to change. Sometimes overt resistance. Sometimes covert. But you can be sure resistance will be there. Here are three of the most common forms of resistance that we have seen:

- Been there, done that!
- We're fresh out of heroes around here!
- We're too small to tackle such a monster!

Been There, Done That

"We've done plenty of change programs already. We don't need another one."
In the last 20 years, almost every organization in the world has either
adopted or been exposed to dozens of change programs or problem-
solving tools. Wave after wave of panaceas have rolled across the corporate landscape, each one promising to bring its adopters into the
glorious perfection of health and balance. Untold billions of dollars
have been spent on quality circles, total-quality programs, reengineering, lean manufacturing, enterprise systems, and hosts of other programs and technologies.[1] And though almost all of these programs have
powerful elements, none of them are universal cure-alls. None of them
alone will lead an organization to perfection. In fact, some research has
shown that the more organizations spend on such corporate programs,
the less successful they are.[2]

Unfortunately, many senior executives still continue to adopt new
programs almost like the "flavor of the month." This faddish tendency
often masks the uncertainty that executives have about how to really
change their organizations, how to deal with performance shortfalls and
strategic challenges. It is often easier to hire a consultant or business
guru rather than to slog through the difficult work of managing organizational change and insisting on results.

In organizations where there have been many such programs, then,
Work-Out could easily be seen as just another fad. Program-weary
managers could quite logically (and rightly) say that they do not need
another program, especially when people are probably not fully exploiting the tools they already have.

If this is the case in your organization, there are several things you
can do. First, keep in mind that Work-Out is not a program or activity.
It is a methodology to support organizational change, solve problems,
and help managers get results. But it is not an end in and of itself.
Whether your organization has been through lots of programs or
not, Work-Out should never be positioned in terms of, "We need to do
Work-Out!"—as though the activity itself is a result. Instead, Work-
Out needs to be positioned in the context of achieving a business result
that needs to be achieved anyway, or attacking a problem that needs to
be solved in any case. The idea is not to do Work-Out just to do Work-
Out; it's to *use* Work-Out to bust bureaucracy, reduce costs, speed cycle

times, increase quality, accelerate new-product development, or address any of a host of other business issues.

Second, take a look at the other programs, activities, or tools that already exist in the organization, or have been introduced previously. Is there a way to create a compelling logic around the sequence of change initiatives and tools? Can you retrospectively show how they build on one another so that Work-Out is then adding to the tool kit rather than appearing as another disconnected activity. For example, quality circles began to give employees a voice; total quality added a focus on customers; reengineering provided tools for taking a systems perspective and asking "what-if" questions; enterprise software provided data to compare results across the organizational system; and Six Sigma added more-rigorous measurement and analytical tools. Given all this— Work-Out could be positioned as a process by which people use the earlier tools and perspectives to reach consensus across boundaries and accelerate the decision about what to do next.

Finally, try to avoid the temptation to start Work-Out everywhere with everyone. If your organization has already had lots of "corporate" programs that have involved hundreds or thousands of people, then don't continue this pattern with Work-Out. Start using Work-Out on a smaller scale. Think of it as an experiment. Try it with one or two low-key sessions, perhaps under the radar screen. In this way, nobody will complain about another corporate program. For example, when Patrick O'Sullivan became CEO of Eagle Star Insurance (which later became part of Zurich Financial Services UK), he found an organization that had tried every program that existed and had used dozens of consultants and gurus. People were highly skeptical of "another big thing" that would take lots of time and money and not get any results. Rather than try to fight the skepticism, O'Sullivan decided to start Work-Out with a small group that was already working on a "brand initiative" in a location far from the center of the company's operations. When participants there were enthusiastic, it then became far easier to try Work-Out in other locations, and eventually throughout the company.

We're Fresh Out of Heroes Around Here

"Our CEO doesn't have the right personality or skills to manage a Town Meeting. There's no reason to even think about taking that approach." Work-

Out clearly requires a senior executive who is ready, willing, and able to chair a Town Meeting and make on-the-spot decisions. This requirement is at the very heart of Work-Out. So what do you do if you think your senior executive is not up to the task?

First of all, it is important to recognize that no organization has the perfect senior executive with all the right skills to run a model Town Meeting. The Town Meeting itself is an intense developmental experience that always has as much learning in it for the senior executive as it does for the other participants. Every manager who runs a Town Meeting, for the first time or for the fiftieth time, always wishes for a chance to replay some part of the tape, to change an answer or a question or an inflection. Like any other unscripted human task, Town Meetings involve hundreds of unknown variables and no "one right way" to do things. So just as there is no senior executive who can run a perfect Town Meeting, there is no senior executive who cannot run an imperfect one. In other words, since they are all imperfect anyway, anyone can run one.

This isn't nearly as flippant as it sounds. The point is that the Town Meeting needs to be demystified for senior executives. One reason why senior executives sometimes resist participating is that they have built it up in their minds as some sort of high-stakes, Carnegie Hall performance that is far beyond the capability of ordinary human beings. With that image in mind, it is perfectly logical for a senior executive to find reasons why it's not the right time, or not the right issues, or not something that "will work for us." A few candid and open executives might even say that they don't have the right skills.

If you and other managers in your organization think of Town Meetings in this light, then one step you can take is to ratchet down the image. Play up the notion of imperfection and learning. And create a safe environment to practice. For example, at Armstrong World Industries, CEO Mike Lockhart wanted each of his senior executives to sponsor a Work-Out session and run a Town Meeting. But, realizing that many of them were anxious about it and didn't have a clear image in mind about what this really meant, Lockhart joined the first couple of managers at their Town Meetings and co-led the sessions. He modeled for them and with them what was involved in running a Town Meeting and stimulating dialogue. And afterwards, he debriefed with them about how it went and—most importantly—what he (and they) could have done differently. In other words, Lockhart made the Town Meeting a learning experience rather than a trial, and thus reduced the pressure to perform perfectly.

But what if you don't have a Mike Lockhart who can model the process? What if the Town Meeting is foreign territory to everyone? And what if you don't have a Jack Welch at the helm who is telling everyone to do it, whether they want to or not?

In this case, you can create some ways for managers to learn more about running a Town Meeting, and hopefully reduce their anxiety. For example, you can arrange for a senior manager to talk with another manager who has run a Town Meeting, perhaps in another company or another part of your company, and learn from that experience. You can arrange for a coach who has been through the process as a facilitator and can talk to you and your managers about the method. And you can practice on a small scale—with small groups addressing narrow or highly focused problems, such as how to get bills out earlier or how to reduce some category of administrative expenses.

Remember also that Work-Out does not need to start from the top and cascade down. If the CEO does not want to get involved, at least initially, look for other managers who have business issues to resolve, and who might be open to a Work-Out approach. For example, when GE Capital began Work-Out, CEO Gary Wendt was skeptical of the process, and he did not want to force his managers to do it. Two other managers in GE Capital, the CFO and the head of the Commercial Real Estate business, however, both heard about Work-Out and worked with the outside consultants to give it a try. And while their initial experiences were mixed, they saw enough positives that they were willing to encourage their boss, and their peers, to try it out. In fact, at a key meeting of the GE Capital executive team (its CEC), Wendt suggested that perhaps Capital should not participate in "Welch's Work-Out" and asked if anyone felt differently. The two executives who had experimented with it raised their hands and eloquently made the case to expand the process throughout Capital. Based on an extended debate, Wendt then encouraged others to try it—which opened up the process throughout the company.

Whatever you do, remember that the Town Meeting is a learning experience. As with golf or tennis, the only way to get better is to get out and play. Hit lots of balls. Practice the swing. So after each Town

Meeting, get some feedback—from participants, other managers, consultants. Was I overbearing? Did I listen enough? Did I solicit others' views sufficiently? Did I ask provocative questions and help people think through the issues, rather than just tell them my opinion? Did I encourage and reinforce good thinking? Did I help people understand why some recommendations could not be approved?

In essence, then, the most important skill for leading Work-Out is openness to learning. But if you don't have that, you are probably not reading this book.

We're Too Small to Tackle Such a Monster

"We can't afford to spend the time. . . . We don't have the resources of a GE. Work-Out is just too expensive for us." At first glance, Work-Out can appear intimidating. There is planning time. There may be food, facilities, and travel costs. There might be a need for outside consulting. And most of all, there is the lost time involved when you take large numbers of people out of their jobs for one, two, or three days at a time. So indeed, looking at the expense line alone can be intimidating.

If you want Work-Out to be effective in your organization, however, you need to focus on the other side of the equation—the payoff line. As with any tool for organizational change, you need to make sure that the measurable outcome is greater than the expense. If you cannot envision such a payoff, then you have chosen the wrong focus for Work-Out. In fact, in many organizations that we have worked with, senior managers insist on a 10× payoff—that is, the potential results from a Work-Out need to be 10 times greater than the expense involved.

Focusing on the payoff of a Work-Out means that the topics themselves need to be rich and meaty enough to have plenty of opportunity for gain. As much as possible, they should be stated in terms of measurable results—say, "reduce claims by 50 percent"—that can lead to a rough translation into dollars (or other currency). This also means that most of the individual recommendations from the teams also need to be stated in terms that have a measurable-results goal.

We have found that even simple and straightforward bureaucracy-reduction objectives can be "dollarized" in a way that makes the outcome clear and compelling. For example, in a GE Capital Work-Out, a team recommended that they send automobile-fleet-leasing customers only summary reports of monthly usage, not all the backup detail. In addition to checking with customers about this idea (and finding strong support), the team also calculated the cost savings involved. This included less paper and postage; reductions in computer processing time; labor savings from less handling, checking, and so on; and less customer-service time responding to questions raised by unnecessary data. When this was all added up, it amounted to hundreds of thousands of dollars—which paid for the Work-Out session many times over.

From Resistance to Readiness

Obviously, every organization is unique—with its own business challenges, management processes, and human culture. Therefore, the three types of resistance we have outlined here are probably not universal—and are certainly not exhaustive. You will undoubtedly find additional and different areas of resistance, or at least hesitation, in your own situation.

To help you shape a Work-Out process that can address your unique organizational issues and potential resistance points, we have developed a self-diagnostic that will help you assess areas where Work-Out might be particularly useful—or where you might need to tailor the focus or positioning of Work-Out. The underlying premise is, as we have stated, that every organization has a business need for Work-Out. Readiness, however, depends on whether the pressure for resolving the business need—and addressing other, softer issues—is stronger than the natural tendency to maintain the status quo. This instrument will help you make that determination.

Instructions

The following questionnaire includes nine sections, with three items in each section. For each item, circle a number from 1 to 10, indicating whether the item applies to your organization "somewhat" (1), "regularly" (5), or "fully" (10). When you have completed the questionnaire, add up the separate scores *for each of the nine categories*. After compiling your score for each category, review the scoring guidelines that follow the questionnaire for possible interpretations.

SELF-ASSESSMENT:
IS YOUR ORGANIZATION READY FOR WORK-OUT?

	APPLIES			
	SOMEWHAT	REGULARLY	FULLY	SCORE
1. Business Impetus				
a. We have important business issues that need to be tackled faster than we're likely to get to them.	1 2 3 4 5 6 7 8 9 10			
b. Many of our critical business issues need cross-functional attention.	1 2 3 4 5 6 7 3 9 10			
c. The organization is facing a crisis, but most people don't realize it.	1 2 3 4 5 6 7 8 9 10			
Total: Business Impetus				
2. Information Flow				
a. Employees don't understand the link between what they do and the strategic priorities of the business.	1 2 3 4 5 6 7 8 9 10			
b. The only measures of performance are financial.	1 2 3 4 5 6 7 8 9 10			
c. Detailed knowledge of competitors' performance is concentrated in a few hands, unavailable to parts of the organization that should have it.	1 2 3 4 5 6 7 8 9 10			
Total: Information Flow				
3. Customer Focus				
a. Customer knowledge is confined to pockets of the organization (such as sales, marketing, senior executives).	1 2 3 4 5 6 7 8 9 10			
b. The response to customer demands is usually piecemeal or incomplete.	1 2 3 4 5 6 7 8 9 10			
c. Customers are complaining or leaving, but we don't clearly understand why.	1 2 3 4 5 6 7 3 9 10			
Total: Customer Focus				

	APPLIES			SCORE
	SOMEWHAT	REGULARLY	FULLY	

4. Decision Making

a. Decision making is out of balance—either so concentrated that people run into delays and bottlenecks or so dispersed that accountability or power to make a decision is unclear. 1 2 3 4 5 6 7 8 9 10

b. There is a lot of red tape, with multiple sign-offs required for most nonroutine matters. 1 2 3 4 5 6 7 8 9 10

c. People are afraid to make decisions on their own—so they always buck them up to someone else. 1 2 3 4 5 6 7 8 9 10

Total: Decision Making

5. Leadership

a. Top management's desired future direction doesn't seem to be getting the attention and action it needs. 1 2 3 4 5 6 7 8 9 10

b. We rarely try projects involving a cross-section of front-line employees and managers. 1 2 3 4 5 6 7 8 9 10

c. Senior leaders do not support one another's projects. 1 2 3 4 5 6 7 8 9 10

Total: Leadership

6. Organizational Bureaucracy

a. Our organization has lots of layers. 1 2 3 4 5 6 7 8 9 10

b. We have lots of rules, many of them contradictory or confusing. 1 2 3 4 5 6 7 8 9 10

c. Our organization has a rigid structure that hasn't really changed in years, despite any attempts at paper reorganization. 1 2 3 4 5 6 7 8 9 10

Total: Organizational Bureaucracy

	APPLIES										SCORE
	SOMEWHAT				REGULARLY				FULLY		
7. Communication											
a. We avoid disagreement and debate, especially between levels.	1	2	3	4	5	6	7	8	9	10	
b. Front-line employees think senior leaders are out of touch.	1	2	3	4	5	6	7	8	9	10	
c. The means of communication in our organization run mostly one way.	1	2	3	4	5	6	7	8	9	10	
Total: Communication											
8. Culture											
a. Managers tend to protect their own turf.	1	2	3	4	5	6	7	8	9	10	
b. People tend to avoid accountability for their results.	1	2	3	4	5	6	7	8	9	10	
c. Suggestions are usually greeted with "we've tried that before and it didn't work."	1	2	3	4	5	6	7	8	9	10	
Total: Culture											
9. Innovation											
a. Innovation and change is mandated by senior managers rather than coming from experiments on the front line.	1	2	3	4	5	6	7	8	9	10	
b. Risk-taking is not rewarded.	1	2	3	4	5	6	7	8	9	10	
c. We don't learn and share with each other.	1	2	3	4	5	6	7	8	9	10	
Total: Innovation											

Scoring Guide

As noted, we firmly believe that any organization can benefit from Work-Out if people are willing to give it a real try. Nonetheless, internal conditions will militate for or against the effort, and the project is best presented in terms of an area where either the need for change or the ability to capitalize on the method—or both—can be readily perceived as high. The scores for each area can all be interpreted as favoring Work-Out, but some more directly than others. Here's how we read each of the nine areas:

I. Strength of Business Impetus

Score 3–12: Low pressure for change. For Work-Out to be effective, business leaders might need to communicate a compelling reason for action—perhaps an impending competitive threat or technological breakthrough.

Score 13–21: Moderate pressure for change. Work-Out could be used to speed up the organization's response and increase the level of innovation.

Score 22–30: Acute pressure for change. Work-Out could be used to make a rapid, coordinated response to specific business threats or opportunities.

2. Ease of Information Flow

Score 3–12: Information flow is already good. Work-Out could harness some of the available data for focused action.

Score 13–21: Information flow is constrained. Work-Out could be used to get information flowing more freely across the organization.

Score 22–30: Information flow is severely limited. Work-Out could be used to open up a flow of information between two or three key groups or functions.

3. Degree of Customer Focus

Score 3–12: High level of customer focus and awareness. Perhaps build on this by organizing Work-Out efforts that focus on customers—or even with customers.

Score 13–21: Moderate level of customer focus and awareness. Use Work-Out to sharpen the company's sensitivity to customer issues.

Score 22–30: Low level of customer focus and awareness. Work-Out could start to develop a stronger customer focus.

4. Decision Making

Score 3–12: Decision making is shared and accountability is clear. Work-Out could build on these positives and reinforce them.

Score 13–21: Decision making tends to be fragmented or too narrowly controlled. Work-Out could help broaden the involvement of senior managers and sharpen accountability for the results.

Score 22–30: Decision making is slow and accountability is unclear or too focused on a few overburdened decision makers. Work-Out could be used to get more executives involved and to clarify accountability.

5. Leadership

Score 3–12: Executives are probably ready for a fast-paced effort that crosses organizational boundaries.

Score 13–21: Executives may be ready to see how Work-Out can help break down functional silos and deliver results. Perhaps a couple of executives could join forces to sponsor a Work-Out.

Score 22–30: Executives may find the cross-functional nature of Work-Out a challenge. Identifying a sponsor and high-level champions will be critical to success. Find a first sponsor with wide credibility.

6. Level of Organizational Bureaucracy

Score 3–12: Bureaucracy is under reasonable control. Work-Out can help make sure the weeds are not growing back into the garden.

Score 13–21: Bureaucracy is an issue and Work-Out can help.

Score 22–30: The organization may be getting crushed by its own bureaucracy. Work-Out could be helpful to break through unnecessary rules, procedures, and paperwork.

7. Communication

Score 3–12: Communication is reasonably open. Work-Out is likely to feel natural and comfortable to many participants.

Score 13–21: There is some constraint in communication. Work-Out can help tap resources of employee ingenuity that are currently being neglected, and expand the quality of feedback to senior leaders on the effectiveness of organizational systems.

Score 22–30: Communications are severely blocked, and Work-Out could release a torrent of creativity and innovation. However, it will require strong, overt support, as employees may be wary of participating. Recruitment of a senior sponsor who can encourage and actively listen to employee input will be important to success.

8. Supportiveness of the Culture

Score 3–12: The culture is open to change. Work-Out could be helpful in sharpening accountability and providing a forum for rapid action on a critical business issue—creating some new business heroes in the process.

Score 13–21: The culture is somewhat open to change, but does not have mechanisms to support radical or cross-functional innovation. In these environments, Work-Out can be an effective tool for capturing employees' ideas and showcasing successful change.

Score 22–30: The culture is set into functional silos and discourages people from stepping outside the box. Success with Work-Out could come from presenting it as a safe structure for change and cross-functional experimentation.

9. Strength of Innovation

Score 3–12: Innovation is already evident throughout the organization. Work-Out could be used to anchor that innovation on high-priority issues with a direct impact on the business.

Score 13–21: Innovation exists in pockets but is not broadly encouraged. Work-Out offers a way to increase the quality or speed of innovation in critical areas.

Score 22–30: Change is driven by senior management—and may be too slow. More front-line innovation and risk taking is needed. Work-Out provides a forum for focused experimentation that does not jeopardize the organization or take too long.

A Final Thought

The value of the self-diagnostic instrument in this chapter is not in the numbers themselves—it's in stimulating dialogue about where and how Work-Out might be useful. Therefore, we suggest that you do not just fill in the blanks on your own. Instead, bring together a small group of people in your organization. Have everyone fill it out independently, and then compare your answers. If the group that does this is cross-functional and maybe even cross-level, the discussion might even simulate a Work-Out session.

In any case, use this discussion to think through the issues that might be most appropriate to tackle using Work-Out, and how best to position Work-Out in your organization. Where might there be resistance, and how might you overcome it? How can you show that the payoffs will be greater than the costs? How can Work-Out help you address soft and hard issues?

Once you have had this conversation, you are ready to make use of Part Two of this book—the actual guide to implementing Work-Out. The next chapter provides an overview of how to get started quickly—and subsequent chapters take you through the process step by step.

How to Lead a Fast, Simple Work-Out— When You've Never Done It Before

As WITH ANY change process, the best way to understand Work-Out is to dive in and do it, rather than just talk about it. You can introduce Work-Out to your organization in just a few hours by having an established work group tackle a relatively simple problem, generate ideas for solving it, and immediately present the ideas to a senior leader for a go/no-go decision. When you strip Work-Out down to its barest essentials, it still works—and it becomes its own best advertisement.

One exercise that has proved useful in a fast, simple Work-Out is called "Wasteful Work Practices" (see Figure 4-1). You can hand this exercise to almost any group of managers and employees, in almost any kind of organization, with very little prior preparation or planning. The only preliminary work needed is to arrange the participation of a senior business leader who will agree to make decisions on ideas in the Town Meeting portion of the session.

To run the exercise, start with a brief explanation of Work-Out, its history at your organization (or elsewhere, if you're just starting), and its purpose. Then give participants the Wasteful Work Practices sheet to fill out individually. Almost everyone can identify parts of their daily round that don't make sense. After a few minutes of individual think-

Figure 4-1. Wasteful Work Practices: A Subjective Survey.

Everyone in organizations, at one time or another, finds that there are recurring work practices—reports, approvals, measures, meetings, reviews, procedures, and so on and on—that take time and effort, but don't seem to add real value, or value commensurate with the effort involved.

1. In the space below, please describe a work practice that you or your people have been doing in the past month or two whose value might be questionable.

2. What's your guess about how many people are involved in this work practice across your company?

3. How much total time would you estimate is spent on the practice?

ing, ask people to form several small teams. (The size and number of teams depends on the size of the group—you want at least 3 people on a team but no more than 12, and at least 2 teams but preferably 3 to 5, so as to give a good idea of the variety of the process.) In the teams, members can share their individual answers and generate additional ideas for the wasteful-work-practices list. Then ask the teams each to select one or two practices that, if eliminated or changed, would make the most difference to them. The teams then present these ideas to the senior business leader at the Town Meeting. The whole session, from introductory remarks through final decisions, can fit into a few hours.

Mike Lockhart (a former GE business leader) used this approach to introduce his senior management team to Work-Out when he became

CEO of Armstrong World Industries. Instead of intellectualizing about Work-Out or telling GE stories, he quickly encouraged them to identify streamlining and simplification opportunities in their own backyards. Among other ideas, the team discussed the way their strategic-planning process took months of effort to produce stacks of data binders—none of which was ever used effectively as a basis for making management decisions. When Lockhart gave them the immediate go-ahead to cancel the standard planning process and design something that would be more effective, they quickly understood what Work-Out was all about.

Express Work-Outs

Many issues take more thought than a fast, simple, few-hour Work-Out has room for, but these can still be dealt with briskly. In many organizations, one-day Work-Outs, what we call "express" Work-Outs, are very useful in a location such as a plant, a sales office, or a distribution center. In such cases, sessions can be held on-site, and resources from the location can be brought in on an as-needed basis to help the working teams. Most importantly, the senior-most person at the site—the plant manager, for example—can be the decision maker at the Town Meeting. If that person has the authority needed to make decisions for the site, then there is no need to bring in a more-senior person from regional or corporate headquarters.

To make express sessions effective, some prior planning is necessary to make sure that the problems on the table are within the scope and authority of the participants and the decision maker. You wouldn't want to ask a plant team to focus on product-mix issues if such decisions depended on systemwide capacity, materials, and skills planning—perspectives that are likely to be far beyond the local plant. However, that same plant team could very likely address ways of managing product changeovers more quickly and efficiently so as to improve their own plant's productivity.

Once the focus is decided, participants can then be selected, facilitators assigned, and the session can proceed. If nobody is coming in from out of town, and the session is being held on site, then the cycle time from planning to execution can be a matter of days—even hours. Figure 4-2 provides an example of a typical one-day agenda from an express

Work-Out session at a GE plant. The focus of this session was on reducing internal bureaucracy and improving productivity. The plant manager was the sponsor and decision maker. All participants and facilitators were from the plant, although corporate functional leaders and their staffs at the business-unit headquarters were available to the teams by telephone.

Note that each team assignment in this example was extremely focused and narrow so that participants could indeed make progress in

Figure 4-2. Express Work-Out at a GE Plant.

8:00 A.M.	Business update (Plant manager)
8:30	Work-Out overview, instructions to the teams, and warm-up exercise (Facilitator)
10:00	Work sessions (Teams, meeting in breakout rooms)

- Team 1: **Time Cards:** Do we need them? If not, what is the alternative for ensuring scheduling compliance and proper payroll?

- Team 2: **Engineering Man-Hour Sheets:** Do we need them? If not, how do we track engineering costs?

- Team 3: **Appropriation Requests:** How can we streamline the process and reduce the cycle time for decisions?

- Team 4: **Highlights Reports:** How can we report on our monthly activities more efficiently?

- Team 5: **Meetings:** Which ones do we need, and which can be eliminated or streamlined? How can we make all meetings more efficient?

12:00 P.M.	Working lunch (Everyone sits with people from other teams to share ideas and get input.)
1:00	Work sessions (Team meetings continue; main task is to prepare presentations.)
2:30	Town Meeting (Each team will have up to 20–30 minutes for presentation and discussion.)
5:00	Adjourn

just a few hours. In addition, although team members were from different functions, the topics were familiar to everyone, so the teams didn't need to dig into the background and bring people up to speed. In planning a one-day Work-Out, you need to make sure that the problems being addressed really are narrow enough to attack effectively in the short time available. Giving people their topics ahead of time can also help participants arrive at the session with some preliminary ideas and with input from their colleagues.

One-day designs also require that other agenda topics that might be included in a longer Work-Out (as described in the next section of the book) are either truncated or eliminated altogether. In this example, the plant manager provided a quick (30-minute) business update, but did not make an extended strategy presentation. The teams did not share their preliminary ideas with each other, except during an informal lunch break. And the teams were not expected to polish their presentations or make dry runs with other teams. In other words, there were very few "local" stops on the Work-Out "express."

Using an "Express" Work-Out to Enhance the Productivity of an Existing Team

Express-type Work-Outs, carried out in a day or less with minimal planning, also can be useful for periodically strengthening the functioning of an existing team. All ongoing teams—whether they work together on a shop floor, or provide leadership for an entire organization—fall into patterns that may eventually become inefficient or even counterproductive. When these patterns are not reexamined and refreshed, team members are often frustrated with "the way things work around here" or the "lack of leadership."

Many organizations resort to team-building activities when the frustration level of an existing team starts to rise or there is a sense that the team is not working well together. But focusing on the interpersonal and team dynamics, without also changing the underlying working patterns, usually only creates temporary improvement. People may feel better about each other, and may appreciate each other's styles and differences, but the root causes of much of the frustration—inefficient or poorly designed work processes—remain in place, quickly canceling out the short-term "good feelings." By designing an express Work-Out process for an exist-

(Continued)

ing team, perhaps even combined with more traditional team building, change and improvement can be much more lasting.

The Simmons Graduate School of Management Case

The administrative leadership team of the Simmons Graduate School of Management provides a good example of how an express Work-Out can quickly enhance team performance. Located in Boston's Back Bay, Simmons GSM is the country's premier graduate management program designed especially for women. In the Fall of 2000, Dean Patricia O'Brien and her administrative directors planned a one-day retreat, hoping to improve communications, raise morale, and reduce turnover among the 25 members of the administrative team. At the suggestion of consultant Debbie Burke, who had previously facilitated Work-Outs as an internal staff member at GE, O'Brien and her team agreed to build the retreat around a morning exercise to improve interpersonal communications, followed by an afternoon Work-Out session on administrative processes. O'Brien's hope was that this combination would not only help people feel better about being part of the administrative team, but would also improve the team's overall performance.

In preparation for the Work-Out portion of the retreat, the participants were each asked to identify their key tasks, the conditions that supported their accomplishment, and the obstacles to be overcome—and to write these out on color-coded index cards. At the beginning of the Work-Out session (the afternoon of the retreat), the staff broke into their regular work groups, each of which included a director and up to five people—while Dean O'Brien went back to the office. In these clusters, participants presented their task information to each other and posted their index cards on the wall—sorted (with different colors) by task, helping conditions, and hindering conditions.

At this stage, Debbie Burke asked each participant to rank her tasks according to importance in pursuing the GSM mission—educating women for power and leadership. This lens of "mission criticality" immediately reframed people's understanding of their work. As might happen in any organization, some people found that they spent a lot of time on work that did not directly support or even enhance the mission. When this was realized, each work group would discuss why this was so, and what it meant. Could a line of sight be drawn from a simple task like answering the phone to serving the mission? Yes. The line wiggled a little. It was not as direct as, for example, organizing a student's internship placement or helping a student research an idea for a new business, but it was related to the overall image the school wanted to communicate. In

(Continued)

reviewing and ranking the tasks in each department, all the participants gained a level of clarity about where they were spending their resources—and where they might spend them more effectively. This is a key early step to taking unnecessary work out of an organization.

During this session, people's attention was intensely focused within their own group. As the task rankings were established, people also talked about helping and hindering conditions. Coworkers soon discovered that although helping forces were quite varied, the hindering conditions tended to center around communication (not having the right information at the right time) and technology (not being able to access or manipulate information easily). It didn't take long for the small work groups to start peeking at their colleagues' charts to see if they were identifying the same problems. Nearly all were.

By midafternoon, people were exploring the work terrain of their neighbors by wandering over to other groups. As semi-outsiders, they were able to add helpful observations as their colleagues worked. But more notable, they were able to see similarities among the different groups' actual work and their analyses of it.

After a brief break, Debbie brought the entire group back together so that the departments could quickly present to each other. There was considerable tension and excitement as the work groups presented their analyses. As the reports were given, Debbie began to note recurring themes on the flip charts at the front of the room.

Partway into the reports, it was clear that communication and technology were the key obstacles most tasks bumped into. No one had to sit and analyze this, no great tools or algorithms had to be used to make sense of the data. It bubbled up with obvious strength, so clearly that no negotiations were required when it was time to pick the primary recommendations to make to Dean O'Brien.

The group spent the final hour of the Work-Out session devising specific recommendations based on the problem issues raised during the day. Some things they could deal with on their own in their own departments; others they put in a shape to present to the Dean for her resolution. Information systems problems were identified and reviewed. Some couldn't be fixed immediately because they were generated by universitywide systems characteristics. But people who knew how to work around the problems identified themselves as "expert resources" to whom others could go for help. Other problems could be ameliorated by training, which some staff members agreed to either provide or to arrange for those who needed it. The resolutions to these problems did not require any significant expen-

(Continued)

diture of time or money, just recognition of what was needed and who could provide it.

From Recommendations to Results

In a typical Work-Out session, the leader comes back at the end to receive recommendations in the Town Meeting. Since Dean O'Brien was obliged to attend another meeting, and could not come back, the Simmons GSM Work-Out built in a small hiatus—from the Friday afternoon of the retreat until the regularly scheduled Tuesday directors' meeting the next week. This meeting was expanded in size and time allotment to accommodate the entire staff and was dedicated to reporting the Work-Out's recommendations.

In the Town Meeting, staff members recreated the retreat ambiance by hanging up all the posters and work papers that had been developed the previous Friday. This sustained the feeling as well as the information generated, and served to include Dean O'Brien in the experience.

As in any typical Work-Out Town Meeting, a number of recommendations were identified, justified, and presented to the Dean for her approval. The presentations were made by staff members. Directors had already signed up to be the owners of specific recommendations. The main recommendations, all of which were accepted, are summarized in Figure 4-3.

A year later, O'Brien identified a number of "lasting institutional changes," which she attributes to the Fall 2000 Work-Out retreat:

— *Enhanced communication.* Regular staff meetings assure that people in all departments are apprised of initiatives or problems that cut across departments.
— *Reduced turnover.* Turnover, which had been running high enough to be an ongoing concern, has virtually ceased. The last departures from the administrative staff took place four months after the Work-Out. O'Brien attributes the change to people's increased understanding of their role in fulfilling the school's mission, and their increased ability to work smoothly across departments.
— *Greater adaptability.* The staff has begun to take the initiative individually and as a group, without waiting for their directors to make assignments to them.

In short, by using an express Work-Out, with minimal preparation, as part of a staff retreat, the Simmons GSM administrative team not only improved communications, but created lasting improvements in productivity.

(Continued)

Figure 4-3. Simmons GSM Work-Out Recommendations.

1. *Establish a weekly cross-department staff meeting.*
   - **Problem:** Staff members do not have enough information about what is happening in other departments.
   - **Impact of problem:** Work is unevenly distributed, causing some departments to be overworked while people in others have slack time and would be willing to chip in if they knew their help was needed.
   - **Desired improvement:** Better formal and informal communication across departments; interdepartmental opportunities identified early; work more evenly distributed.
   - **Plan:** Hold the meetings semimonthly and include all members of the staff. Allow any staff member to submit an agenda item. Arrange for items that cannot be resolved within the meeting to be delegated to an appropriate cross-functional team.
   - **Responsibility:** Responsibility for creating the agenda, running the meeting, and circulating follow-up communication will rotate among staff members.
   - **Participation:** All staff members, managers, and directors. Anyone may put items on the agenda. The dean will be invited when her input is required for a decision, and she will also be able to ask to attend when she has information to share.
   - **Owner:** Wendy D'Ambrose, Director of Career Services

2. *Improve training and coaching in communication and database software.*
   - **Problem:** Not everyone is facile in all the key programs. There is no established plan for training new employees when they come aboard. Some programs are old and difficult, and upgrades and informal improvements are not documented.
   - **Impact of problem:** People do not have access to the information they need. They cannot share data easily and feel incompetent if they cannot use the programs.
   - **Desired improvement:** Everyone will be able to do her recurring computer tasks more easily and will know who to go to for help with specific problems. The importance of certain systems improvements will be raised to the College MIS organization.
   - **Plan:** Individuals with expertise are identified as the "go-to" people for questions on each program. Shortcuts and tips for difficult programs will be documented and circulated. Andrea Bruce and Dean O'Brien will work with the college MIS organizion to assure that GSM's required program upgrades and replacements receive higher

(Continued)

Figure 4-3. *(Continued)*

priority. Andrea Bruce will be appointed to the collegewide technology governance committee.
- **Responsibility:** Individual volunteers with specific expertise to offer.
- **Participation:** Everyone, as needed.
- **Owner:** Andrea Bruce, Director of Admissions and Marketing.

3. *Circulate clear communication after directors' meetings.*
   - **Problem:** Staff members do not have as much information as they need from directors about policies and current events.
   - **Impact:** Employees feel left out, or disempowered; rumors fill the vacuum created by too little information.
   - **Desired Improvement:** All staff will feel "in the loop" about what is happening and how they might contribute.
   - **Plan:** Directors will prepare a bulleted list of main points to share from the directors' meeting and will use it to share information with their staffs as soon as practical after the meeting. This will be done face to face immediately, or in the next scheduled departmental staff meeting. In addition, when needed, the directors will prepare a communication e-mail containing the critical "who, what, where, when, and why important" for circulation to the entire staff.
   - **Responsibility:** It is the responsibility of the directors to communicate news from their meetings, and the responsibility of their staffs to ask for the information they need. Responsibility for all-hands written communication will be rotated as appropriate.
   - **Participation:** All directors.
   - **Owner:** Mary Dutkiewicz, Director, MBA/administration.

When Express Is Not Enough: Getting Started Quickly on the Full-Blown Version of Work-Out

Many business topics and challenges, of course, cannot be handled in one day, and might therefore require a full-blown, multiday Work-Out event, along with some amount of follow-up. Part II of this book, beginning in the next chapter, provides a detailed, step-by-step guide for planning, conducting, and following up on this kind of Work-Out. But if you are thinking about Work-Out for the first time, don't be intimidated by the size and detail of Part II. Keep it simple and straightforward. Just pick out the elements that you need, and get started.

That's what Marty Turock did when he headed GE Canada's Silicones business in early 1991. This case study will give you a good role model to follow for your first Work-Out, especially if you also use some of the valuable tools in Appendix A: The Work-Out Leader's Tool Kit.

Planning the Work-Out

In 1991, GE Canada Silicones was a stand-alone division of GE Plastics, employing 80 people in two small factories, a Toronto head office, and several sales offices. Although 1990 had been a good year for the business, Turock wanted 1991 to be more than just good—he wanted it to be a banner year. To that end, he decided to challenge his business team, all 80 people, to achieve their entire 1991 year-end sales and net-income goals early—by October 31st instead of by December 31st. And he used Work-Out to make it happen.

To get started, in February of 1991, Turock held a couple of meetings with one of GE Canada's Work-Out consultants, Suzanne Francis, and his head of Operations, Mike Geisinger. After describing what he wanted to do, the three of them identified the main areas of the business that would have to change in order to close out the year early. For example, the sales force would have to expand sales from existing customers and find several new ones. Manufacturing would need to increase its capacity, without increasing its unit costs. Bills would need to go out faster. Collections would need to accelerate their cycle times. Purchasing would need to source raw materials in response to changing production schedules. Distribution would need to find ways of delivering products faster and with less expense. All in all, they identified nine key areas—largely organized around existing functions. They then assigned all 80 people in the company—managers, professionals, secretaries, and factory workers—to the nine areas (mostly by function) and invited them to a Work-Out that was to be held in early March.

> If you are planning a Work-Out for the first time, start by identifying what you want to achieve—the elimination of bureaucracy, a step-up in sales, or the reduction of cycle times, for example. Think about who will need to be involved in achieving the goal, or goals—regardless of rank or title. Put together some teams to tackle different areas that might make a contribution. Then find a place to hold your Work-Out session, invite the people, and

mark the date. And remember, you don't need to do all of this by yourself—you can find a Work-Out consultant or ask a couple of members of your staff to help you with the design. More detail about how to do this is included in the next section of this book.

Conducting the Work-Out

Marty Turock opened the Silicones Work-Out by reviewing the entire business picture—the numbers from the previous year, what competitors were doing, customer needs, and the financial commitments for 1991. He then challenged the group to deliver early—and told them that while he didn't know how that could be achieved, he believed in them—that they could come up with the answers. Suzanne Francis then gave a brief introduction to the Work-Out process and the agenda for the next two days, and the session was off and running. Turock left and the nine small teams got to work.

As could be expected, Turock's challenge to the business did not meet with universal enthusiasm. Most people in Silicones already felt stretched—believing that the numbers they were committed to achieving for the whole year were already ambitious. The sales people, for example, couldn't imagine that their customers would need to buy more product, or buy it more quickly. And many of the manufacturing people—long-time unionized shop-floor workers—thought that the whole idea was crazy, especially given the antiquated equipment with which they worked.

After giving each team some time to talk about the assignment (and complain in many cases), the facilitators helped each team begin brainstorming possible actions. And much to everyone's amazement, creative solutions started to emerge. The sales team, for example, identified existing customers with the greatest potential for buying additional products, existing customers that might be at risk, and potential new customers that might utilize Silicone's products. They then developed specific "call programs" for meeting with these customers, with clearer accountabilities and short time frames. And they eliminated some administrative processes and paperwork that would give them additional time to make the calls. Similarly, manufacturing came up with several ideas for accelerating equipment change-overs, cleaning equipment faster, and scheduling production runs differently—all to add capacity without requiring an additional shift.

After a full day of brainstorming, prioritizing, developing recommendations, and conducting dry-run presentations, Marty Turock returned for the Town Meeting. Over the course of four hours, he heard 36 specific recommendations, and approved 30 of them. Each recommendation was presented using an LCD projector with a laptop—so as the discussion went on, and changes were made to the recommendation, they were recorded in real time.

At the end of the Town Meeting, Turock had a chart on the wall with all 30 of the approved recommendations, each with its expected results in terms of sales and/or net income acceleration. He then created a rough "scorecard" for the recommendations—marking some of them as "easy to achieve" and others as "difficult." For the "difficult" ones, Turock discounted the expected results by 50 percent—and then added up all the numbers. To his satisfaction, and the satisfaction of the entire Silicones business team, the goal looked achievable. At least on paper, 12 months of results could be delivered in 10.

The Work-Out event itself has several elements, spread over the course of two to three days. If you are the business leader, your job is to kick off the Work-Out by establishing the business "context" and challenge. Help the participants understand the overall goals of the business, and how the Work-Out topic fits in. Then, like Marty Turock, you can leave and return when it's time for the Town Meeting. While you are away, your Work-Out consultant and facilitators will help the participants brainstorm ideas in small groups, prioritize the best ideas, and create recommendations that they will present to you. Before you return, they will dry-run these presentations and try to eliminate the overlap. But it's a real-time process, without a lot of real time. So don't worry if things are a bit messy. In any case, when you return, it will be time for the Town Meeting. At that point, you will have a chance to listen to each recommendation and have a dialogue with the entire group about it. After each idea is presented and discussed, you will need to make a decision—thumbs up or thumbs down. That will be the hardest part—but also the most rewarding. With so many smart and experienced people in the room, representing so many parts of your business, most of the ideas will be pretty good.

Following Up on Recommendations

Translating results from a paper chart to a bottom line, however, requires more than just good ideas. To make sure that the recommendations really happened at Silicones, Turock created a follow-up process that he called the "breakfast of champions." Every other week, Turock held a breakfast meeting in his office with the "champions" for each recommendation. After serving Wheaties and milk, Turock went around the table and reviewed each idea—what was working, what problems were emerging, and what else could be done. Based on this meeting, Turock then updated his "scorecard" of recommendations—tracking actual results that everyone in the business could see, and adding new ideas as they bubbled up.

Eventually, even the most skeptical of Silicone's people came on board and started to contribute. Sales people found new applications for their products with existing customers and won several new and significant new customers. The plants ramped up their productivity and increased their manufacturing flexibility, without adding to their unit costs. The finance organization developed electronic invoicing and payment programs to accelerate billings and collections. Success bred success, and by the Fall, the goals for the year were within reach. When they were actually achieved and booked on October 31st, Turock held a gala "New Year's" party for the entire Silicones team—a new year that came two months early.

> **Work-Out does not end when the event concludes. After any Work-Out session, there is a need for follow-up. As a business leader, you should organize some sort of regular review process with the champions or sponsors of the various ideas. Sometimes they will run into brick walls in trying to make things happen, and they will need your support and guidance about how to proceed. Other times, they will find that ideas at the Work-Out session need to be modified or adjusted, and they will want to talk about that too. And at other times, they will just want encouragement, reinforcement, and recognition—natural human desires. The important thing, however, is to keep the follow-up grounded as a disciplined business process—what was intended, what was really done, what results were achieved, and what was**

learned. Asking those questions ensures that Work-Out is treated as an ongoing opportunity to improve the business, and not just an isolated, one-time event. To reinforce that further, the follow-up should also include some broader communication to the entire organization (like Turock's scorecard), and of course, some time to celebrate.

Making It Easy

The purpose of this chapter was to help you get started quickly down the Work-Out pathway, by giving you several illustrations of how you can just "plunge in"—either with a few hours of Work-Out, a one-day session, or a multiple-day design. In all three cases, Work-Out still has the same basics—a group of people that gets together quickly, solves business problems, presents them to a business leader for "yes-no" decisions, and then follows up to make them happen.

Part II of this book gives you complete details about how to plan, conduct, and follow up on a full-blown Work-Out, as well as a number of ideas and examples for variations in different situations. But if you want to skip all the detail and cut to the chase, Figure 4.4 provides a quick reference guide that can help you get through the process—fast.

The "Plan" Stage

1. Select a business problem for the Work-Out (bureaucracy-busting, process improvement, supply-chain integration, etc.) The written goal should include:
   - The estimated impact if the improvements are achieved.
   - Several likely improvement opportunities, or problem areas.
   - a 12-week or shorter timeline for implementation
2. Get organizational and senior-management support for the Work-Out:
   - Get the senior manager (the Sponsor) on board and make sure he or she is ready to listen to and openly discuss improvement recommendations at the Town Meeting, then make a

---

Figure 4-4. A Work-Out Reference Guide.

decision on the spot, in public. The Sponsor should plan the agenda with the design team and oversee the preparation and follow-up of the Work-Out, or delegate this work to a "Champion."

- Organize a design team, led by the Champion, to plan the Work-Out, create a work-flow chart or process map of the issues involved, and delegate areas of the problem to the Work-Out teams.
- Recruit cross-functional teams of employees and managers close to the problem. These teams do the core work of the Work-Out: brainstorming and selecting improvement ideas, making recommendations to the Sponsor at the Town Meeting, and implementing the recommendations that are approved.

3. Arrange the logistics for the Work-Out event, including:
   - Team facilitators
   - Location

The "Conduct" Stage

The Work-Out Event typically consists of five sessions that take place over the course of one to three days, depending on your "design."

1. Introduction: Brief participants on the business strategy, the goals and agenda for the Work-Out, and the culminating event: the Town Meeting. Review the process and ground rules (no sacred cows, no "turf-defending," no blaming, no pulling rank by managers, no complaining; focus on solutions).
2. Brainstorming: Multiple cross-functional teams each brainstorm a different aspect of the problem. Each team creates a list of top 10 ideas for achieving the team's assigned goal. Use the "Pay-Off Matrix" in Chapter 7 to prioritize ideas.
3. The Gallery of Ideas: Each Work-Out team presents its 10 best ideas to the rest of the Work-Out participants. Participants vote on the best 3–4 ideas worth implementing from each team's top 10.
4. Generate Action Plans: Teams use the remaining time to develop an action plan for implementing the selected ideas, and to prepare a presentation, including supporting data, requesting approval for the idea from the Sponsor at the Town Meeting. Each idea must have an "owner" who will take responsibility for seeing it through implementation if it is approved.
5. The Town Meeting: Teams present their recommendations to the Sponsor. The Sponsor dialogues with the team and other partici-

Figure 4-4. *(Continued)*

pants about the viability of the idea, and asks for input from managers who will be affected by the team's recommendation, before making a "yes/no" decision, on the spot.

The "Implement" Stage

1. Action recommendations are implemented by project owners and teams within 12 weeks—to meet the goal established at the outset of the Work-Out.
2. The Sponsor organizes a review process of some sort to track progress and help the project owners with any problems they might encounter.
3. Results of the Work-Out and progress along the way are communicated to the entire organization.
4. The impact of all action recommendations is assessed for the entire Work-Out.
5. A closure work session is held. The next steps for extending improvement initiatives are decided on and communicated.

Figure 4-4. *(Continued)*

PART II

Making Work-Out Happen: Implementing the Full-Featured Version

CHAPTER

V

A Work-Out Road Map

ORK-OUT IS A journey that's better to take fast than slow. If you spend six months planning and designing your first session, what you'll wind up with won't be Work-Out—people will either be locked in to a solution or they'll have forgotten about the problem and will just go through the motions of yet another management fad. So to help you travel quickly and comfortably, this chapter provides a road map to the whole process.

The main highways of Work-Out run through three distinct territories:

- Plan
- Conduct
- Implement

After the overview in this chapter, the next three chapters will dig into the details—giving you the street maps and building plans for a full-length Work-Out.

Before beginning the journey, we want to reiterate what we said in Chapter 2—that describing something almost inevitably freezes it—as though the description is the only reality. With Work-Out, that's especially dangerous. Once you get past a very few key points, Work-Out's most important feature is that it is really suited to the group and the matter at hand, and that will almost inevitably mean that your Work-Out will be different from all other Work-Out efforts, including the one described here.

So with that in mind, let's begin—starting with a travelogue of sorts. The experience of Acme Industries (a fictional company based on many real ones) and its staff brings to life the main features of a full-blown, three-day Work-Out trip.

> **Acme Industries' Household Products division sells a variety of housewares—some manufactured in-house and some assembled or bought ready-made—to large and small retailers, ranging from Wal-Mart to the neighborhood hardware store. Sales are growing, but lately customer complaints, returns, and claims have grown even faster. Margins are eroding, and—even more worrisome—sales reps are reporting that customers are losing confidence in the quality of Acme products.**
>
> **Jan Murphy, the president of Household Products, cannot put her finger on any one single cause of this claims problem. There seem to be a lot of factors spread across the division—manufacturing problems, design issues, poor training of retailers, installation faults, and more. Despite all the data about these problems, nothing anyone has tried has done anything to stem the flow of complaints.**
>
> **Jan decides it's time to take action. Because the issues are interrelated and the accountability crosses all of the division's functions, Jan decides that GE's Work-Out process will help break the logjam and get some positive results. Jan arranges to meet with Gordon Peterson, a Work-Out expert, on Monday morning to talk about how to get started.**

Like a great many businesses and other organizations, Acme faces an identifiable problem—in this case, a host of unhappy customers—but can't trace it to an easily defined cause. If Jan knew exactly what was wrong and why, she wouldn't need Work-Out; she could just go ahead and fix whatever was broken and move on. All too often, however, the visible symptoms of a problem don't point to specific causes, and a company could pour millions into a fix that fixes nothing because it doesn't deal with what's really wrong. Work-Out works because it focuses on business results—but does so in a way that brings the people who have information to fix the problem together, and thus reduces the chance of lingering "gotchas" and unintended consequences.

The kind of business you run or belong to, or the kind of problem you face, may be quite different from the one presented here. But the basic architecture and roles, steps, decisions, and activities should be similar. Once you've traveled with Jan and Acme, you'll know the layout of the Work-Out approach and will be able to see how it could be adapted to your specific situation.

Stage 1: Plan the Work-Out

In the first stage, designing a Work-Out, a senior leader pulls together a small "design" team to agree on the key issues to be tackled, identify participants, communicate expectations of what people will do at the Work-Out event, and prepare business leaders for their role. The design team can also pull together data analyzing root causes and quantifying the potential gains in different areas of the Work-Out.

> **Jan Murphy and Gordon Peterson meet over coffee early Monday morning. "The first thing we need to do," he says, "is nail down a goal and several focused issues for the Work-Out."**
>
> **"Isn't that clear? Our margins are shrinking and quality's down the toilet! We have to jump on that!"**
>
> **"Well, that's what you need to deal with," he replies, "but it's too broad for a Work-Out team—we need things a group could address in concrete terms. What you're after are one or two focused issues that affect margins and quality where your people could pick a course of action and get moving fast."**
>
> **"That's the whole problem," Jan replies. "See those stacks of reports and complaints? If I knew where to start, I'd get started!"**

"Don't worry—you don't have to do everything at once. You'll see; the starting point is in there somewhere."

So Gordon and Jan meet a couple of times over the next few days and start to narrow down the focus for the Work-Out. It seems like customer complaints that require Acme to provide free repairs or replacement products are the point of greatest concern and potentially have the biggest impact on the corporation. Margins are shrinking mainly because these kinds of claims have gone through the roof in the past six months.

At Gordon's suggestion, Jan calls in a few of her managers and a couple of junior people on the "high potential" list to help design the Work-Out. Her quality director, Joe Thompson, brings to the meeting a stack of data on the underlying causes of all recent claims, complaints, and returns. Apparently, problems are cropping up throughout the production and marketing process, from design through manufacturing, retailer training, and installation.

"No wonder you're in the tank," Gordon says. "Nobody can survive with an 18-percent claims rate. What you need is more like 2 percent. That's got to be the goal. And you need it fast—say, within four months."

"What are you smoking?" Joe snaps. "We'd have to do a whole plant transplant to get close to that level!"

"No, you can do it," replies Gordon. "But you have to shake people up. You have to draw a line in the sand and force some major rethinking. Incremental improvements won't be enough—Acme needs some radical new approaches." Gordon reassures Joe and Jan and the rest of the design team that a successful Work-Out often starts with a goal that's such a stretch it knocks people out of their usual mindset.

"Well," says Jan, "This will sure turn up the heat. We'll need some impressive breakthroughs in a few areas to pull this one off."

Having chosen the overall goal for the Work-Out, the design team then identifies several focus areas that can be addressed. One focus is a particular product that seems to be generating an especially large percentage of claims. A second focus will be on shipping and distribution, since it seems that many of the claims stem from breakage that occurs in transit. A third team will look at the quality process in the plant to see if there are better ways to prevent defects at the source.

The next day, the design team reconvenes and selects about 40 people who might make an input to the three focus areas, representing all the functions that are involved in the process. Gordon then helps Jan draft an e-mail message to senior managers, telling them about the Work-Out and the goal that will be targeted. They send another e-mail message to the selected participants, inviting them to the Work-Out event and handing out some preliminary assignments to start preparing for the session. Joe agrees to put together a data kit for participants that covers all that's known about the claims problem. Finally, Jan sends a general announcement to all staff. In less than a week, Jan feels she is about to unleash a major effort to get fast action on claims.

In the design stage, selecting the improvement opportunity is the critical first step—because all the action of the Work-Out and the changes that follow it must be oriented toward a valuable business outcome. Doing Work-Out to do Work-Out is never the goal. Sometimes selecting an improvement opportunity is straightforward—you've got a distinctive challenge due to some unmet customer demand, looming competitive threat, or obvious internal weakness. In other cases, selecting the improvement opportunity means sifting through a number of alternatives and choosing the one that offers the greatest potential payoff. And sometimes the conclusion may be that the Work-Out itself is the best venue for sifting the options and identifying what the company really needs. But the preliminary work helps ensure that all the subsequent effort of the Work-Out is focused on engaging employees to deliver a bottom-line improvement.

Jan was able to take action so fast because she was in a position to get quick participation. As division president, she had both authority to act and responsibility for performance. All she needed was the willingness and ability to try something new. In addition, involving members of her senior team was key to getting the ball rolling.

It helped that Acme was sufficiently hierarchical so Jan's decision to do Work-Out could be put into action without much debate or second-guessing. The organization of your company may be different. Even in the early days of Work-Out at GE, even with Jack Welch's direction and corporate provision of a consultant, many business leaders questioned or postponed action, waiting to see which way the wind was blowing, if Work-Out was for real, or if it would blow away.

As the one who decides to introduce Work-Out into your organization, you may need political savvy to convince key stakeholders to participate. You're asking for a major commitment of time and talent, because a Work-Out event is a workshop lasting anywhere from one to three days and involving up to 80 people—or even more. The aim is to concentrate the organization's resources on generating concrete ideas for improvement, and then capturing those ideas in a project-team structure for rapid implementation. Work-Out's strength as a vehicle for large-scale change is that it enables lots of people—from multiple functions and perspectives—to generate ideas together, prioritize them, and get fast approval for action.

To get this process organized, the design team not only selects the improvement focus and the participants, but also it shapes an agenda for the Work-Out event. It also organizes prework, prepares facilitators to work with teams, and oversees the logistics of getting everyone together. Ideally, by the end of the design stage, most of the deliverables in Figure 5-1 are in place.

Stage 2: Conduct the Work-Out Event

The workshop is both the visible beginning of a Work-Out and its pivotal event. Ideally lasting two to three days, the workshop pulls together senior managers, members of staff functions, and people from the operating front line.

> **As the Work-Out participants assemble, Jan Murphy notices a distinct buzz in the room. People have been talking about this session for days, ever since the invitations went out. Some of**

Figure 5-1.   The "Plan" Stage of a Work-Out.

1. Select a business problem for the Work-Out (bureaucracy bust-ing, process improvement, supply-chain integration, etc.) The written goal should include:
   * The estimated impact if the improvements are achieved
   * Several likely improvement opportunities, or problem areas
   * A 12-week or shorter timeline for implementation
2. Get organizational and senior management support for the Work-Out:
   * Get the senior manager (the Sponsor) on board and make sure he or she is ready to listen to and openly discuss improvement recommendations at the Town Meeting, then make a decision on the spot, in public. The Sponsor should plan the agenda with the design team and oversee the preparation and follow-up of the Work-Out, or delegate this work to a "Champion."
   * Organize a design team, led by the Champion, to plan the Work-Out, create a work-flow chart or process map of the issues involved, and delegate areas of the problem to the Work-Out teams.
   * Recruit cross-functional teams of employees and managers close to the problem. These teams do the core work of the Work-Out: brainstorming and selecting improvement ideas, making recommendations to the Sponsor at the Town Meeting, and implementing the recommendations that are approved.

them, she's heard, have been analyzing the data on their assigned aspect of the claims issue. Many are openly talking about this as a chance to implement some long-overdue changes. Jan senses others are keeping their more radical ideas in reserve, waiting to see whether there'll be real interest from management.

It's 8:00 on Tuesday morning. Time to get started. Jan steps to the front of the room and starts her introduction. Using simple charts, she identifies the worrying signs that the business is slip-ping and highlights the financial impact of the recent decline in quality. For a total of 30 minutes, she points to the data showing problems throughout the production and distribution process and the need to tackle the claims issue with a coordinated push. "The bottom line," she says, "is that we need to get our claims rate down to one-tenth of where it is now, and we need to do it within three months. Your challenge is to come up with workable ideas for making that happen."

For a moment, there is stunned silence. Slash the claims rate by a factor of ten in three months? Participants telegraph their skepticism to each other with looks and nods. The tension in the room is thick enough to taste. Jan walks to the refreshment table and grabs a cup of coffee, hoping she looks as confident as she'd like to feel.

Then the show begins in earnest. Gordon Peterson, acting as lead facilitator for this event, strides to the front of the room and— sounding a bit like a coach for a team going into its big game— gets everyone's attention. He gives clear directions about what will take place throughout the day and the two that follow. He lists activities and timetables quickly and without much reference to Jan or anyone else. He also notes that the schedule will remain flexible, except for the final Town Meeting (the last two hours of the session) where the decisions will be made. He introduces the facilitators who will work with each breakout team. Each facilitator waves a confident and enthusiastic "hello" when introduced.

Gordon then launches a brief warm-up exercise. To demonstrate, he has one of the three teams stand in a circle and toss a tennis ball around, setting up a pattern that the ball always travels. After all the teams have their own patterns, which he points out are like business processes, he has each team time itself—then try the same pattern with three balls instead of one and see what effect that has on time and quality (defined as keeping the balls off the floor). Then he tells them they have a mystery competitor who can do the same process flawlessly in a tenth the time, and turns them loose to figure out how to get the balls from hand to hand in the prescribed order without dropping any of them. Tossing balls harder clearly doesn't work, and new ideas begin to flow.

The teams rearrange themselves, crowd together, and the time keeps dropping.... The exercise not only illustrates how processes can be improved, but seems to break some of the tension that Jan sensed at the beginning.

Gordon then announces where each breakout team will meet, and tells them that the facilitators will join them in the rooms in ten minutes to give them directions on what to do next. He tells them that when they return to the main room after lunch, they will present their first round of ideas.

Jan heads back to her office to attempt to work on something else, hoping that the teams really will generate ideas that will make a difference. She is confident that there are good people involved and that the process will work—but she knows that she'll be on pins and needles until she actually hears what they come up with. "This empowerment stuff is hard," she thinks.

The participants sort themselves into their three preassigned groups and spend the rest of the morning discussing the issues and brainstorming ideas. Suggestions come from every angle, the data on claims is pored over and dissected, and participants piggyback on each other's contributions. Each group has its own leader, plus a facilitator who is trained to help a group keep the brainstorming flowing and then sift and prioritize the ideas so they'll be able to present the most important ones to the other teams.

After lunch, the participants return to the main room, and each group spends about 20 minutes sketching out its most promising ideas to the whole session and fielding questions to make it clear what they have in mind.

Gordon takes in the mix of questioning and confidence, excitement and exhilaration, eagerness and reservations that people seem to be feeling, and smiles to himself, sensing that the ideas are starting to jell. After each of the team presentations, he leads a discussion and feedback session, with some further incorporation of ideas from people in other groups.

As the groups present their top-priority ideas, some patterns begin to emerge. The potential confusion of over 30 different "bright ideas" dissipates as similar ideas are consolidated. There is some discussion about the scope of the ideas—some are intended to be narrow and some broad, some simple and some more complicated. A few teams take their pride of authorship too far at first, but with the facilitators' guidance and the suggestions of the members of other teams, eventually everyone supports the melding of their ideas with similar ones. The facilitators then orchestrate a priority-voting process that reveals 20 improvement ideas that teams will develop for presentation to Jan and her leadership panel on Thursday morning.

The groups then buckle down to work. Some stay up late Tuesday night; all gather early Wednesday morning and work on into the evening—performing dry runs of their presentations at the end of the day. In the process, they find some ideas that simply don't seem worth developing, and others that can be further combined. Eventually the team leaders report that, between the 3 groups, there are 16 ideas on the table that promise immediate and valuable results. Every one of these ideas has someone on the team who is willing to accept "ownership" of it and make sure it really gets implemented if Jan authorizes the effort.

Thursday morning the Town Meeting opens back in the main room. Jan, as the Work-Out Sponsor, has organized six of her senior managers to join her as panelists, to help her listen to the teams' recommendations and decide which should be given the go-ahead.

"This is pretty pressured," she thinks. The teams have been told they each have one hour to present their whole list of improvement ideas. In that short time, they must cover each issue by presenting their analysis of root causes, their recommendations for action, and their assessment of the potential payoff.

Her management panel asks questions to probe the chances of success and the likely benefits of each recommendation. Lots of people seem to be getting involved in the dialogue, Jan realizes. She's struck by how much passion there is behind these ideas. At the end of each presentation, the team members look up expectantly, waiting for a decision. Some recommendations are no-brainers, because the improvement will be immediate or the potential payoff is so obvious. And there are a couple of obvious no-go's as well—where the cost of implementation just wouldn't be worth it. Others are less clear. And old habits of decision making—like, "take your time," "weigh the numbers," "it never hurts to find out a bit more"—are deeply entrenched. When her senior managers stall on taking a position, Jan steps in.

In some cases she asks a couple of questions to prompt her staff to reach a conclusion, which she then confirms and finalizes. In a few cases, she just makes the decision herself. After three-and-a-half hours, 12 improvement ideas have been approved, and specific individuals have volunteered to drive each idea to implementation. If the pay-off estimates are correct, the claims rate should be down to 2 percent or less in three months, yielding savings of several million dollars this fiscal year. If this happens, the stretch goal Jan set will be met in plenty of time.

A Work-Out event usually consists of five sessions, as summarized in Figure 5-2:

- Work-Out introduction
- Small-group idea generation
- Whole-group idea assessment—what we like to call the 'Gallery of Ideas"
- Small-group recommendation development
- Final-decision session—the "Town Meeting"

In the last session, the Sponsor and other invited senior managers listen to action ideas put forward by teams—and make a decision on the spot on those to be implemented in the final stage of Work-Out.

Figure 5-2. The "Conduct" Stage of a Work-Out.

The Work-Out Event typically consists of five sessions that take place over the course of one to three days:

1. Introduction: Brief participants on the goals and agenda for the Work-Out, and the culminating event: the Town Meeting. Review the process and ground rules (no sacred cows, no "turf-defending," no blaming, no pulling rank by managers, no complaining; focus on solutions).
2. Brainstorming: Multiple cross-functional teams each brainstorm a different aspect of the problem. Each team creates a list of top 10 ideas for achieving the team's assigned goal. Use the "Pay-Off Matrix" in Chapter 7 to prioritize ideas.
3. The Gallery of Ideas: Each Work-Out team presents its 10 best ideas to the rest of the Work-Out participants. Participants vote on the best 3–4 ideas worth implementing from each team's top 10.
4. Generate Action Plans: Teams use the remaining time to develop an action plan for implementing the selected ideas, and then prepare a presentation, with supporting data, requesting approval for the idea from the Sponsor at the Town Meeting. Each idea must have an "owner" who will take responsibility for seeing it through implementation if it is approved.
5. The Town Meeting: Teams present their recommendations to the Sponsor. The Sponsor dialogues with the team and other participants about the viability of the idea, and asks for input from managers who will be affected by the team's recommendation, before making a "yes/no" decision on the spot.

The main objectives of the Work-Out event are to maximize the number of high-quality ideas for change and to carve out a doable list of actions that will deliver fast results on the improvement opportunity. In this quick overview, we've concentrated on the way Work-Out can address management concerns; in practice, you'll find that it also brings new things to the fore. The people on the front lines have their own concerns, and things they know need attention often haven't impinged on the perceptions of management. Sometimes addressing those concerns can provide even more long-term benefit to the organization.

Stage 3: Implement the Work-Out Recommendations

The final stage of a Work-Out cycle implements the action ideas. Many recommendations will have decisions that can be made on the spot (say, reduce a report or eliminate an approval) and thereby save time or reduce costs immediately. They just need a watchful eye to make sure they really do get implemented. Others will require a series of steps to begin to generate real results, and each of those ideas needs to be shepherded to completion.

Gordon and his crew of facilitators help each of the 12 "recommendation owners"—one Work-Out participant for each of the approved ideas—get up and running immediately after the Work-Out. Each owner, some of them with teams to help, has three months to make the assigned action recommendation a reality.

To smooth their way, Jan sends out an announcement the day after the Town Meeting, telling her staff what was approved and listing the projects that are being kicked off. She makes it clear that the owners and their teams have the power to do whatever it takes to get their assigned action recommendation in place in the specified time, and that they have her full backing.

Most of the key senior managers were present at the Town Meeting and joined in her decisions, but to lock in their support for the 12 projects she now starts every management meeting—and most of her informal conversations—with a report on Work-Out progress.

The owners give their first update two weeks into the projects. A couple of them are having a tough start, but the others look to be in good shape. Three of the projects are particularly promising. Jan is reassured by one of Gordon's comments: "Don't expect all the projects to be winners. The idea is to launch enough, on enough fronts, that you'll generate the overall result you're looking for. It's better to be mostly right and fast than to be completely right and slow."

Four weeks after the Work-Out, the Household Products Division is jumping with energy. "They got the go-ahead from senior man-

agement at the Town Meeting," thinks Jan, "and so far, they are running with it hard. Some teams are meeting at least weekly and are dealing directly with any problems or barriers they encounter. I've been asked to intervene only three times—not bad, considering we've got 12 little projects with people running around trying to change some long-entrenched processes. At this rate, we might actually hit our target."

The implementation process starts with getting the word out on what was decided at the Town Meeting. It includes making sure that project owners and teams have some support so they can successfully deliver on their action recommendations. It also includes tracking owners' progress and assessing the overall impact of the Work-Out across all projects. And finally, it means deciding what steps must be taken next to lock in or even extend the gains from the Work-Out. Figure 5-3 illustrates what the implementation process is designed to accomplish.

Figure 5-3. The "Implement" Stage of a Work-Out.

1. Action recommendations implemented by project owners and teams within 12 weeks—should meet the goal established at the outset of the Work-Out.
2. Impact of all action recommendations assessed for the entire Work-Out.
3. Closure work session held. Next steps for extending improvement initiatives decided and communicated.

Key Roles in the Work-Out Process

Like a script for a Broadway play, a Work-Out has a defined cast of characters, all of whom are essential for getting from Act I through to the conclusion. And although—like plays—Work-Outs can differ in length, tone, and topic, they all have three main clusters of roles that need to be played out: leadership, facilitation, and participation. The emphasis on each role varies as the Work-Out progresses. Each role can also be carried out by a cast of starring and supporting players. Figure 5-4 charts the three roles in the three stages of the program.

	Leadership	Facilitation	Participation
Initial Approach	Make the decision to use Work-Out. Select lead facilitator. Select additional leaders (champions, Town Meeting panelists). Pick the best place to start— organization, function, process, customer. Call the meeting. Communicate!	Build relationships with Sponsor and other key leaders. Educate leaders about Work-Out essentials and leadership roles. Consult with leaders on communication to organization. Become familiar with the organization, its key issues, and key players.	Participate in focus groups or discussions to identify • Key issues • Best starting point
Design	Collaborate with lead facilitator on all aspects. Determine scope and focus. Work with additional leaders. Identify participants (or participant groups). Set logistics— location, dates. Invite participants. Communicate!	Design specifics of the Work-Out event (schedule, activities, tools, output forms). Train facilitation team. Establish clear communication method, schedule, and signals with leaders and facilitators. Consult with leaders on communication to organization. Identify analysts and resources, and prepare to answer teams' questions during session.	Participate in design discussions if appropriate.

Figure 5-4. Work-Out Roles: Who Does What?

	Leadership	Facilitation	Participation
		Take care of logistics and administration: • Invite participants. • Reserve location. • Prepare location. • Provide equipment and tools.	
Conduct	Launch the session with some context, information, and the charge (what is to be accomplished). Leave the session during most of the Work-Out event. Collaborate behind the scenes with facilitators and other leaders as appropriate. Return to last session to hear and approve or reject participant recommendations.	Lead facilitator: • Serve as master of ceremonies— run all large-group sessions. • Check with other facilitators to assure that all teams are on track. • Provide support to other facilitators as necessary. • Conduct team-debrief session at end of each day. • Collaborate with leaders to minimize their anxiety and maximize their effectiveness. Facilitation team members: • Work with each breakout team.	Participate fully in all activities, according to design and at direction of facilitators. As needed, serve as team representatives to present recommendations. Identify and provide (if possible) data, information, and resources to support analysis and recommendations. Volunteer to take ownership of specific recommendations.

Figure 5-4. *(Continued)*

	Leadership	Facilitation	Participation
		• Assure that teams accomplish tasks on time. • Take pulse of teams and individual members.	
Implement	Assure that teams are supported with resources and access to key people and information. Monitor and support team progress. Congratulate success. Communicate!	Lead facilitator: • Assure that leaders support implementation process. • Develop implementation-monitoring process. • May continue to work with leaders to develop their new roles. Other facilitators: • Continue to work with teams as needed.	Team members may continue to work on projects, or may hand them off to other Work-Out teams for implementation.
Next Cycle	Identify target opportunity, organization, and leaders for the next Work-Out cycle. Review best practices from first cycle. Launch the next cycle.	Work with leaders to create the next cycle.	Participate in focus groups or discussions to identify • Key issues • Best starting point Participate in design discussions if appropriate.

Figure 5-4. *(Continued)*

Leadership

The job of leadership is to drive for improved results by introducing Work-Out to the organization and convening the Town Meeting. The star leadership role is the *Sponsor,* sometimes supported by a *champion.* Usually the Sponsor is the top leader of the business or the business unit, but it may also be someone with a more limited scope. The Sponsor's role is to demand real-time results and then assure that the organization actually does the work prior to and during the Work-Out process to achieve them. The Sponsor lays out the terrain for the Work-Out with the design team, hosts the Work-Out event, and then supports the process, gives political cover, and ensures that communication is thorough. A champion is typically a next-level manager who is selected to drive the day-to-day follow-up on the ideas created in the Town Meeting.

Facilitation

Facilitation is all the work that is needed to oil the wheels of the Work-Out. People who are usually enlisted to provide this support might include an outside or internal consultant acting as *designer,* plus *facilitators, experts, analysts,* and an *administrator.* At least at first, it's useful to involve at least one external consultant, so as to provide experience with the Work-Out process and an objective counterweight to the prevailing culture. Particularly in hierarchical organizations, it is often difficult for internal people to challenge senior leaders or coach them on how to play new, more participative roles. So in those cases, a credible external Work-Out expert is essential.

Facilitators are also critical for working with the Work-Out teams, to help them challenge prevailing assumptions, stay with the flow of the process, and support positive group dynamics. This role can be played by skillful internal people—often as a developmental experience—but is best left in the hands of someone who isn't directly involved in the business issue that forms the Work-Out topic.

Participation

The real work of Work-Out is done by *participants at the Work-Out event* and senior managers who attend as *Town Meeting advisers.* After the event, participation in the follow-up stage is driven by *recommendation owners (who stepped forward at the Work-Out and volunteered to take charge*), and *team members* (*some of whom may have been recruited by the recommendation owners after the Work-Out event*). The senior managers help the Sponsor make the final decisions at the Town Meeting, then clear the way for the implementation owners and teams to do the agreed-upon work. The rest of the participants at the Work-Out event gather information if needed and discuss the problems posed to them. Some present ideas at the Town Meeting, with the advice and support of the rest of their groups.

A Wild Journey

Is your organization ready to take off down the Work-Out road? To help you decide, you might want to take another look at the assessment tools at the end of Chapter 3. If you've got some ideas for an improvement opportunity or problem that needs urgent action across functional lines, you could be ready for Work-Out. If you see the broad direction your organization needs to go, but need the injection of ideas from a wide cross-section of your people to give that direction specific form and committed effort, you could be ready for Work-Out. If you have the appetite for rapid action on many fronts at once, you could be ready for Work-Out. If you are willing to test out your strategy on the run, gathering more data as you go and refining the plan *in situ*, then Work-Out could be for you. Figure 5-5 provides a time line—a marked-up map—for the journey.

Days

1	30	33	60	90	120

Plan Stage (30 Days)

Participants: Sponsor, lead facilitator, champion, others as invited

Goals: Select theme, set date, design session, pick and invite team leaders, team members, team facilitators, Town Meeting panelists, administrator, and resource people

Conduct Stage (1–3 Days)

Participants: Sponsor and/or champion (at kick-off and Town Meeting), lead facilitator, team leaders, team members, team facilitators, resource people, administrator, and Town Meeting panelists (Town Meeting only)

Goals: Analyze situation; come up with recommendations; get yes-or-no decisions, approve action plans;

Implement Stage (90 Days, Punctuated by 3 reviews)

Participants: Recommendation owners, others recruited to participate in implementation

Goals: Carry out action plans and get results

Follow-up reviews should take place every 30 days

Participants in a Review: Sponsor, recommendation owners, others as invited

Goals for a Review: Check progress, resolve problems

Figure 5-5. Sample Time Line for a Full-Length Work-Out.

VI

Planning a Work-Out

W HETHER YOU'RE BUILDING a house or organizing a Work-Out session you need good plans. Architects say that good design has function and form that work together and please the eye. Work-Out plans should do just that. Their function—to make business improvements quickly—and their form—participatory and active—work together to engage everyone who takes part, and foster both organizational and personal growth. At the end of the Town Meeting, participants should feel proud of what they've done.

Once you decide to go ahead with Work-Out, you have three design challenges to address before the session opens:

- *What* business issue to work on.
- *Who* is going to participate—both in the planning process and in the Work-Out itself.
- *How* to load the process for success.

Once these challenges are met, you can then determine *when* to get started.

The WHAT: Selecting a Business Issue for a Work-Out

It's inevitable—every organization has many . . . call them *opportunities for performance improvement:* staff suggestions—and frustrations too deep for suggestions; failures in meeting customer expectations—and successes that could be built upon; complaints of bureaucracy—and employees who feel too stifled to risk complaining; performance that falls short of plans and budgets—and planned achievement well below what managers believe is actually possible.

When you face a chronic deficiency or an immediate competitive threat, selecting a target for your Work-Out may be straightforward. Otherwise, you may need to look around before deciding on a focus. If things are very unsettled and it isn't clear why, sometimes just bringing employees who have a common interest (a shared customer or a process they all work on, for example) together to figure out the issues can become the focus of an extremely effective Work-Out event. Otherwise, the first step is to generate a list of possible business issues. Then the business issue that will provide the greatest payoff can be identified.

There are a number of ways to generate a list of business issues:

- Identify performance gaps against business plans, budgets, or key performance measures.
- Interview customers (internal or external) to clarify service expectations and find out how service might be improved.
- Meet with managers of other areas to review processes that cut across functional boundaries.
- Benchmark performance against competitors.
- Get staff together and ask what is limiting business results—find out what is keeping them awake at night.

What Makes a Good Work-Out Target?

Nobody is going to catch fire over your paper clip distribution policy. To sustain a Work-Out, you need an *urgent and compelling business issue.* The closer your target fits this description, the more ready and willing everyone will be to commit their time, energy, and talents to the achievement of the goal.

From the list of business opportunities that you might have generated, Work-Out targets should meet these criteria:

- The business goal is important and urgent. It is not just a "nice to do" objective, but rather something that will make a real difference to the organization.
- The topic is broad enough for brainstorming—not a single, well-defined task or narrowly stated problem—but still concrete enough that a measurable goal can be defined.
- The objective is an improvement in actual performance, not just an improvement in planning, training, measurement, and documentation.
- There are aspects of the improvement opportunity that can yield results right away—either immediately or in three to six months at the most. It will not take years of investment before the change will bear fruit.

What you're after in this planning phase is to answer one question: What is the objective of this Work-Out, in bottom-line business terms? The more clearly you can communicate your intentions and expectations, the better the results you will get. Too often, improvement efforts begin either with a vaguely defined business issue, resulting in confusion and activity that is off the mark, or with a narrowly defined task that allows for no empowerment of the team or no real impact on business results.

For example, "improving customer service" through Work-Out is too vague and unclear. It could mean almost anything, from call answering to on-time deliveries. On the other end of the spectrum, "implementing the predetermined customer-response 'script' for all telephone calls" may be too narrow—and may not allow room for creative thinking. By the same token, "reducing bureaucracy" may be too broad and vague for a starting point, while "eliminating the monthly activity report" would be too narrow. Work-Out planning needs to find the sweet spot in between—leaving plenty of room for participants to bring up things that are important to them even though management may not have noticed the specific need, but without dumping the participants around a table to stare at each other and wonder what they're doing in the session at all.

Selecting a Business Issue

The process of identifying business issues varies with every situation, and it is important to consider the needs of both the organization and its customers or clients. Sometimes pressures for improvement are internal to the organization. Your costs are out of line. You're not earning an adequate return. Your competitors seem to be better able to customize their products. Sometimes the needs of the customer drive the change effort, as when an important customer threatens to go elsewhere, or when customer feedback identifies a crucial area of weakness. And sometimes there is no pressure for change at all—except from your own vision of new opportunities that might be possible to capture.

Identifying and describing a specific opportunity might take an hour or two of discussion with a Work-Out consultant, or it might take a couple of weeks and involve a number of managers and employees. These dialogues usually begin with one of the following three scenarios:

SCENARIO #1: YOU WANT TO IMPLEMENT A SPECIFIC SOLUTION TO A PROBLEM: *You've already defined a specific solution to a particular problem*—which might involve changing a process, developing a new system, or installing a new piece of equipment. To begin the dialogue, either with a Work-Out consultant or with your management team, you might first step back from the solution and define the business objective to be achieved. What larger benefit will be derived from this particular solution? Is this a specific task to be completed, or is it one possible solution, among many alternatives, for a long-standing business issue?

If, after this discussion, you still feel that you have the right solution, and therefore a one-time, well-defined task, the challenge is how to implement the solution in a way that achieves the business results, and gains the "buy-in" of the people that will need to use the new approach. For example, when GE Lighting wanted to extend its order-entry system to include its Canadian business, the technical issues were straightforward (although difficult). The U.S. system needed to be modified to convert Canadian currency, extended to Canadian facilities, and made accessible in French. However, to get the real business value, there had to be changes in the way that employees on both sides of the border used the system. Therefore, a multifunctional Work-Out, involving people from systems, customer service, distribution, manufacturing, sales, and finance was organized, aimed not just at implementing a new system—but at achieving a 20-percent cost reduction and a 20-percent improvement in key service indicators within 6 months.

SCENARIO #2: YOU WANT TO DEVELOP A SOLUTION TO A PROBLEM: *You have a general business problem*—say, poor on-time delivery, large work backlogs, too many employee injuries—but do not yet have a specific solution. Perhaps the problem has existed for a while but hasn't quite risen to the top of the pile, or it has just become more urgent because of internal or external pressure. In any case, it is probably a business problem that requires multiple perspectives and will involve different groups both to develop and implement a solution. In this instance, some discussion may be required to narrow down the focus to find an achievable goal or goals, or a specific subset of the issue. For example, the Work-Out might be focused on how the problem can be addressed in terms of one major customer, or a category of customers, one major market or a geographical region, an office or plant, or one or more products or services, or the like.

The former AlliedSignal Automotive Business (now Honeywell) provides a good illustration of this "narrowing down" process. Several years ago, the problem they faced in the Heavy Vehicle Division was how to improve the introduction and commercialization of new products. This is a very broad topic that potentially involves research, engineering, marketing, manufacturing, sales, finance, distribution, and more. To design a Work-Out that could make a difference in the short term, the head of the division, after discussion with a Work-Out consultant, decided to focus the problem around one particular new brake product. The goal was to get the new product to market and generate a specific amount of revenue within four months (which meant accelerating the entire process by more than 30 percent). Work-Out teams were formed to work on key aspects of the process (ramping up manufacturing, developing marketing and sales materials, gearing up distribution). And while the teams focused on this particular product, they also provided ideas that could then be applied to other products—thus improving the entire commercialization process.

SCENARIO #3: YOU WANT TO DEFINE A PROBLEM: *You see a lot of challenges and are convinced that the organization can perform more effectively, but it isn't clear where to start the improvement process.* Perhaps there are a number of equally important issues, but no one "burning platform;" or perhaps you are not clear which problems will yield the most results, or where people are most ready to dig in and get started. In these cases, there are several ways to proceed.

First, you might ask a Work-Out consultant to conduct a series of interviews with managers and employees about where they see opportunities for improvement. Where do they think change is needed or possible? What is most urgent from their perspectives? Where do they have ideas and energy to get started? If they were running the business, what would they focus on? Based on these interviews, you can then have a working session with those who were interviewed to feed back the interview results and discuss which business issues might be focused on first. This small group could then become a "design team" for Work-Out.

A second way to proceed might be to interview customers—to get their views on opportunities for improvement. What changes would they like to see? How could you help them be more successful? What gets in the way of a better business relationship? Again, you might gather a small team of people in your organization to conduct these interviews. That team could then become a "design team" for Work-Out.

A third way to define a Work-Out problem or focus is to have a working session with a Work-Out consultant, and perhaps a few colleagues, to review the mission of the group and its performance against its critical goals. Where are the biggest gaps? What is causing particular shortfalls? Where are you most at risk? Based on this discussion, some problems for Work-Out might emerge—and then be further shaped by the "design team."

In the absence of a clear business problem, it is also possible to use the first part of a Work-Out session as a "problem-definition" vehicle. For example, at GE Power Systems, the business leader did not want to impose his views about priority problems on a team that had been dictated to previously on a host of issues. Instead, he began by listing some of the business issues that "kept him up at night," and then asked each of the participants to make their own lists. In small groups, people debated and prioritized the issues and problems, and then the entire group voted on which were the top five. These problems then became the topics for the Work-Out session.

Working with a Work-Out Consultant

In all three of the scenarios listed here, we have suggested that a Work-Out consultant might be involved in the process of selecting a business focus and a Work-Out goal. We'll say more about this role in the next section, but at this point all you need to know is that by *Work-Out consultant,* we mean someone who can help a manager think through the alternatives to select a Work-Out goal. This person could be an external consultant, an internal consultant, a human resources manager, or a trusted colleague. The key is to have someone—because it is very difficult for a manager—at any level—to shape a Work-Out without talking through the details with someone else.

In selecting a Work-Out consultant, make sure it is someone who has the insight and the courage to "push back" at you (hopefully in a pleasant way). As comforting as it is to be agreed with, be leery of a consultant who takes your initial statement of a problem at face value. Few people find it easy to engage a senior manager in a discussion of underlying goals—but important business issues are missed when this exploration doesn't happen. You want a consultant who will think like a good automotive services manager when someone drives up and says, "My car needs a tune-up." The service manager who wants to avoid unnecessary or misdirected repair work will reply, "Great, we can do that. But first, tell me, have you come in for regular maintenance or has the car been having some problems . . ." The Work-Out consultant too should question what you are trying to achieve and why.

Second, use the Work-Out consultant to avoid the very natural tendency to want to define exactly what a group should do and how it should do it. This pattern is particularly tempting when you're facing a raft of performance problems and large work backlogs. The more trouble the organization is in, the more you may want to manage directly all aspects of the work. It can be tough to shift from trying to control everything to presenting a team with an opportunity and an expectation for results. A good Work-Out consultant will help you make this shift and stay focused on the benefits of empowering a group through the Work-Out process. Remember that a good Work-Out goal specifies what is to be achieved—but does not specify a particular pathway for getting there.

Criteria for a Work-Out Goal

Once you have agreed on the business focus for Work-Out, you need to define an overall goal that the Work-Out teams should aim to achieve. This goal should be expressed using a *SMART* goal statement—that is, one that presents the goal in these terms:

Stretch
Measurable
Achievable
Realistic
Time-related

Here are some examples of SMART Work-Out goals from a variety of organizations:

- Reduce average costs per repair by 10 percent over the same period as last year, without reducing customer satisfaction, within 100 days.
- Reduce litigation costs by at least $30 million this year without increasing average claims-settlement costs.
- Increase productivity by 20 percent while consistently achieving service standards, within 3 months.
- Maximize sales opportunities and increase revenue by $500,000 within the 12-week Work-Out implementation period.
- Save 2.5 to 5 million dollars in Direct Claims costs, and increase productivity by 10 percent by end of the year.
- Reduce cycle time for client-proposal preparation by 50 percent within 4 weeks.

Defining the Business Impact of a Work-Out

To double-check that you have defined a SMART goal for Work-Out, you should try to estimate the business impact that will be derived from achieving the goal. The business impact of Work-Out is an estimate of the bottom-line impact to be achieved if the Work-Out is successful. While there could be other areas of potentially major impact for the organization, typically such estimation falls into at least one of four major categories:

- Reduction of a cost or expense
- Improvement in some aspect of profitability
- Improved customer service or satisfaction
- Improved productivity or efficiency in the way work is being done

Try to be as specific as possible when quantifying the estimated impact. Even when the expected business impact is great, it may initially seem hard to quantify. However, we encourage you to spend some time at this stage exploring different ways to quantify the Work-Out's estimated financial impact, and deciding on a measure that is relevant and compelling. For example, if the Work-Out goal is to reduce average costs per repair by 10 percent, you can calculate the business impact as follows:

a. Determine the average cost per repair
b. Determine the average number of repairs per month
c. Multiply a × b × 12—which gives you the average repair costs for the year
d. Take 10 percent of this number (c)

This overall business-impact number then provides motivation and excitement to the Work-Out participants. It helps them see that they are not just engaging in activity, but helping to put some real money (or other key measure) on the bottom line.

If you are unable to make this calculation—even with rough estimates and surrogate measures—then the goal you selected may not be SMART. Or if the number is too small or insignificant, it may not be the kind of goal that will really make a difference to the organization. In that case, go back to the goal and try to reformulate it.

Planning for Work-Out: The Faster the Better

One of the ways to load Work-Out for success is to keep the planning process as short as possible. Planning for Work-Out should not be a major analytical or intellectual exercise. Think about possible issues. Discuss them with a Work-Out consultant. Get some additional input if necessary, let a design team flesh out the details and the logistics—then move into action. Think in terms of weeks or days rather than months.

When you are planning a Work-Out, remember that the aim is to have a rapid impact on an urgent business issue. Therefore, if the process of getting ready for the Work-Out takes more than a month, ask yourself these questions:

- Is there a more pressing business issue that could be addressed more quickly? Is there another issue that is more central to the performance of the business and that we can move on more quickly?
- Is the Work-Out topic too complex? If so, could the Work-Out be reduced in scope, or tackled on a smaller scale, so that it can be launched faster?

The aim, again, is to select a business issue and define a Work-Out goal that can drive the achievement of an immediate improvement in results. If it takes longer than a month, it isn't *immediate* anymore, and if the idea sits around too long, people will grow too set in their ways to take proper advantage of the Work-Out when it finally arrives.

The WHO: The Cast of Characters for Work-Out

As described in Chapter 5, the Work-Out cast includes leaders, facilitators, and participants. Within these three categories of cast members, however, are a number of possible roles, some mandatory and some optional. In planning the Work-Out, it is important to be clear about which roles will be needed, and who will play them.

Leadership Roles

Sponsor (Mandatory)

The *Sponsor* is the senior manager responsible for all the parts of the organization that are involved in the Work-Out. The Sponsor selects the focus area—the business topic and goal—and essentially commissions the Work-Out. The Sponsor then attends the Town Meeting, makes the final yes-or-no decisions on each idea proposed, and holds people accountable for follow-up implementation. The Sponsor also selects the champion (if there is one), and helps select the other participants. Finally, the Sponsor issues the formal invitations to participants asking them to take part in the Work-Out.

Champion (Optional)

The *champion* is a business manager who represents the Sponsor at the Work-Out, taking responsibility for the detailed preparation and follow-up to the Work-Out session. (The Sponsor may choose to take on the role of champion as well.) If the roles are separated, the champion plans the agenda, works with the design team to develop the overall plan for the session, and coordinates and oversees the preparations. These typically include the following:

- Assisting with the preparation of invitations for participants
- Collecting background information and data
- Overseeing coordination of logistics

After the Work-Out, the champion organizes review sessions at regular intervals (usually 30, 60, and 90 days), helps overcome barriers to implementation, and helps track the progress of the Work-Out ideas.

Facilitation Roles

Work-Out Consultant (Mandatory)

The *Work-Out consultant* is a person with experience in the Work-Out process who helps the Sponsor make the initial decisions about the objectives, then works with the Sponsor (and champion, if any) to design the Work-Out and organize its logistics. The Work-Out consultant also works with the team leaders, facilitators, and other members of the supporting cast, to run and follow up on the Work-Out session. Other tasks for the Work-Out consultant include:

- Working with the champion to select and convene a design team (as needed) and then helping to create the specific design for the Work-Out.
- Facilitating design-team meetings (as needed).
- Helping the champion design the follow-up process (after the Work-Out).
- Helping to brief and prepare the champion, Sponsor, and others needed for their opening remarks, and on their roles in the Town Meeting.
- Help the Sponsor or champion agree on methods for tracking Work-Out results and measuring its impact on the business.

Organizations that are new to Work-Out almost always use an external person as a Work-Out consultant, at least initially. Particularly in hierarchical organizations, it is difficult for an internal person, no matter how skillful, to push back at powerful senior leaders and help them to shift their behaviors in alignment with what's needed for Work-Out to succeed. At the same time, one of the goals of an external Work-Out consultant should be to coach senior people so that Work-Out leadership behaviors become more natural and embedded, and the need for outside push-back is lessened. A good external consultant also helps to coach and train internal Work-Out consultants and facilitators who can, over time, take on most or all of the tasks that the external person had performed. In fact, in almost all of the GE businesses, the external consultants paired up with internal consultants to form a Work-Out consulting team.

Analyst (Optional)

Some organizations have designated a person to serve as an *analyst* to support the implementation of Work-Out recommendations and track progress against the goal. This means both doing the work of collecting data and providing constant reminders, as needed, to keep the rest of the participants aware of the importance of planning and establishing meaningful tracking measures. The analyst participates in design-team meetings and prepares and validates the contents of the data pack that is distributed to teams for use during the Work-Out.

Facilitators (Mandatory)

The *facilitators* help the Work-Out consultant (who often acts as lead facilitator) to prepare for and run the Work-Out session. They should be trained in Work-Out methods and have strong skills in facilitating group processes. Before the Work-Out session, the facilitators:

- Attend a preliminary briefing session with the lead facilitator.
- Meet with the team leaders to plan the Work-Out team sessions.

Expert Resources (Optional)

The *expert resources* are people who are available during the Work-Out session to provide background to the team in particular functional or technical areas (for example, IT, finance, or marketing). They are not members of the team but are expected to help the team, if needed, to shape a work plan for the 12-week time frame. Before the Work-Out session, expert resources, if utilized, can:

- Prepare data packs for the teams to use during the Work-Out. Each data pack should contain data and other information that might be useful in providing input to the teams (for example, on the feasibility of implementing ideas, the resources that might be required, or the way the problem is addressed in other firms).
- Alert colleagues to be prepared to be available by phone during the Work-Out session to provide further details as needed.

Administrator (Optional)

Some organizations have found it useful to designate a specific person as the administrator. The *administrator* organizes the logistics of the Work-Out event. This is a highly detailed but crucial role—time frames are short and deadlines have to be met. The administrator has the responsibility of sending out invitations, organizing venues, helping with the Town Meeting presentation, ensuring all documentation is recorded and distributed, and dealing with the many other tasks involved in making a large gathering run smoothly. The administrator works closely with the lead facilitator to ensure that all information is shared.

Participation Roles

Team Leaders (Mandatory)

The *team leaders* take responsibility for preparing each team for the Work-Out, leading it through the process of idea generation, action planning, and Town Meeting presentation, as well as ensuring the implementation of the work plan. They also work as a group to report back on progress and learnings.

If possible, team leaders should be selected and notified about their roles before the Work-Out takes place. This will give them time to meet with the design team to go over the background for the Work-Out, the likely team goals, and the agenda for the Work-Out. Team membership is also usually decided at this stage. The team leaders sometimes play a part in identifying team members, and sometimes simply take on teams that have already been assigned.

After meeting with the design team, the team leaders have the primary job of getting the teams ready for the main session. In some cases, team leaders will hold preliminary meetings with their teams prior to the Work-Out, to talk through the goals and assemble any background data needed. For complex process issues, it can be useful for the team to sit down and map current processes in advance. However, team leaders need to make sure that these preliminary meetings focus on understanding the context of the goal and gathering data and do not get into the brainstorming and problem-solving mode that is the focus of the Work-Out. Otherwise, the Work-Out itself might not be fresh and productive.

In some cases, team leaders may just want to talk with team members individually prior to the Work-Out event and ask them to go off to collect information. At the same time, team leaders also need to talk with other colleagues to gather their ideas and input. It is helpful to involve as many people as possible in this, so they will be involved in the Work-Out even if they are not attending on the day.

Team Members (Mandatory)

The *team members* are, of course, at the core of Work-Out. They may gather data and do some preliminary thinking prior to the Work-Out event. Their main role, however, kicks in when the Work-Out event is convened. Their job then is to be part of a team that solves a business problem through brainstorming, selection of ideas, and presentation of recommendations. Once ideas have been given the green light by a sponsor, some team members become "recommendation owners" who are empowered and accountable for delivery on their ideas.

Most people find it exciting to take part in a Work-Out. It can be exhilarating to take time out from a regular job and sit down to think creatively about specific short-term improvements that can be made. It is a chance to think more widely, to get exposure to people from different parts of the organization, to share opinions as to how things should be done, and to help drive changes that will realize tangible business gains for the organization and remove frustrations on the job. Despite these "positives," team members often need reassurance that the effort involved in Work-Out (which can be considerable) will be worthwhile—that senior management really will listen "this time," and that the regular workload will be dealt with without requiring heroic measures on their part. To facilitate this positive spirit, it is important that they understand what will be happening both before and after the Work-Out, as well as the goals and objectives of the Work-Out and the goals for the team. They should be encouraged to talk about their participation with colleagues who are not attending the Work-Out, and to seek others' views and opinions to add to their own.

Selecting Team Members. To select specific team members for a Work-Out, think through what input is needed and why, in order to accomplish the Work-Out goal:

- Is there a need for particular information and expertise?
- Should we build in user, recipient, or customer perspective, particularly if it was excluded in past improvement efforts?
- Who are the potential implementers of recommendations?
- Will some employees or managers benefit from participation in terms of observation, education, professional development, or broadening awareness? In particular, are there well-respected cynics who might be converted to supporters by participation in the process?

In addition to answering these questions, also define participants by function or position first, then identify the individuals in those categories who are likeliest to further the goals of the Work-Out. For example, if the Work-Out goal involves reducing product defects, then you will probably need people who come from areas such as product management, manufacturing, finance, quality, distribution, IT, and customer service.

Include those business units and functions that will make a contribution to developing recommendations and those that will be affected by the work, and thus need to be involved in implementing the recommendations. You also want representatives from any units in a position to provide critical information or unique perspectives on the problem. When determining which business units and functions should be represented in each team, it is often helpful to create an organizational map around each challenge. The mapping process should identify the following points:

- The underlying process and the business units or functions that it cuts across
- Related areas that are not currently involved in the process but could or should be
- Who will benefit most from achievement of the challenge goal
- Who else may need to be involved in the thinking or the implementation

When making specific selections, avoid putting bosses and their own subordinates on the same team, if possible. Also remember that you want people who will be in a position to implement ideas the team may come up with—which means the right mix of frontline and management people. It's also useful to have people with strong linkages outside the group, and people who will find each other to be compatible company. Eight to ten people on a team is the optimum number.

Town Meeting Participants (Optional)

The *Town Meeting participants* are other senior managers representing key functional areas, who may be invited to the Town Meeting to hear team recommendations and give the Sponsor their opinions, input, and counsel. While it is optional to invite such managers, our experience is that if they're not invited, they are apt to "wander in" anyway, "just passing by," because of overriding curiosity about what's happening.

By making them a formal part of the process, you give yourself an opportunity to brief them about the part they can play in it and thus greatly improve your chances of a productive Town Meeting. They need to understand that the Sponsor has the responsibility for making the final decision on the recommendations presented at the Town Meeting. The other managers who attend the Town Meeting as participants representing key functional areas often do not share in the decision making, but they always have an important role to play by helping to evaluate and comment on recommendations put forward by teams.

Putting Together the Cast of Characters

The basic Work-Out roles are simple and straightforward—leadership, facilitation, and participation. To help you visualize how these roles play out over the course of a Work-Out process, Figure 6-1 summarizes the Work-Out cast. This chart will be repeated in the next few chapters as different roles come to the forefront.

The HOW: Designing Work-Out for Success

Earlier in this chapter, we referred to a "design team" that would take the Work-Out business goal and move the process forward. Such a design team typically consists of—at minimum—the Work-Out consultant and the Sponsor or champion. In most cases, the design team also

Figure 6-1. Key Players in Designing a Work-Out.

includes several others who can make a major contribution to the Work-Out design (such as key managers or experts in the Work-Out target area, or people with a great deal of Work-Out expertise). If employees are represented by a union, it may be important for union representatives to be members of the design team as well.

Prior to the Work-Out event, the design team helps the Sponsor clarify the selected Work-Out opportunity and (as described earlier in this chapter) focus in on an overall Work-Out goal that is defined in SMART terms. Once the overall goal is determined, the design team roughs out a work-flow or process map related to the goal, in order to portray graphically the issues involved. This should not be a major analytical exercise but rather a high-level view to help determine how best to select subteams that each have a specific focus.

Based on the high-level map, these are the design team's main tasks:

- Define the Work-Out subgoals, that is, logical areas of focus or process phases to divide among Work-Out teams.
- Flesh out the subgoals with preliminary assignments and thought-starter questions for each work group.
- Pick the specific participants—including both team members and team leaders.
- Set the date for the Work-Out and make sure the meeting logistics are taken care of.
- Review data related to the performance issues in question, including historical data and benchmarking data, and if appropriate, provide "data packs" in advance for the teams.

The product of a typical design team should be a one-page summary of the Work-Out goal, subteams, and thought-starter questions. Figure 6-2 provides several examples of goal summaries from different organizations.

How Much Planning Do You Need?

Each organization that uses Work-Out will have its own twist on the planning phase. We've seen the whole gamut of preparation levels, ranging from putting people in the room with common interests and enabling them to make decisions, on the spot, to long and complex, carefully orchestrated planning processes. You should strive for a level of planning that's "just right" for your organization. That depends on the particular culture you have now—and the one you intend to create. But if you do err, we recommend that you do it on the side of simplicity. It's better to get moving with a minimum of planning than to get stuck before the process even gets started.

Here's a cautionary tale about getting stuck in the planning rut: Some years ago the CEO of a $4 billion chemical company played a round of golf with Jack Welch. The next day, the quality manager got a call that resulted in the directive to "do Work-Out." The quality manager began a research period during which he talked to many members of his long list of business contacts, including consultants and former graduate school professors. At the time, Work-Out had not yet been chronicled in the business press, and information about it was closely held in the GE circle. The chemical company, characterized by a cautious, risk-averse, and analytical culture, applied that same cautiousness to Work-Out planning. After a year of thinking and talking and planning and considering various topics, the quality manager (who was still on the hook to "do Work-Out") had not been able to move the ball forward at all. The only progress he had made was to train the company's cadre of internal quality people to become Work-Out facilitators. So after a year, they were all "dressed up" but had nowhere to go. The CEO (golf game now comfortably in the past) did not drive the effort, and the otherwise well-meaning quality manager was constrained by needing to navigate political waters where all the big fish were most interested in maintaining the status quo. Eventually, however, he used his newly trained facilitators to launch a modest Work-Out that he kept below the organization's radar. After over a year of planning, the impact of the effort was minimal, and the effort was dropped because, as people said, "Work-Out doesn't work for us."

At the other end of the scale from the chemical company just described, many GE units have had great success designing their Work-Outs with minimal fuss. The extent of their preparation might be to book a conference room, borrow a facilitator from down the hall, order paper, pens, and post-it notes, and send out an e-mail note asking people to bring their ideas and coffee cups next Tuesday morning. This approach can be vastly comforting, especially when Work-Out is new and people are afraid that it's a new way to reduce the workforce—the informality, lack of preparation, and lack of management steering toward any topic, all reassure people that it's safe to proceed, and the small scale produces ideas that can be implemented on the spot, without complex process mapping and heavy commitments of resources. And when Work-Out is old hat—when all the key players are skilled at working together, can communicate clearly with one another, and have a bias for action—this approach can produce even more dramatic results with not much more effort or investment.

Your organization's design phase will no doubt fall somewhere between these two extremes. But if in doubt, keep it simple. Keep it focused. And make it fast. And then turn to the next chapter to see what happens in a real Work-Out event.

6-2a Armstrong Work-Out Goals
Overall Objective for the Work-Out: Making Customer Service a Competitive Advantage

Team Topic	1. Pricing/Billing	2. Product and Promotional Information	3. Claims Resolution	4. Claim Reduction
Goal	Quote accurate prices to customers in all cases on the first request, and eliminate billing errors due to incorrect prices, by April 15.	Satisfactorily answer on the first call all requests for information on new or dropped products, promotions beginning with product changes, and promotions in April.	Resolve 95 percent of claims within 30 days of receipt of the complaint (by either Customer Service, the retailer, or distributor) by April 15.	Reduce the average number of weekly claims by 30 percent beginning the week of April 9.
Participants	• Pricing • Sales • Marketing • Customer Financial Group • Customer Service • Finance • IT	• Sales • Marketing • Customer Service • R&D • Finance	• Marketing • Customer Service • Company rep • Distributor rep • IT • Finance • R&D	• Marketing • Customer Service • Company rep • Distributor rep • IT • Finance • R&D
Thought-Starter Questions	• What could be done to ensure that Customer Service Reps (CSRs) always have the prices for new products? • What could be done to ensure that CSRs are aware of all the special-price lists? • What other changes in communication or processes would help ensure that CSRs always have accurate price information?	• What could be done to ensure that CSRs are apprised of new products early in the development cycle? • What training might help CSRs handle any calls about new products? • How could CSRs be used more effectively to proactively support promotional activities? • What support tools might help CSRs on the call?	• How might we expedite the process of deciding which claims are legitimate? • How might we take more advantage of the Retailer Self-Inspection program to expedite claims resolution? • How might we expedite the process of dealing with claims that are outside the RSI limit?	• How might we reduce claims that could have been anticipated in the presale or sale process? • How might we reduce claims due to faulty installation? • How might we reduce other common causes of claims? • What trends are there (e.g., by product, region, or distributor) and what changes do these suggest?

Figure 6-2. Sample Work-Out Design Goals and Starter Questions for Problem-Solving Teams.

	6-2b Allied Signal Work-Out Starter Questions			
Key Goals: Accelerate the product commercialization				
Ensure achievement of cost/quality/performance expectations				
Team #1 **Product/Process** **Planning**	**Team #2** **Project** **Management**	**Team #3** **Product/Process** **Quality**	**Team #4** **Cost**	**Team #5** **Measurements/** **Rewards**
How might we best determine whether new-product intro-ductions are really needed and all objectives are clearly defined?	How do we ensure that the right resources (e.g., leadership, skills, training, capital expenses, etc.) are involved/used at the right times?	What can be done to mini-mize unproven technology risk?	How can we do a better job of dis-tinguishing between program and product costs?	What measure-ments should/-shouldn't we track that are unnecessary (or need change) to improve product development?
How can we include all perti-nent (internal and external) customer and supplier requirements in product/process planning?	How can we bet-ter define team-member roles and responsibili-ties, including leadership?	How can we ensure that all (internal and external) cus-tomer and supplier require-ments are met?	Given volumes and costs, how can we better define target costs?	What changes might be made in the incentive and rewards sys-tem to improve the product-development cycle?
What could be done to improve the analyses of competitive products and processes?	What might be done to reconcile the differences (e.g., in author-ity, approvals, accountability, documentation, etc.) between dis-ciplines and the project team?	During develop-ment, what can be done to achieve customer satisfaction and confidence (con-sider design, FMEA, tests, and risk of recall)?	What opportuni-ties exist to improve the accuracy of product-unit costs such that targets are met?	What are the aspects of our culture that, if changed, would add value to product development?
How can we make sure that there are suffi-cient resources (i.e., manpower, capital, facilities, and material expenses) available?	How do we improve project management (i.e., planning, control, review, audit, and deci-sion-making) to meet project parameters of cost, timing, and investment?	How do we ensure product manufacturabil-ity? And, how can the product be best manufac-tured (internally/externally)?	How do we achieve better integrity in capi-tal justification? How should we better manage resources (e.g., expense, tooling, capital, start-up inventories, and cash flow) dur-ing the project?	
	How can we bet-ter maintain team (member) continuity?	How can we improve the qual-ity plan to reduce reject rates and field failures?	How do we mini-mize the number of product/program changes that are costly?	
		What changes and/or alterna-tives to audit procedures (e.g., EN0050) would demonstrate improved launch readiness?		
		How could we improve product delivery and service?		

Figure 6-2. *(Continued)*

6-2c Wal-Mart Work-Out Starter Questions			
Customer Service	**Store Productivity**	**Home Office "Roadblocks"**	**Night and Weekend Business**
How do we stay ahead of the competition?	How do we get the "dumb" out of our store jobs?	How can Home Office stop getting in the way?	How do we improve our night and weekend business?

6-2d   GE Capital Real-Estate Financing Work-Out Starter Questions

The following are thought-starter questions to each team. Please review and be prepared to discuss so we can make the sessions as productive as possible.

Managing New Business—Is there a better way?
What are our products and are they changing? Who are our customers, and how do we market and service them better? Are we handling new deals as efficiently as possible? Are there ways to improve communication within our office? With Stamford? Can we eliminate or modify current paper flow? Could Due Diligence/closing process be improved? What ways can Central Region Production add to new-business-product development? How can production affect portfolio ROI in the short run to maximize returns? Are there areas in which we lack proper training and/or staffing?

Managing Our Existing Portfolio—Back to basics
The focus of this team will be to re-examine and recommend improvements in the way we manage our existing portfolio of businesses: What steps must be taken with every property in the portfolio to ensure that we maintain good control, information flow (including portfolio reviews, valuations, etc.), and income generation? Is it clear who does what, and why, and when each step needs to take place? Are there ways to streamline the process without compromising controls? What is the paper flow involved, and can it be improved? Are there ways to utilize production and project-management people to increase production? How do we improve the closing process—are we serving the clients properly? How do we ensure that early action is taken on properties that may be on the verge of trouble? How should we communicate most effectively within the region, with our customers, and with Stamford? What skills or procedures might need to be improved to do a better job in this area in the current business environment? Are there areas in which we lack proper training and/or staffing?

Modifications, REO Management, and Disposition
The focus of the team will be to examine and recommend improvements in the way we (a) handle problem properties, (b) develop and implement the strategy for disposition, and (c) handle the interim management process: What is the priority of steps which must be taken to ensure that 1) the proper personnel and controls are in place to proactively identify troubled properties, 2) we effectively manage and monitor troubled properties and REO, 3) liabilities associated with GECC's ownership are minimized, and 4) development and implementation of the disposition strategy are on the most timely and prudent course possible to minimize GECC's holding period and owned operating expenses? How does Work-Out/REO effectively work with Production to marry REO properties to product in the market in need of mortgage money? Is the responsibility for each step clearly defined, as to Operations, Work-Out, and AMO? Should the REO management team be expanded to include Production personnel for market information and customer relationships? When should the REO management team become involved in the loan process to maximize turnaround of the asset? How should we communicate most effectively within the region and with Stamford? What is the paper flow involved, and can it be improved? Are there areas in which we lack proper training and/or staffing? How can we minimize ROI?

Figure 6-2. *(Continued)*

Conducting a Work-Out

Now you know the theory of Work-Out. You've thought about how to engage employees to deal with business opportunities through Work-Out in your organization, and you've considered what a Work-Out design might look like. But what actually happens during the two or three days of a Work-Out event? What is the agenda? How are ideas generated? How is the Town Meeting structured? How does the Work-Out event make its breakthroughs?

This chapter provides you with an outline and preliminary tool kit for conducting a Work-Out event. It will walk you through a typical agenda and share techniques and approaches for a successful Work-Out. We'll even give you an opportunity to sit in on part of a Town Meeting, and we'll review some of the pitfalls that you should avoid.

In reading this chapter, however, keep in mind that there really is no such thing as a *typical* Work-Out event. Every event starts with a different focus and a different cast of characters, and every event is embedded in a different organizational culture. Just as no two human faces are exactly alike, no two Work-Outs will be just the same. But all faces are composed of the same elements—and all Work-Outs have a core set of building blocks. So while the proportions might be different, the core is always there to build from. This chapter, then, will provide you with the building blocks for constructing your own Work-Out. What you make of it after that is up to you.

Core Building Blocks of the Work-Out Agenda

No matter the scope, scale, focus, or duration, the Work-Out event always includes five core agenda elements. Each of these elements can be expanded or contracted, depending on organizational experience and the complexity of the session. Other elements can be added. But these five steps of the process must be present in some form for a Work-Out to be successful:

1. **Work-Out introduction.** Brief participants on the business issues and opportunities, review the objectives and agenda for Work-Out, and introduce the overall Work-Out process.
2. **Small-group idea generation.** Set up sessions to create an initial array of ideas and opportunities that can be further focused during the course of the Work-Out.
3. **Gallery of Ideas.** Have the entire Work-Out community meet to prioritize and select ideas and opportunities for further work.
4. **Small-group recommendation development.** Split up and turn initial high-level ideas and opportunities into specific recommendations with measures of success and accountable owners.
5. **Town Meeting.** Present the recommendations to the senior management Sponsor for yes-or-no decisions.

It's useful to go through each of these elements one at a time, then put them together to create a Work-Out agenda.

Element 1: Work-Out Introduction

The purpose of the opening session is to launch the Work-Out and get it going on an enthusiastic note. Specifically, it aims to set the business context as to why this Work-Out is being held. In case any of the attendees are new to the process, it explains the benefits of Work-Out, what it seeks to achieve, and what is involved in taking part in it. It will also present the Work-Out goals and challenges to the participants, introduce the cast of characters and their roles, and set the teams off on their first work session.

The opening session at the Work-Out usually consists of these elements:

- Welcome by lead facilitator and introduction of the Sponsor
- Opening remarks by the Sponsor, on the purpose and importance of the Work-Out
- Further remarks by the Sponsor or a designate (a Work-Out "champion") on the business issue to be addressed: background information, team assignments, introduction of team leaders, facilitators, and expert resources
- Overview of the Work-Out process, agenda, and ground rules by the lead facilitator
- Warm-up exercise

Sponsor's Opening Remarks

As described earlier, the Work-Out Sponsor is usually a senior leader— sometimes the CEO of the business unit or the head of a division or function. This is the same person who will return at the end of the Work-Out event to host or cohost the Town Meeting and make yes-or- no decisions. At the beginning of the Work-Out, the Sponsor's opening remarks typically include:

- Greetings and welcome
- Comments on the breadth of representation at the session (differ- ent functions, branches, regions, business units, and so on)
- Remarks about the business issues that the Work-Out is address- ing and the reasons for focusing on the selected topic
- Any remarks the Sponsor would like to make about Work-Out, based on personal knowledge and experience
- Comments on the Work-Out goal and the Sponsor's expectations of the teams
- Expectations for the Town Meeting
- A reminder to focus on "hard," bottom-line results or savings, and to focus on decisions that can be made here and now
- Encouragement to the teams that they are the ones who are clos- est to the work and can best say how to improve it—and a chal- lenge to them to not be afraid to generate radical, innovative ideas

- A reminder that participants' contribution won't necessarily stop at the end of the Work-Out—they may be involved throughout the implementation period that follows

Champion's Opening Remarks

Sometimes the Sponsor will designate another senior manager, typically a direct report, to be the champion for this specific Work-Out. The champion is the senior manager who will have hands-on accountability for following up on the recommendations that receive a "yes" at the Town Meeting, and making sure that they are implemented. Sometimes there will be more than one champion.

At GE Lighting, the president of the company, John Opie, sponsored many of the early Work-Out sessions. For specific topics, however, he would designate one of his direct reports as the champion—and if the topic cut across business units or functions, there would be multiple champions. This sent a powerful signal to the participants that if their bosses could collaborate, then they could as well. For example, one of these Work-Out sessions was focused on improving certain aspects of customer-delivery performance—which required collaboration between Marketing, Customer Service, Distribution, and Manufacturing. Because of the multifunctional nature, Opie asked two of his vice presidents—who had a history of not working well together—to colead the session. At the Town Meeting, Opie and his two VPs made the decisions together.

People filling this champion role should also make some general introductory and welcoming remarks. This might include reference to this being an opportunity to work together (say, across different parts of the business), and to be creative and innovative in developing recommendations.

If the Sponsor hasn't done so, the champion should present the overall Work-Out goal and the specific team assignments. Each team will be assigned a specific goal that is usually one aspect of the issue for the Work-Out. In doing this, the champion needs to be clear as to what limitations there are on the scope (if any), and should review any key data and issues relating to the Work-Out topic.

Finally, the champion should introduce the team leaders and facilitators, and introduce and explain the role of any expert resources, analysts, and others in attendance. A picture of the cast of key players who could be present at the Work-Out is shown in Figure 7-1. A champion

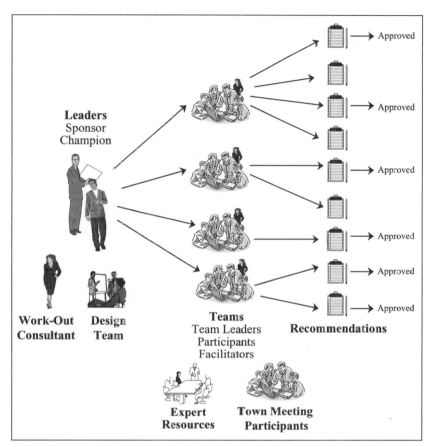

Figure 7-1. Key Players in Running a Work-Out.

who plans to sit in throughout the session should explain that it will be to listen and provide expert advice as needed, without influencing or guiding the discussion.

> **In general, we strongly recommend that neither the champion nor the Sponsor remain at the Work-Out session after the teams begin their work. The session tends to run most smoothly if they leave then and don't return until the Town Meeting.**

In most organizations, even the most adroit senior people exert subtle influence on participants—either inhibiting certain ideas or channeling the thinking in a particular direction. Part of the power of Work-Out is that senior people get to hear relatively unadulterated, unfiltered ideas—and not just what they want to hear, or what people expect them to want to hear. Furthermore, additional power in Work-Out is created when the Sponsor and champion hear ideas for the first time—on the spot—without preparation, at the Town Meeting. If the champion or Sponsor hang around, then that dynamic is compromised.

Facilitator Overview

After the Sponsor and champion have introduced the content of the Work-Out session, the lead facilitator should review the process of the session. For organizations or units that are new to Work-Out, this review might include a more extensive overview of the history of Work-Out at GE and elsewhere, why Work-Out works, and some of the key principles and ground rules for the session. If the participants are generally familiar with Work-Out, then the facilitator's overview might just mention where else in the company Work-Out has been used—and then remind people about the ground rules. In both cases, the facilitator should also review the agenda and timing for the session, as well as logistics, room assignments, and other mundane details that people need to know to work smoothly.

Part of the facilitator's overview should include a review of key ground rules that make the Work-Out session work:

- No "sacred cows:" Anything is open to question, and phrases such as "we've always done it that way" are invitations for challenging assumptions.
- No "turf:" People should not defend functional boundaries, but should instead look at issues from a process and customer perspective, regardless of their functional "home."
- No "blaming:" Work-Out is about making things better, not searching for the villains who got things into the shape they're in.
- No "stripes:" Rank has no privilege in a Work-Out session, and ideas from all sources should be respected.
- No "complaining:" An observation about something that needs to be fixed is just a complaint unless it comes with everything needed to fix it—a recommendation, an action plan, a timeline, and an accountable owner to see that the correction comes to pass. Work-Out is not a complaint session.

The other part of the facilitator's overview that is crucial is the description of the Town Meeting. Participants need to have an image, ahead of time, about how the Town Meeting will work. They need to know that real decisions will be made there, in real time, based on real dialogue. This up-front picture injects a sense of urgency and excitement into the Work-Out session. It is at that point that participants realize that the work they are doing is for real, that it will truly change the organization, and that there is a time limit for their efforts. If done well, this introduction ups the ante and starts to charge the collective batteries.

Warming Up the Troops

Before sending people off to develop ideas, there is one additional introductory activity that many organizations find useful—a warm-up exercise. In the early days of Work-Out at GE, doing a warm-up exercise lightened what often began as a tense and anxious atmosphere. In many cases, the exercise served to start building a sense of team and community among the participants, many of whom did not know each other or had not worked with each other before. In addition, the exercise was used to stimulate thinking about the Work-Out topic and get people in a mood for open, creative thinking.

Though warm-up exercises are usually conducted with the entire Work-Out community, they tend to be most effective if each Work-Out team needs to do something as a unit. This provides an initial opportunity for the team members to meet each other and have some quick fun together, before getting to work. For example, at a Work-Out session focused on customer service and packaging in GE Lighting, the initial warm-up exercise required teams to construct a "shipping package" for a raw egg—which could meet the specification of protecting the egg when it was dropped from a six-foot ladder. Teams were given materials to make their packages within a 30-minute time limit. At the end of the time, the eggs were packed in the containers and dropped from the ladder (onto a plastic sheet to protect the floor). Each team then spent a few minutes with its facilitator debriefing how they worked together—and thinking about the implications for the packaging of light bulbs. And with that experience in mind, the teams were off and running. Some cynical managers started by wondering what they were doing playing games, but they soon found that such exercises opened the team to new ideas and to engaging with each other in solving problems.

There are innumerable warm-up exercises that can be used at the beginning of a Work-Out. In general, such exercises should meet these criteria:

- Give the team members an opportunity to do something together.
- Help team members and facilitators gain some quick insight into the team's dynamics and interpersonal relationships.
- Create an atmosphere of innovation and teamwork.
- Stimulate ideas about the Work-Out topic.
- Run quickly (in 15 to 45 minutes) so as not to take too much time away from the Work-Out agenda.

We have found two exercises particularly useful in helping to launch Work-Out sessions. Both can be done quickly with large groups, and both meet the listed criteria. One is to ask each team to create a collage out of magazines and other materials that portrays what their organization or unit might look like if the Work-Out is highly successful. This exercise helps teams begin to articulate aspirations and expectations for what their work can produce. The other exercise involves passing tennis balls around a circle to simulate a process flow—and then adding more tennis balls as the volume increases. The team then needs to redesign its process flow to handle the increased volume while dramatically reducing the cycle time of the process. Figures 7-2 and 7-3 provide instructions to facilitators for how to run these exercises.

Element 2: Small-Group Idea Generation

Following the introductory session, it is time for the Work-Out teams to get to work. Their first objective—and the aim of this element of the Work-Out—is to identify a top-10 list of possible ideas or opportunities for achieving the team's assigned goal. The notion is to get a wide array of possible ideas identified quickly, based on participants' prior thinking and initial discussions. Once the ideas are on the table, the team can narrow them down to those that seem to have the most potential to make a difference, and then share them with the wider Work-Out community. This sharing, in the Gallery of Ideas described in following sections, will help avoid duplication, and will also stimulate new possibilities.

In a Work-Out session with a very broad or loosely defined topic, or no particular topic, the focus of this initial brainstorming is to define the

Facilitator Note

Participants construct collages that represent how their organization or unit might look if the Work-Out is highly successful. Each team is given a large piece of art board on which to construct the collage, as well as scissors, glue, and a diverse selection of magazines and other art materials (things like twine and sparkles). It is helpful if each team has a separate work space so that one team's discussion does not distract the other teams.

Steps

1. Introduce the exercise. Explain that the exercise explores the participants' visions of what their organization or unit might look like if the Work-Out is highly successful.

2. Divide participants into their Work-Out teams. Ask each team to construct a vision collage, using images from the magazines and other materials that represents how people imagine or hope the future will be different if the Work-Out is successful. Allow approximately 45 minutes for this.

Reconvene the larger group and ask each team to present its post-Work-Out vision. You can stimulate discussion of each vision with the following questions:

1. Explain why you put the images that you did in your collage. What do they represent?

2. What did you decide to leave out, and why?

What does this vision say about your organization or unit's strategic priorities? The capabilities it will require? The challenges it will face?

Figure 7-2. Collage Exercise Instructions.

topics or opportunities that the Work-Out session can address. These ideas must be as specific as possible. In some early GE Work-outs, much of the focus was "removing bureaucracy," and individuals were encouraged to identify reports, approvals, meetings, measures, policies, and practices (the RAMMPP matrix) that kept them from being effective. As individuals identified specific items, they could share them in their teams. At other times, as with the GE Power Systems Work-Outs described in Chapter 6, the theme was possible threats—the things that

Facilitator Note

You will need three tennis balls and a timing watch for each team. Try to build humor and fun into this demonstration. The exercise will be more successful if you can make some jokes along the way.

Steps

1. Ask each team to form a circle with plenty of space to toss a tennis ball around. Designate two people from the team, one as a *ball feeder* and one as a *timer.*

2. Tell them you will first demonstrate with one group.
    *   Use one ball only.
    *   Toss it to someone on the opposite side of the circle from where you are standing.
    *   Tell that person to toss it to someone else, but to remember who that someone is.
    *   Have the next person toss to someone new (not a direct neighbor in the circle), remembering who, and so on.
    *   When the last person gets it, have them start again, always passing the ball from person to person in the same order.

3. Ask the other groups (if any) to try it with one ball.

4. Ask the "timer" in each group to time how long it takes for the team to finish one complete cycle of passing the ball in that order. Depending on the size of the group, it typically takes 8 to 10 seconds.

5. Note to the group that this now represents a "process:" material or information being passed through a series of steps in a particular order.

6. Now ask the group to increase the "volume" of the process that is being handled—by passing three tennis balls instead of just one. Teams should stay where they are, and the balls must continue to move, one at a time, from person to person in the standard order. Timers should record the time and also observe if "quality" (keeping the ball in the air rather than dropping it) declines.

7. Ask the teams how fast they think they can do the process with three balls, without changing anything else. This repre-

Figure 7-3. Tennis Ball Exercise Instructions.

sents trying to do a process faster and harder—but not necessarily any differently.

8. Now tell them that a competitor can do the same process in less than one second—and that they should figure out how to meet that competitive challenge. Teams will now start to reconfigure, move around, and experiment with different ways of moving the balls. (The best solution we have seen is to create a "funnel" with team members' hands and use gravity to let the balls pass through.)

9. After teams have had a few minutes of fun in trying to speed the process, engage the group in a quick debriefing with questions such as these:
   - What were the factors that helped you dramatically improve the process (competitive threat, teamwork, innovation, process analysis)?
   - How well did the team work together? Did everyone listen to each other's ideas?

10. Conclude the exercise with a comment about how this is a microcosm of the Work-Out process—face a stretch challenge, take a fresh look at a process, use the team to come up with new ideas, try things quickly, and improve results.

Figure 7-3.   *(Continued)*

kept people up at night—and the teams brainstormed lists of possibilities that they categorized, prioritized, and brought to the Gallery of Ideas for discussion with the full group. Then, based on the voting of the whole group, Work-Out topics were developed, and teams were formed around them. In these open-ended sessions, the ideas generated are less tied to any one goal and the process is meant more to allow employees to put parameters on what can and should be done.

When Work-Out topics have been preassigned, the teams in this part of the Work-Out session need to do the following:

- Review and discuss the team's assigned goal, pertinent background data, and process maps. This is the first chance for the team to sit down together (after the warm-up exercise). So this is the first substantive discussion of the goal and prework that has been done in regard to it.

- Have some discussion of the key issues and root causes that are getting in the way of achieving the goal. This should not be a deeply analytical discussion, but rather a chance for the participants to talk about the potential barriers and issues that are affecting organizational performance.
- Brainstorm action ideas for addressing these issues and root causes. There are many techniques and approaches to brainstorming, any of which can be used here. We often find it valuable to hand out pads of post-it notes and ask everyone first to write down their own ideas individually (one per post-it note). This helps the quiet ones think and come up with ideas, without the pressure of having to jump into a hot and heavy discussion.
- Once people have written down their own ideas, then we begin the traditional brainstorming, with people adding ideas and building on one another's. Each idea gets stuck on a wall, where it will then be easier to move ideas around, combine them, and figure out what they mean.
- Categorize and prioritize these ideas—some people call this "affinity mapping"—to select the "top 10" for presentation to the main group.

A simple but powerful tool for prioritizing ideas or possible actions is the "payoff matrix." Teams use the payoff matrix to assess each idea in terms of two criteria: How easy or difficult will it be to implement the idea or opportunity? (*Easy to implement* means eight weeks or less, and with minimal new resources; *tough to implement* means more than eight weeks, or lots of additional resources, or both.) And what's the size of the expected payoff? (As in *large* or *small*—no need for much detail at this point.)

Plotting each action idea on the four quadrants of the payoff matrix, shown again in Figure 7-4 for your convenience, highlights the "Bonus Opportunities" that offer the most bang for the buck—the easy-to-implement, high-payoff ideas. These will typically become the team's top-priority actions. It also shows the "Quick Wins" and the "Special Effort" actions. Teams will typically want to pursue some of these ideas as well. The "Time Wasters"—low-payoff and tough-to-implement ideas—should, of course, be avoided.

	EASY TO IMPLEMENT	TOUGH TO IMPLEMENT
SMALL PAY-OFF	**Quick Wins! (QW)**	**Time Wasters (TW)**
BIG PAY-OFF	**Bonus Opportunities (BO)**	**Special Efforts (SE)**

Figure 7-4. Payoff Matrix.

Facilitators usually work with each team to help them brainstorm and organize their ideas. Teams often need help to avoid getting too bogged down in detailed analysis of data or processes. They also tend to want to do group brainstorming immediately rather than allowing all the members to do their own thinking first. Once they do start talking together, the facilitator needs to keep them from things like rushing to solutions before being clear on the problems and root causes, judging and debating each idea when still in the brainstorming phase, and losing sight of the goal—and whether the ideas relate to that goal.

Left to themselves, Work-Out groups have a tendency to combine too many ideas that are similar—but not identical—into one. They leave themselves without enough time to work through the categorization of ideas using the payoff matrix, and they want to work too many ideas—and especially too many "Special Effort" ideas.

Of course teams can also struggle with group dynamics at this stage, including a team member who dominates the group, or team members who show resistance to the goal or to the process. It poses particular problems if a team winds up with a team leader who is too passive to keep things moving smoothly or to keep an expert resource from driving the discussion. It's even worse to have a facilitator who is too passive—or, conversely, one who wants to contribute to the subject-matter discussion. Experienced facilitators can help teams overcome these hurdles—and can avoid presenting any hurdles of their own.

Once the team has identified its top-10 list for the Gallery of Ideas, one of its members should write out the list on a series of flip charts or posters. We recommend placing two ideas on each large chart—leaving room between them for people to make comments and place votes. In the Gallery session, the objective is for the full group to get a sense of each team's preliminary ideas and to deal with any overlap or conflict in the ideas being developed. A long or formal presentation is not required. One or two people should, however, be designated to explain the ideas quickly.

Element 3: The Gallery of Ideas

The Gallery of Ideas is when each of the small Work-Out teams share preliminary ideas and opportunities with the rest of the Work-Out community. The purpose of this session is to allow everyone an opportunity to see the main ideas that the other teams have identified so far, to indicate their preferences for the ideas that should go forward to the Town Meeting, and to resolve ownership of any duplicate, overlapping, or conflicting ideas and, then reassign ideas and team members as needed.

Process Overview

Before the session starts, each team should post charts containing its top 10 ideas or opportunities on the wall of the large meeting room. The session can then proceed as follows. Allow about 5 minutes for the introduction to the session, and 20 minutes per team—10 for the team's presentation, followed by another 10 minutes or so for questions before moving on to the next team. At the end of the session, allow 10 minutes, if needed, for resolving duplication or overlap issues, and another 10 minutes for voting on the ideas.

Introduction and Team Presentations

After a brief introduction by the facilitator, the first team comes to the front of the room. A spokesperson reminds the rest of the group of the team's assignment and gives a brief review of their top ideas. In doing this, the spokesperson should briefly explain each idea, the rationale behind it, and something about the potential payoff. (The facilitator needs to watch the time and encourage people to move faster if they are taking too long. This should just be a brief explanation—not a formal presentation or sales pitch.)

After the team has reviewed all of its ideas, the floor is opened for questions. These should be questions of clarification—for example, explain the idea further if someone does not fully understand the nature or content of the idea, or how it relates to the goal. This is not the time for the group to debate or to work the ideas. They can convey their views during the voting, and the ideas will be worked more thoroughly during the next session. The facilitator needs to use judgment with other kinds of comments—for example, if someone sees a major risk with an idea that will need to be addressed, or if someone has a concept for how to significantly improve on an idea, it may be appropriate to allow this dialogue.

The process is then repeated with each of the other teams.

Resolving Duplication or Overlap of Ideas

As the team presentations are being made, participants should identify where there is any duplication or overlapping of ideas.

The groups should try to reach agreement as to which team should take ownership of ideas that could be claimed by more than one team. Team leaders should take the lead in doing this, with help from the facilitator. If there is no immediate agreement, the ideas can be arbitrarily assigned to one team or the other for the purpose of the voting. Once the voting is completed, the group can revisit the question of which team should take up which idea.

If ideas are similar but not identical, they can be left on their original team list for the voting—and revisited after everyone has seen the scores.

Voting

In some cases, teams come to the Gallery of Ideas with one big idea, or with just a few reasonably substantial ideas. In such cases, it is not necessary to go through a voting process. In other cases, teams might come to the Gallery of Ideas with a large number of "quick hits." These may also not need to be voted on since the team itself can parcel them out. In other words, the objective here is not to constrain the teams or dampen their enthusiasm in any way. Instead, the voting is designed to help each team narrow down its preliminary list of approximately 10 ideas to 3 or 4.

One of the ground rules for this part of the session is that the teams need not feel bound by the results of the voting. The purpose is to give them a sense of the entire group's view of the best ideas.

The voting itself works as follows:

- Participants get a number of dots or stickers to cast their votes (usually four times as many dots as there are teams).

- Participants can use their dots to vote for the top four ideas for each team, including their own teams. (With two teams, that means everyone can vote for the top four ideas for team one and the top four for team two.)
- No one can put more than one dot on an idea.
- No one has to use all the dots.

Once people have voted, the facilitator and team leaders (or other volunteers) should quickly count the votes for each team so everyone has a snapshot of the ideas that the entire group thought were most worth pursuing. This helps to create a total sense of community ownership for the ideas. This collective ownership will reemerge during the Town Meeting when recommendations are presented and discussed by the whole Work-Out community; teams often support each other in the debates.

When this process is completed, if ownership of any high-scoring, duplicate ideas is still unresolved, the team leaders and the facilitator should agree on who will take them forward.

Realigning the Teams and Their Assignments

Sometimes it becomes necessary to consider realigning the teams based on the ideas presented and the outcome of the voting. For example:

- If two or more teams have the same idea, the teams that will not have ownership of the idea for the rest of the session may want to assign one of their own team members to join the team that does have ownership of the idea. This will improve the recommendation by adding to the perspectives brought to bear upon it.
- If two teams have clearly conflicting ideas, it may make sense to have one team work on both of them and move some team members over from the other team.
- If two teams have an overlapping idea and there is enough substance to it, it may make sense to consider forming a separate small team, with members drawn from the original teams, to work on it. If this impromptu team completes its work before the Town Meeting, its members can rejoin their original teams at that point, to help out.

Element 4: Generating Specific Action Recommendations

For the balance of the time leading up to the Town Meeting, participants work in their teams to think through and develop the selected ideas in more detail, and to prepare the presentation for the Town Meeting. We have found that it is useful to have a standard format for the presentation—but how each team makes the presentation, who does it, and in what the order, should be up to them. The reason for the standard format is twofold: it helps each team be sure to touch on key points that will help the Sponsor or champion make a decision, and it makes it easier for the Sponsor or champion—and all the other participants at the Town Meeting—to follow the various ideas. Facilitators should review this presentation format with participants at the start of this session so everyone knows the endpoint at which they need to arrive.

Figure 7-5 shows a Work-Out presentation format that we have found useful. Facilitators should also go over with the teams what they can expect to happen in the Town Meeting, including:

- Who will attend
- The time allotted for each team
- The process and ground rules for the question-and-answer, dialogue, and decision-making sessions

In the most successful Work-Outs that we have seen, the teams are not limited in the number of recommendations they can present to the Sponsor. They are limited, however, in the amount of time available. Therefore, the teams will need to decide how many recommendations—including time for dialogue—they can make in the allocated time. They may want, for example, to present 10 quick-hit, no-brainer ideas that will probably require very little discussion—and just 1 or 2 big ideas that will require debate. Or they may just want to focus on one really big idea that has multiple parts. It is totally up to them. But knowing this ahead of time will help the team figure out their presentation strategy.

Participants should also be informed up front by their facilitators that they can expect the managers to ask some tough questions and to challenge them about risks and payoffs—so they need to try to anticipate what will come up and be ready with their answers. In that context, they should be reminded that this is a team effort and the dialogue is between

Town Meeting Presentation

Team: _____

QH	TW
BO	SE

Issue: _____
_____

Recommendation: _____
_____
_____
_____

Pay-Off and Risks: _____
_____
_____

Action(s) (what):   Responsibilities (who):   Dates (when):
_____
_____
_____
_____
_____
_____
_____
_____
_____
_____

Plans for Tracking Progress (what to track and how often):
_____
_____

Team Leader: _____
Sponsor: _____

Figure 7-5. Town Meeting Presentation Worksheet.

the teams and the management group, not just an individual presenter. Thus, any member of the team should be ready to help answer questions—even when not at the front of the room doing the presentation.

The teams might also be encouraged to allow themselves time to do dry runs of their presentations. We have found it helpful for teams to pair off and try out their presentations on each other before the Town Meeting. If time allows, it can produce even better results to have the teams do full presentations to the whole group—full-scale dry runs—before the Sponsor and other managers show up for the Town Meeting. This enhances the support for all the ideas that go forward in the Town Meeting and helps build enthusiasm. At GE Power Systems, Sponsors went to great lengths to get the participants together: Steve Kerr would tell them, "The leadership panel outranks you but you outnumber them, so it's a fair fight—but only if you stand together during the final presentations. So if you hear something you don't like, the time to say so is during the rehearsal, not later on." To bolster this, Power Systems used to give everyone on each team a colored jacket at the start—so they had the blue team, the red team, and so on. But after the dress rehearsal, they had everyone turn their jackets inside out. The linings of all the jackets were rainbow striped with the colors of all the teams, and that's what everyone wore to the final presentations. Likewise, they coached the presenters always to say "we" recommend, never "I recommend."

All this information, and discussion about it, should be conveyed to the teams at the beginning of this session. This will help the teams allocate their time and monitor their progress over the course of the hours that remain before the Town Meeting.

Selecting and Developing Action Recommendations

Once the teams understand the endpoint and the overall timetable for getting there, they need to start shaping specific action recommendations for presentation at the Town Meeting. These steps usually lead to a workable list:

1. Review the discussion during the Gallery of Ideas session, and consider any possible implications for reshaping ideas or opportunities.
2. Select the top 3 or 4 ideas from the original list of 10. These 3 or 4 are the ideas that the group will further develop for the Town

Meeting. Most groups focus on those ideas from their own list that received the most votes in the Gallery of Ideas session. However, there are often a couple of other ideas that someone feels passionately about, or that have such significant potential payoff that the team elects to work on them anyway—even if they did not receive the highest number of votes.

3. Assuming that there are several rich ideas or opportunities to pursue, the team might then decide to work in subgroups to ensure that enough time is spent exploring each idea and developing the specific recommendation. When groups decide to take this approach, it is effective to allow some time for the entire team to discuss each idea or opportunity first—before splitting into subteams. This is almost like a second round of brainstorming, focused on the specific idea. Without debating each comment, the entire team can provide input to the subgroup on what it will take to turn this idea into action, where the idea might first be tested, possible objections or resistance that might be encountered, related ideas that might be included, and so on. The subgroups can then take this input and factor it into their thinking.

The subgroup work is at the core of a Work-Out event, for it is there that ideas are narrowed down into realistic recommendations that are clear enough for a senior leader to simply say yes or no. It is thus crucial that the subgroups avoid vague platitudes and be as specific as possible. For example, when a team wants to recommend that a certain report no longer be produced and distributed, it cannot simply say, "Let's kill it." In addition, the team needs to be able to discuss the original purpose of the report, how that original purpose might have changed, the consequences of not producing it any more, who (if anyone) uses the report, what they would do if it wasn't available, who would need to be informed about no longer providing the data and creating the report, how people would spend their time if they were not producing the report, and so on and so on. And they need to be able to say what the organizational benefit or payoff would be for not producing the report.

On a more complex issue or idea, this level of specificity is even more important. For example, at a Work-Out in GE Supply—a unit that distributes electrical and other types of equipment—a subteam focused on a recommendation for "empowering the sales force." While this is a worthy goal, it lacks specificity. Thus, the Sponsor at the Town Meeting said he couldn't argue with the intent, but he still could not say yes because it was not clear what the team was actually proposing. What would be different? Eventually, the subteam refocused on the idea of salespeople being able to make pricing decisions on the spot with customers—instead of the current practice of having to call a central pricing department or coming back to the customer days (or weeks) later with a quote. To enable salespeople to make such quotes, the team recommended the creation of a sales "decision tree"—a set of pricing guidelines that would cover almost all situations and contingencies. They also recommended an enhanced communication process between field sales and the home office so that salespeople had daily updates of current product and price information. And, longer-term, they recommended technology solutions that would connect salespeople to the headquarters in real time. These much-more-specific recommendations were then presented at the next Town Meeting and won a warm reception.

Making Recommendations Specific

After the subteams have spent some time working on their ideas or opportunities, it is useful to bring them back together to review or develop one recommendation as an entire team so that everyone can see what a strong presentation looks like. Then the team can be divided back into subgroups to tackle the remaining recommendations.

The subteams should use the Town Meeting presentation format as a guide in this work, as follows:

1. Each subgroup starts by talking about the steps on the first part of the Town Meeting presentation format—discussing issues, payoffs and risks, and the other factors. One person from the subteam should make notes that can be incorporated into the presentation.
2. For the second part, the draft action plan, the subgroup might split up and have each person spend five minutes writing up a list of action steps and approvals required to implement the recommendation.
3. The team should then list these ideas on a flip chart and discuss them. They can then develop these steps into an action plan as outlined on the second part of the presentation format. As part of this, they need to identify resources and time frames for making

each step occur. At this point all the work plan needs is a rough estimate—meant to provide a sense of what it will take to implement the idea. After the Town Meeting, if the recommendation is approved, then the action plan will need to be further vetted, strengthened, tested with others, and turned into a real commitment to action.

One of the main purposes of doing a preliminary action plan at this point is to help sharpen the thinking about the recommendation. If a subteam cannot clearly think through the steps for implementation, then they probably do not have a clear sense of what they are really recommending. Doing the draft action plan forces this thinking.

Once the subteams have developed their draft presentations, the entire team should reassemble to hear and critique the work of each subteam. In listening to each subteam, the team should consider the following questions:

- Is the implementation of the recommendations well within the appropriate time frame? Are there ways to accelerate action? Is the timing realistic, given everyone's ongoing responsibilities? As a senior HR manager at GE used to say, "Don't forget that everyone still has day jobs!"
- Are there other ways to improve the recommendation or the action plan—to make it more complete or more compelling? The team could use the worksheet "Strengthening Action Plans" to test the completeness and quality of the plan. (See Figure 7-6.)
- Are there steps built into the plan to track and measure progress?
- What are some of the likely objections or questions that might be raised at the Town Meeting? How might these be addressed?

At the end of this discussion, the team needs to select one or two people who will make the actual presentations at the Town Meeting. Some teams like to give every team member a chance to present or be part of the presentation. While this is sometimes feasible, it often makes the Town Meeting drag on too long—and it is distracting to have people coming and going in the front of the room. Moreover, if just one or two people make the whole presentation, they will more easily convey the connections between recommendations.

Questions to Strengthen an Action Plan

What is the probability of success? Are there ways to increase it?

_____

_____

_____

_____

_____

Are the dates realistic, given other commitments and priorities?

_____

_____

_____

_____

_____

Have you considered key risks and weak spots? Can you build steps into the plan to address these?

_____

_____

_____

_____

_____

Who do you need to share the plan with? How will you communicate what you may do to those affected? Are there people who should become part of an "extended team"—that is, asked to help with some parts of your project?

_____

_____

_____

_____

Can you build some "zest" into the effort?

_____

_____

_____

_____

_____

Figure 7-6. Worksheet: Strengthening Action Plans.

In the early days of Work-Out at GE, most presentations were made with flip charts and hand-written transparencies for visual aids at the Town Meeting. These continue to be excellent means of presenting because they engage the audience intensely—as opposed to PowerPoint presentations, which seem more formal and detached from the audience. Whichever medium the team is using, the next step is to finalize the presentations based on the subteam work and the critiques.

As noted earlier, once the presentations have been prepared, it is useful to give the presenters a chance to practice—do a dry run—with the friendly audience of the team and perhaps one or more of the other teams. It is important here not to overrehearse the presentations—the Town Meeting dialogue works best when it is mostly spontaneous. But for people who are not used to presenting ideas to very senior managers, the opportunity to do a dry run is very important for reducing anxiety and sharpening the key messages to be delivered.

If time remains, the team can then select additional ideas from the original list and develop these into action plans and recommendations.

Common Struggles of Work-Out Teams

The heart of a Work-Out event is hard work. Participants move back and forth between a team, its subgroups, and the entire Work-Out community. In various forums, they brainstorm, prioritize, focus, sharpen, and iterate their ideas. Many participants have likened the process to "moving down a funnel"—from a broad topic to more-and-more specific ideas—while still maintaining the line of sight back to the overall goal. In many cases, teams and subteams work late into the evenings.

Given this intensity—and the high stakes of the Town Meeting that is to follow—it's no surprise that teams run into a number of common "process" problems during this portion of the Work-Out event. Facilitators and team leaders should be alert to the following problems and try to avoid them or make corrections as needed:

- Dividing up into small groups too quickly—before the group has learned how to recognize a robust recommendation by working on one together.
- Not being sharp and clear enough in describing the recommended action idea—or the issue that the action is designed to address.

- Confusing the recommended action *idea* with action *plans* for implementing the idea.
- Being reluctant to estimate payoffs—or not knowing how to go about estimating.
- Wanting to present all the background detail and calculations supporting the estimated payoff—rather than showing the number and the key assumptions and simply referring to the pages of the calculations.
- Losing sight of the goal.
- Including too much detail and having too lengthy a presentation.
- Wanting to work too many ideas.
- Staying with an idea too long. Some teams find—as they work the idea through in more depth—that they should discard the idea because it does not have as much merit or will not result in as much payoff as originally thought. Yet they are reluctant to let go, so they waste time going down a blind alley.
- Not having enough fun as they go through the process. Intensity is a good thing, but it is important to keep a sense of humor and perspective throughout the sessions.

Element 5: The Town Meeting

The Town Meeting is one of the most crucial and distinguishing features of the Work-Out process. The purpose is to enable each team to present its recommendations and action plans to the Sponsor, champion, and other key business managers—and for the Sponsor to make needed decisions on the spot.

The Town Meeting takes place at the end of the Work-Out session. It is essentially a forum for decision making by the Sponsor with the teams and the other attending managers. The facilitator helps keep things running smoothly and makes sure everyone stays focused on getting decisions made.

During the Town Meeting, each team first presents the actions it would like to implement over the coming weeks to achieve its stated goals. The presentation includes the specific recommendation, the issue that the recommendation addresses, the financial payoff and other benefits, the risks, the way results will be tracked and measured, and the action plan for implementing the recommendation—including the name of the person on the team who has volunteered to oversee the work. In addition, each team will make recommendations for any changes in ways of working, or for any additional help that it feels is needed to achieve the goals and needs business-leader approval (for example, increasing the authority of claims handlers to resolve certain types of claims).

Questions are held until the end of each presentation (or each idea), when the lead facilitator will then open the meeting for questions or comments. At this point the Sponsor and attending managers should ask clarifying questions, as needed, to ensure that they understand precisely what change is being recommended, and to make sure the team has explored all the available options. (For example, they might ask, "Do you know how often we face these types of claims and what the impact is likely to be financially if we expand the authority of claims handlers?") They should also encourage the team to be bolder when appropriate. (For example, "Why not expand the authority of the front-line representatives even further—to $X level?") In the process, they should be candid—but constructive—in expressing any concerns or reservations. It is important that the Sponsor has the benefit of everyone's views, so that an informed decision can be made.

After the question-and-answer session, the Sponsor then has the task of making or arranging for a yes-or-no decision on that particular recommendation. Some of the decisions can be made on the spot and actions implemented; other decisions will lead to short-term, focused task teams who will implement in the next 90 days. At GE Power Systems, Steve Kerr used to invite the immediate superiors of every Work-Out participant to attend the final presentations. That way they could see the excitement in the room and the level of support given to their subordinates (if their subordinates volunteered to take ownership of recommendations) by the heads of the business. This increased the likelihood that they would support the owner, or at least not grouse about time taken from normal duties. He also briefed the panel to ask of a potential owner who was volunteering for unusually time-consuming work: "Who's your boss? Charlie? Charlie, are you in favor of this idea? Do you see any problems with Sally being its owner?" (If Charlie didn't claim to have a problem then, he was less likely to develop one later.)

The Work-Out process aims for as many "yes" decisions as possible—since the work of the teams over the previous two days has been to develop realistic plans and to highlight legitimate obstacles and areas where help is needed. However, occasionally the Sponsor may need to say "no". If this is the case, the Sponsor should explain the reasoning to the team, so that the team can understand the rationale behind the decision. Occasionally the Sponsor may need to ask the team to do more analysis or planning before receiving an unqualified yes. If this is the case, there needs to be a specific, *short* time frame set for completing this work and making the final decision. (For example, "I want to say yes, but we really need the financial implications to be spelled out more clearly. Get the numbers and let's meet tomorrow at 8:00, and if they look good, my decision will definitely be yes.") Though in general the Sponsor makes most of the decisions, the senior officers acting as the panel discuss things among themselves—always openly, never in an executive session—and sometimes the one most nearly affected will give the answer. The only absolute is that there has to be an answer; indefinite deferral to further study is not an option.

Typical Work-Out Dialogue

Work-Out generates a lot of its real power during the Town Meeting, particularly because the decision dialogue that occurs is unscripted and spontaneous—and thus becomes a wonderfully rich learning experience for everyone. In that context, some senior leaders use it like an advanced graduate seminar in business economics. As ideas are presented, they help the entire room walk through the logic of how to explore the issue, how to weigh the pros and cons, how to solicit different viewpoints, and ultimately how to reach a decision. Other senior leaders use it as a "spark box" to stimulate controversy and stir up emotions—and then commitment—toward changing the organization.

In all cases, senior leaders who are running Town Meetings need to set the tone and kick off the dialogue. Here are three typical "tone-setting statements" from GE Capital business leaders:

> **Leader #1: "OK, why don't we get started here, keeping in mind our strategy statement. How can we bring more value to the customer? What do they want? What can we provide, given the way we're organized and the constraints that we have?"**

Note that this leader immediately focused the participants on the customer and signaled that the main decision screen would be the customer and the business strategy.

Leader #2: "What we're trying to do today is for you to go and talk among yourselves and come back and tell us and tell me and all these guys who are supposedly running the company what we can do better, how we can do these things better!"

The second leader, from a business that had a history of top-down command and control, emphasized that the Town Meeting would be an opportunity to reverse the traditional paradigm of the business culture.

Leader #3: "The reasons these sessions work is because of you people in the audience, that you have conveyed the ideas from all the people in the organization, and that you have actually put them into action. I guarantee you, as good ideas come up, we're going to take action on them."

The third leader stressed faith in the Town Meeting participants to come up with good ideas, and commitment to put them into practice.

After these opening statements, the presentations begin. After each presentation, the senior leader stimulates a discussion by asking questions, making comments, and soliciting others to respond.

Here is a typical snippet of dialogue from a session at GE Capital's Fleet Leasing business:

Presenter: *What we'd like to do in order to further protect our security interest and reduce our interaction from a paper-and-collection standpoint on our titles, is try tracking individuals by state. Specifically in states where we have high concentrations of vehicles, we should get someone to actually handle this process for us.*

Business Leader: *I think that's a great idea. It lets us protect the security interests of the vehicle.*

Presenter: *It really would be all-round beneficial, especially if we could get a substantial fee out of it.* [group laughter]

In this dialogue, the business leader not only supported the idea, but built upon it (adding "security" as a benefit). The presenter was then encouraged to go even further with the idea by suggesting that it could be a fee-based service. Thus, even from this small sample of dialogue, it is possible to see how the Town Meeting can begin to fly, taking a good idea and making it even better.

The meeting becomes even more powerful when a number of people participate in the dialogue, some of whom are challenged—in public—to deal with their resistance to change. Here is a conversation that took place in an equipment leasing business of GE Capital:[1]

> **Presenter:** *Let's eliminate the regional manager's signature on all the paperwork when we have to liquidate an asset coming off lease. . . . We can let the branch manager sign off. It takes an extra 30 minutes for the regional manager to sign all the papers for each unit. It's at least 40 hours per month for each regional manager—not to mention the slowdown of our processing.*

> **Business Leader:** *What value does the regional manager's signature add?*

> **A Regional Manager:** *There are some cost considerations here regarding the price for liquidation. It's got to be a management-controlled decision.*

> **Business Leader:** *Do the regional managers pay any real attention to what they are signing? In other words, do they ever not sign, or change the price, or anything?*

> **Another Regional Manager:** *It's basically a rubber stamp. We never look at the numbers; we just sign.*

> **Business Leader:** *Let's do it!*

> **Group:** [Loud cheers]

As this dialogue shows, the first regional manager was probably threatened by the recommendation of the team, perhaps feeling that it would erode his authority. He had grown up in an environment where control was important, and this recommendation suggested that he would lose control. The Town Meeting dialogue smoked out this resistance and brought it to the light of day. The business leader did a masterful job of not confronting the regional manager's need for control directly, but rather testing whether that control had any business benefit. And when it became apparent that there was no added value by having regional managers control the process—and that the process could be speeded up by eliminating that step—the decision became obvious.

Tuning the Meeting

Most Town Meetings are successful no matter what people do. Putting committed Work-Out participants in direct dialogue with a senior business leader is almost always beneficial. But you can do two things that are more or less guaranteed to make it even more successful: brief the extra participants, and set up the environment to help maintain the focus.

BRIEF TOWN MEETING PARTICIPANTS: Besides the people who have been meeting since the beginning of the Work-Out and the Sponsor or champion who will make decisions, a number of other managers often join the Town Meeting. These are typically heads of other business units, functional heads, and other middle and senior managers who might be affected by the Work-Out recommendations.

In our experience, these people tend to be the ones most threatened by Work-Out and the Town Meeting process. Sometimes they are challenged in public. Their direct reports have an opportunity to tell their bosses how they would like to do things differently, which might reflect on the bosses. And sometimes the recommendations test the very assumptions upon which their careers have been built—the old management standbys of "command and control," "information is power," "never admit weakness," and the rest.

An open and transparent Town Meeting can do a great deal to turn this instinctive reaction into acceptance or even support. We strongly recommend that middle and senior managers who have not been part of the three-day process be invited in. As we've said before, you may as well invite them; if you don't, they're apt to show up anyway—out of pure self-interest, if not curiosity, and they'll be in a much better frame of mind if they don't feel like they're gate-crashing. For example, at some of the first Work-Out sessions at Zurich Financial Services UK, the Town Meetings were standing-room-only events because so many middle and senior managers wanted to attend.

Given the likely attendance of other managers, we recommend that the lead facilitator or perhaps a couple of the team leaders take about 15 minutes before the Town Meeting commences to brief these newcomers. It's useful to begin by welcoming the managers and checking to see how many have attended a Town Meeting before. The more first-timers or known opponents of the process you have to deal with, the more care the rest of the introduction will require. Explain the purpose of the Town Meeting and the process it will follow, covering at least these points:

- Who will act as facilitator for the meeting.
- How each team in turn will present its recommendations.
- How questions will be addressed. (The options are to ask everyone to hold questions either until the end of each team's whole presentation or until the end of the presentation of each idea. This point should be decided before the Town Meeting, based on the nature of the ideas and the preferences of the teams.)
- That any and all relevant questions are permissible once the floor is open. (Make it clear that they can speak up if they do not understand what is being proposed, or if they want to be sure the team has thought through the risks adequately, or if they would like to challenge the recommendation in some way—but ask them to try to phrase their questions and comments in a positive way.)
- That there will not be time for philosophical debate, some issues may need to be taken off-line, and the facilitator will help guide this or cut off discussion.
- That the Sponsor will be the one to make the final decision or to delegate it to someone else. (Explain that the Town Meeting does not involve voting or consensus decision making—but the purpose of having the other managers there, and encouraging them to raise questions and concerns, is so the Sponsor can make an informed decision at the end of the discussion.)

Make it clear that the Sponsor will be asked to make or request a yes-or-no answer on each idea presented, and to explain any rejections clearly enough that the team can understand—and accept—that there is sound reasoning behind the decision. Also make it clear that occasionally it may be necessary for the Sponsor to qualify a yes by asking for more work to be done before giving a final decision—but with a very short time frame for this work and the ultimate decision to be made.

After making these points, check for questions—then move on to review the overall goal and the team assignments. Be upbeat in telling everyone that the teams have worked extremely hard over the course of the session—but also flag any key challenges the teams faced in coming up with ideas.

Emphasize that, because the teams have worked so hard and are impassioned about their ideas, it is important that the managers be positive in what they say, how they say it, and in their body language.

Finally, caution the managers that the presentations may not be as polished as they are used to, that many of the presenters will not have done anything like this before, and that some are very nervous. Ask them to be as understanding and supportive as possible—and also encourage them to focus on the content of the presentation rather than the way it is presented.

SET UP THE TOWN MEETING FOR SUCCESS: Logistically, before the Town Meeting, you should set up two flip charts, both headed, "TOWN MEETING." On the first, draw three columns, headed, "RECOMMENDATION," "PAYOFF," and "DECISION." On the second, draw two columns headed, "RECOMMENDATION," and "QUESTIONS/ COMMENTS/ISSUES."

Ask a facilitator for each team to be prepared to take the notes on the flip charts during the Town Meeting discussion after their team's presentation. Even though this is a low-tech way of tracking the decisions, it is useful for the senior business leader and all the participants to see a running record of what the Work-Out community has accomplished. Afterwards, this can form the basis of a communication both to the Work-Out participants and to others in the organization.

Since the Town Meeting is meant as a forum for dialogue, you should try to arrange the room in a way that makes it easy for people to talk with each other. Teams usually like to sit together at round tables, rather than in a classroom-style setting. Try to have chairs that can swivel or move around so that people can look at others no matter where they are in the room. Managers who are attending the Town Meeting but did not participate in the small group sessions should be interspersed among the teams—rather than sitting in the back like a judgmental jury. And the Sponsor who is making decisions should sit up front, but with the flexibility to walk around if desired. It is also helpful to make sure that the acoustics allow for good interaction—or to have hand-held microphones available so that everyone can be heard. You also need to make sure that the screen (or whatever you are using to present ideas) is visible to everyone.

Facilitating the Town Meeting

Here are a few guidelines for the Town Meeting facilitator that will help things run smoothly:

- Allow five minutes or so for introduction, and (usually) one hour for each of the team presentations, including time for questions and answers. Remember that some teams will be covering many recommendations in that time, while others will be asking for in-depth discussion of just one or two recommendations. A successful Town Meeting depends on very disciplined time keeping, so every team has an equal chance to be heard.
- Welcome everyone to the Town Meeting.
- Introduce the managers who are present for the meeting, or—if you don't know them—ask them to introduce themselves.
- Quickly review the process and ground rules for the Town Meeting and check for any questions. (Build in the detailed points covered in the "Brief Town Meeting Participants" section if you have people there other than the Sponsor who haven't sat in on the subgroup meetings.)
- Ask the first team to come up and present.
- Watch the time and, if needed, signal them—tactfully—to speed up.
- Either after each idea, or at the end of the entire presentation (whichever option you have decided on ahead of time), ask for questions and comments.
- Watch the time—and cut off the discussion as needed.
- Now ask for a decision on the idea (or each idea if the decisions have been deferred to the end of the team's presentation).
- Move on to the next team and continue the process.

Throughout the meeting, watch the time—and intervene to move things along (you can agree with the teams and presenters ahead of time on signals you will use to indicate that they need to speed up). Stand up to facilitate the question-and-answer and decision-making activities. Your main job is to enforce the ground rules—being assertive, but using humor when possible. Cut off philosophical or irrelevant discussion—politely, and always either while watching for or getting an approval signal (for example, by eye contact) from the Sponsor. If you are not sure if the question or discussion is relevant, check with the group—or ask the champion or Sponsor.

Be sensitive to the need for a break—for example, if the presentations are getting to be lengthy, somewhat boring, or if people are getting restless and leaving the room. Listen to the dialogue and be sure the people working the flip charts are capturing the comments and decisions in a timely and accurate manner—if this is not happening, either go up to the flip chart yourself and add the additional text or quietly guide the writer as to what to add.

Be "sensitively tough" with the Sponsor in clarifying the decisions, explaining any no decisions, and pinning down the timetable for further work. If the Sponsor is clearly going to have a difficult time making a decision, or if you sense that the Sponsor is becoming uncomfortable with the dialogue, call for a break. Discuss the possible courses of action with the Sponsor without the pressure of group attention. It is important to find some process that will enable some form of immediate decision to be made. (It can be tough to do—but sometimes the Sponsor may need to do a public poll to ask each of the managers present whether they support the idea or not. After that, the decision must be made.)

Sponsor's Remarks and Behavior in the Town Meeting[2]

The Town Meeting is one of the best opportunities business leaders have to exercise leadership in front of a large number of people, relatively unconstrained by reporting relationships, channels of communication, and other barriers. This is where they can live the vision, "walk the talk," provide examples of openness and frank discussion, promote empowerment, and break down organizational barriers.

Here are the most effective things Sponsors can do in a Town Meeting:

- Challenge groups to move beyond their recommendations. ("Why just a $5,000 limit? Why not $50,000? Why not eliminate that report instead of modifying it?")
- Accept some degree of risk. ("We don't know exactly how much it is going to cost, but the payback is obviously big and fast—we'll do it and cost it out later.")
- Ask others at the session who may not have been part of the group actually making a recommendation what they think of the proposal. ("Sally—this will affect your business area, what do you think? Does anyone have any ideas for improving this further?")
- Express enthusiasm for recommendations and recognition of employees. ("That's a terrific idea—it took you folks who actually maintain these machines to make us realize just how much time could be saved by replacing parts instead of cleaning them.")
- Provide clear reasons for saying no. ("It's a great idea, but the current regulatory environment makes it difficult to get all the right approvals.")
- Involve other managers in the acceptance, rejection, or modification of the recommendations. ("Bill, this really affects your distribution costs—what do you think? Should we do it?")
- For very contentious recommendations, insist on getting a very clear reaction from each of the assembled managers. ("This recommendation clearly has some risks and has evoked some strong views—both for and against. To help me make a decision, I'd like to poll each of the managers here. If it were up to you, would you say yes or no?")
- Challenge other members of the assembled management team when they raise objections to recommendations. ("I understand that elimination of this check increases the credit risk, but is it really a material risk?" "I realize that having to give up first-class travel may be difficult for some of us, but we need to significantly reduce our overhead costs, and our management team needs to display some leadership in this area.")
- Make sure there is a management sponsor when needed for approved recommendations. ("Mary, will you agree to help Fred's team move this ahead?")

Here are some behaviors to beware of:

- Physically disengaging from the process by leaving to attend meetings or by taking phone calls.
- Denigrating presentations. ("This is trivial." "We thought of this many years ago but didn't do it because. . . ." "This is not a new idea.")
- Exercising sole personal power of approval, and not entertaining the views of other managers. ("I agree to this [implying *and I don't care what anybody else says*].")
- Excessive deferment to further study. ("It looks OK, but we'll have to run some numbers on it, and I'll let you know.")
- Excessively defensive behavior, particularly when personal criticism is involved. ("OK, I know you want me to consult more on decisions, but there isn't always time to do this, and anyway, you say we have too many meetings now.")
- Impassive, nonreactive acceptance of recommendations. ("I agree," as opposed to "Wow! Terrific! Let's do it!")

Champion's Role in the Town Meeting

The champion should sit in on the briefing of Town Meeting attendees before the session begins, and add any comments, as needed, to those made by the lead facilitator. After that, the champion's role is to participate in the Town Meeting in the same way as any other manager—but if needed, help to clarify any points of understanding for the Sponsor. At the end of the Town Meeting, the champion closes the meeting with remarks along these lines:

- Thank the participants for their hard work and comment positively on the quality of the recommendations.
- Thank the facilitators and expert resources.
- Advise team members that they may be involved in working with their team leader or another "owner" of that recommendation to implement action ideas.
- Comment on the follow-up process, which will include initial, midpoint, and final review meetings when everyone will reconvene to hear the progress and results of the actions taken.

- Ask the team leaders, facilitators, and any other recommendation owners to stay back for a short briefing session on the follow-up process.

Putting the Elements Together to Create an Agenda

Do not try to use a highly structured agenda and timetable. Work-Out sessions cannot be structured to follow a rigid track. Stay flexible and be ready to allow for more or less time as needed in the work sessions or the Gallery of Ideas, depending on the complexity of the subject and the pace at which the groups are able to work. The only exception to this is that the Town Meeting should be kept to the planned start and finish times.

Even though you're planning to stay flexible, of course, it helps to make up a rough timetable and share it with the group. After all, though the details can and probably will vary a bit, the overall shape can't change all that much in the time available. Figure 7-7 illustrates the sort of agenda document the group is likely to find reassuring.

In reviewing the agenda for the group at the beginning of a Work-Out, explain that the sessions will not be held to a rigid time frame—except for the Town Meeting. Note that participants can expect to work into the evening to be able to complete the work leading up to the Town Meeting. Be clear that this is old-fashioned flex time—how late people want to work in the evening and how early they want to start in the morning is up to them. Make sure they understand the basic logistics—the times for meals (and drinks, if applicable) and the location, and the room assignments (and locations) for each team. Note that they will find the session to be hard work—but they should also find it fun as well.

In the early months after the introduction of Work-Out, the majority of people will not have attended one, so you will need to give a full overview of the process and the agenda. Once Work-Out becomes well-established in your organization, more people will have been involved and a shorter overview of Work-Out may be possible.

Day One

8:00 A.M.	Session 1: Work-Out Introduction	
8:30	Welcome and Introductions	Lead Facilitator
8:45	Sponsor's Opening Remarks	Sponsor
9:30	Champion's Opening Remarks	Champion
9:45	Overview of the Work-Out Process, Agenda, and Ground Rules	Lead Facilitator
10:15	Break	
10:30	Warm-Up Exercise	Lead Facilitator
11:00	Session 2: Small-Group Idea Generation	Work in Teams
1:00 P.M.	Lunch	
2:00	Session 3: Gallery of Ideas	
3:30	Session 4: Generating Specific Action Ideas	
	Work on Recommendations	
6:00	Dinner Available	

Day Two

8:00 A.M.	Generating Specific Action Recommendations (Continued)	Work in Teams
12:00 P.M.	Lunch Available for Teams	
4:00	Town Meeting Preparation and Practice (dry-runs with other teams)	
6:00	Dinner Available for Teams	

Figure 7-7.   A Three-Day Work-Out Agenda.

Day Three

8:00 A.M.	Final Preparation for Teams	
9:30	Session 5: Town Meeting	
	Welcome	Lead Facilitator
	Team 1 Presentation	Team Leader for Team 1
	Team 2 Presentation	Team Leader for Team 2
	Team 3 Presentation	Team Leader for Team 3
	Sponsor's Closing Remarks	Sponsor
	Champion's Closing Remarks	Champion
	Wrap-Up	Lead Facilitator
1:00 P.M.	Lunch and Adjourn	
2:00	Follow-Up Session for Champion, Facilitators, and Recommendation Owners (can also be held the next day)	
1 Hour	*Debrief for Sponsor, Champions, Lead Facilitator, Team Leaders, other Recommendation Owners.*	
Up to 2 Hours	*Work-Planning Session: Team Leaders, Recommendation Owners, Champions, Facilitators.*	

Figure 7-7. *(Continued).*

Running a Work-Out: Enjoy the Ride

This chapter has provided you with the essential elements for running a "typical" two-to-three-day Work-Out—from the introductory session through to the Town Meeting. Chapter 9—"Customizing Work-Out"—will help you develop and implement variations on this format.

Running the event itself however, is not the end of Work-Out, it's merely one stage in an ongoing process of change. It is the opportunity to let the genie out of the bottle—to empower and energize people to change the organization and improve results. But once the genie is loose and people are charged up about change, you need to face the next challenge of how to translate this energy, and all of the Work-Out ideas, into results. And that is the subject of Chapter 8.

Implementing Work-Out Recommendations

T AKE A MENTAL JUMP, and assume you've held your Work-Out. Let's assume everything went well. . . .

Now the Town Meeting is winding down, and you've approved an ambitious list of actions and recommendations. Everyone is astonished at the number and quality of the improvement ideas put forward. The team leaders who led the discussions and helped shape the recommendations are exhilarated that their ideas have been approved. The newly appointed recommendation owners are now keen to get past the talk, seize the mandate for change, and get into action.

As the Town Meeting disbands, you can see people in huddles all over the conference center, still working on details and sketching out next steps. Some recommendation owners are working the phones, calling key people back on the job who will need to move on some of the recommendations. Out at the office and the plant, word has already spread that some major changes are going down. The business is buzzing with Work-Out energy.

This scenario is not the end of a successful Work-Out; it's the beginning. The power of Work-Out lies in taking the ideas and energy unleashed in the Town Meeting and translating them into real organizational change and real results. This chapter walks you through key elements of the follow-up phase, showing who needs to do what, and when, so that the potential of the Work-Out event will be transformed into bottom-line business results. Although many of the recommendations approved in the Town Meeting will be quick and easy to implement, even these require follow-up to ensure that they stick—that they really occur. Other recommendations will need sustained effort, and for them the follow-up (and the reports of success on other recommendations) will be crucial to sustaining the momentum generated by the Work-Out event.

There are four elements in the follow-up phase. First, immediately after the Work-Out, there is the task of making accountability stick. This means confirming quickly who will be accountable at the grassroots level for implementing each recommendation. It means pulling together the team that will drive the effort—the champion, team leaders, and recommendation owners who will be on the hook for the next 8 to 12 weeks to deliver on the Work-Out's promise. And it means getting them moving on a work plan while the adrenaline is high and the issues are still fresh. The key players who will be involved in implementing the Work-Out are shown in Figure 8-1.

The second follow-up element is the ongoing challenge of managing the organization's cycle of energy. As effective as Work-Out is at initiating a rush of ideas and adrenaline, few organizations can sustain that high. Understanding the predictable ebb and flow of energy that people will go through during the follow-up phase is a crucial step in supporting and coaching them through the challenges and obstacles they'll face in making change.

The third aspect of the follow-up phase comes back on the job, translating ideas into action. This means clarifying and, if necessary, sharpening the goals to be achieved in the next weeks, involving any other people who will be needed to tackle the bigger or more complex recommendations, and developing a detailed work plan to keep the momentum going.

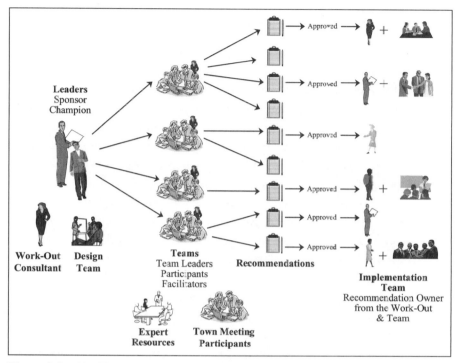

Figure 8-1. Key Players in Implementing a Work-Out.

Finally, there is management oversight and support of the implementation effort. This means planning to get the work done—establishing the discipline of regular reviews in ongoing management meetings, stepping up to the leadership opportunity, and making sure that communication is happening on multiple fronts, using multiple modes. Figure 8-2 summarizes these four elements.

- Making accountability stick
- Managing the organization's cycle of energy
- Translating ideas into action
- Providing management oversight and support

Figure 8-2. Four Elements for Translating Work-Out Recommendations into Results.

Making Accountability Stick

Immediately after a Work-Out there is a magnificent "Work-Out afterglow." You can capture these vibes to help people move into action. Implementation can start the moment the Town Meeting is over. It can start before people leave the room, if there is time left in the day. Or it can start with a planning session the very next morning, while people are still immersed in the issues and energy of the Work-Out event. And at the latest, it can start with an implementation workshop within one week of the Work-Out, to follow up with the accountabilities for each recommendation, along with a detailed work plan to guide implementation. Making accountability stick starts with laying out the first steps to be taken when returning from the Work-Out, reaffirming who will be responsible for each step and by when, and reviewing the plan for involving any other people who will need to contribute.

During this period there are two crucial elements for success. The first is to confirm which people—from the Work-Out teams—will take ownership of implementing each recommendation. These "recommendation owners" are the Work-Out participants who accepted responsibility for making the ideas happen. A best practice is to let these people self-nominate during the Town Meeting, in the context of each recommendation. In fact, in most companies, a ground rule for Work-Out teams is that they cannot make a recommendation unless one person from the team is willing to be the "owner" if that recommendation is approved.

After the Town Meeting, the Sponsor or champion needs to confirm these assignments—so there is one individual who has accountability for each approved idea. Sometimes these people are organizationally in the right position to get rid of a barrier, cut some wasteful process, or make a quick change—so the assignment is obvious. Sometimes the recommendation owner does not have direct authority over the area being changed, but is well-enough connected to be able to pull together a team to deliver on the change. In other cases, the recommendation owner is a Work-Out team member who has some passion for the idea, but who will need to go beyond the usual bounds of authority and relationships to make it happen. In those situations, the recommendation owner may have to stretch and learn how to operate outside a usual comfort zone.

All recommendation owners should have a stake in the business issue being addressed and understand the performance issue they need to tackle. If they are being asked to lead a team effort, they will also need the ability to work well with other people. The bottom line is that the recommendation owners are the people who will be accountable for making the Work-Out recommendations into reality, and there should be no ambiguity about who they are.

The second element for success is to move immediately into work planning. We will have more to say about work planning later in this chapter—but it's worth noting here that immediately after the Town Meeting, the champion's job is to get the work planning process under way. The champion should aim, straight after the Work-Out, to convene a preliminary work-planning session with team leaders, recommendation owners, and anyone else who can help sketch out what needs to be done to get each implementation moving fast. The champion and facilitators should encourage recommendation owners to work with anyone available from the Work-Out to sketch out their work plans. Team leaders and facilitators can help owners with this. Team leaders can also help the champion pull together the work plans for multiple recommendations, building an early picture of the overall implementation plan.

At Zurich UK, Armstrong World Industries, and a number of units in GE, two-hour work-planning sessions take place immediately after the Town Meeting—before people can get back to their offices and e-mail systems or run out to the airports. Any recommendation owner who cannot stay on for the session leaves with some quick instructions about crafting a work plan and the assignment to send one back to the champion within 24 hours. This ensures that implementing the Work-Out recommendations stays "top of mind" and does not get buried under all of the usual organizational busy-ness.

Managing the Cycle of Organizational Energy

The buzz that starts at the Work-Out can last a few days, even a couple of weeks after people have gone back to work. However, champions and recommendation owners should not be surprised to see the organization's energy ebb soon after the hard work of implementation kicks in. This is a part of a predictable cycle of team energy illustrated in Figure 8-3.

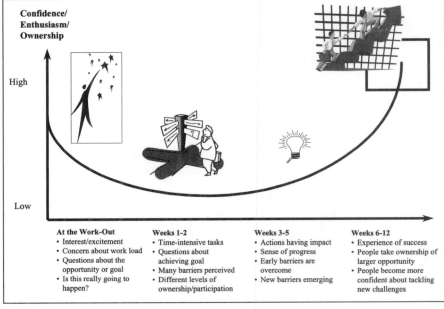

Figure 8-3. Dynamics of Team Performance.

As people get moving on change, they will hit barriers. Some roadblocks will look like outright opposition based on people protecting their turf, trying to preserve existing relationships or power, or simply fearing change. Some roadblocks will be more subtle, based on political maneuvering, delay, and the call for more study or data. Even people who nodded in agreement at the Work-Out can turn out to be less supportive of change once back in their day-to-day routines.

Consider the following case: One of the first Work-Out sessions at Armstrong World Industries focused on speeding claims resolution on flooring products—for example, when a piece of tile was improperly installed or damaged in some way. One recommendation that was given the go-ahead at the Town Meeting was to increase the dollar limits on claims that local retailers could inspect and approve themselves—thus reducing the number of consumer claims that had to be reviewed by Armstrong's own customer-service organization, and thereby speeding up the entire process.

Despite the fact that this recommendation was thoroughly discussed at the Town Meeting—in front of all the key functional managers—the recommendation owner discovered that some managers had doubts about the wisdom of the idea. In the weeks following the Work-Out session, these managers (who considerably outranked the recommendation owner) insisted that additional analysis be conducted before moving forward. They wanted to know break points on claims amounts for different types of products. They asked about claims statistics in different regions of the country. They wanted to examine patterns of claims among different retailers. The only thing they didn't want to do was implement the recommendation.

Problems like these can be very discouraging. However, they are entirely predictable, and can be anticipated by the leaders of the Work-Out. If there is no resistance to change, then the ideas probably were not bold enough. In fact, the Sponsor and champion should view Work-Out as an opportunity to play a new kind of role in leading change. They can position themselves as supporters, teachers, and coaches for the individuals and teams that have taken on the tough work of making change happen. For example, the Sponsor or champion may need to help a recommendation owner clarify or refocus a goal, navigate political barriers, or pull in key resources.

In the Armstrong case, the recommendation owner talked with the champion, Frank Ready, about his frustration and his inability to implement the retail self-inspection idea. Frank's first reaction was to go talk to the resistant managers (who were his peers) himself, or to get their boss, who had sponsored the Work-Out, to "lean on them" and force them to allow the recommendation to go forward. Frank's Work-Out consultant, Elaine Mandrish from RHS&A, however, suggested instead that Frank coach the recommendation owner about how he could influence these managers, without resorting to hierarchical authority. Eventually, the recommendation owner and Frank met together with the managers, listened to their issues, and broke the logjam. In this way, not only was the claims-resolution process improved, but a number of key people—at different levels in the organization—learned valuable lessons about how to orchestrate change.

Translating Ideas into Action

Some recommendations approved for action at the Town Meeting will have a clear scope and narrow goal. Examples include scrapping a study or pilot test, or eliminating the requirement for a report to be produced or a form to be filled out.

Sometimes, however, the Town Meeting approves action on a recommendation that involves major progress on a complex issue in a very short time frame. Two to three months is nothing in the life span of an organization. An implementation team could be pulled together to push the idea forward, without necessarily having the benefit of detailed analysis, study, or supporting infrastructure. And the idea might be a radically new one that is supported by some in the organization but regarded with deep skepticism by others.

Clarifying the Goal

If a recommendation has this kind of complexity or political volatility, it may be necessary for the champion to work with the recommendation owner to drill down to a more tightly framed goal that can realistically be delivered in the time available. Problems during follow-up often trace back to confusion over what a Town Meeting recommendation might actually mean in terms of results in 8 to 12 weeks or less. The owner of the recommendation may need to work with the champion to spell out a narrower goal that nevertheless links to the original business rationale for change. This could mean agreeing with the champion on an achievable goal that moves the organization in the right direction—for example, by introducing a new system in one unit or geographic location. It could mean agreeing to focus effort on parts of the organization that are ready to move, rather than those that are already distracted by other major changes or are likely to put up stiff opposition. It could also mean trying out a new system for a defined period—say a month.

Another example from Armstrong illustrates this dynamic. An additional recommendation from the Work-Out on flooring-product claims was to develop a nationwide "installer certification" program. This would involve training local flooring contractors across the country in proper installation methods and then "certifying" them for various products. Certification would help those contractors gain additional business while the additional training would reduce claims caused by improper installation—a win-win proposition.

Although this recommendation was approved at the Town Meeting, afterwards it became clear that the program was far too large to be implemented across the entire country in 12 weeks. Materials had to be developed, criteria for selecting contractors needed to be agreed upon, trainers had to be recruited and prepared, training locations had to be secured, other contractor programs had to be coordinated with, retailers had to be queried and notified, and more. Rather than try to move all of this forward at once, the Work-Out champion instead suggested to the recommendation owner that he focus on one or two major metropolitan areas first—and get the program up and running there. Then, based on what was learned, he could develop a rollout schedule for the coming year.

The champion should be alert to recommendations that are likely to be too large for full implementation in 12 weeks, and ready to work with the recommendation owner to shape a sharper goal. It's easy to be very ambitious while the Work-Out is in progress. Without allowing momentum to dissipate, the champion should keep an eye on each goal to make sure it has a clear time frame that is reasonably tight—and a clear reference to the business rationale for the change and the expected business impact, stated in bottom-line metrics, such as costs saved, revenues generated, and so on.

Getting Teams Organized

Often, implementing a Work-Out recommendation will require effort from a team of people. This may or may not be the same group that worked on shaping the recommendation at the Work-Out event. Some people won't be available for the follow-up work. Others may not have the skills and connections needed. During the work-planning session immediately after the Work-Out, the owner of that recommendation should be thinking about who should be on the team and any other people who should be asked to offer support or resources.

Some team members will have been at the Work-Out event. For them, the first task on returning to the workplace is to talk to other colleagues about their experience. They will need to report to their colleagues on which ideas were discussed, what the outcomes of the Work-Out were, and what steps will be taken next.

Once this is done, team members will be working to carry out the ideas approved in the Town Meeting. They will be held accountable for completing any specific tasks they are assigned, by the agreed date, and for helping other team members complete their tasks. Usually, team members will be asked to attend weekly team meetings (in person for local people, on the phone for those from other locations) and participate in scheduled reviews, when all the teams get together with the Work-Out Sponsor and champions.

The weeks following the Work-Out are extremely busy for most team members. Often they will be involved in tasks that take them away from their immediate job responsibilities and create pressures on their time. This has to be managed, and they will need to be sensitive to the reactions of colleagues who, as a consequence, may be taking on more work. But because Work-Out implementation represents a terrific opportunity to get involved in an exciting project, to meet colleagues from other parts of the business, to learn new skills, and to be part of the achievement of some real business results, most people put in this extra time without complaint. In fact, in many cases, the high value of Work-Out-implementation activities forces people to reprioritize their day-to-day routines—and often drives out lower-value-added work.

Selecting implementation team members is much like selecting people to attend the Work-Out itself. The team needs people with characteristics like these:

- They have jobs close enough to the front line to allow them to fully understand the technical aspects of the Work-Out subject matter, the related work processes, the issues, and the potential opportunities. Most of the people on the implementation team should be from the particular business unit or function that is having the Work-Out. However, it is often useful to include some people on the team who deal with the same subject matter or the same function, but are from a different business unit.
- They have the potential to challenge the status quo and be innovative and creative in generating improvement ideas.
- They are likely to participate actively and work effectively in a team without dominating it, being dominated, or driving their own agenda.
- They are strongly oriented towards action and results.

Identifying Other Key Players

Not every task needed to implement a Work-Out recommendation will fall to a team. Often, there will be tasks that can be handed off to individuals to implement as part of their regular jobs. The owner responsible for the recommendation will need to manage communication with these people and ensure that deadlines are met.

Sometimes highly specialized tasks will need to be done by functional experts who are not team members. The recommendation owner should move quickly to recruit these people as supporters and allies. The Sponsor and champion may be asked to help get these people on board.

As this section suggests, one of the innovative aspects of Work-Out is that it positions frontline organizational members as "change leaders." Recommendation owners, who can be middle-level managers or shop-floor workers, take on the responsibility of leading change—even if it involves recruiting people from other parts of the organization, or "managing" people who are higher in the organizational structure than they are. For example, another of the Armstrong recommendation owners in the claims Work-Out was responsible for establishing a full-time "quality" leader for the flooring business. This involved not only creating the position description and goals for the quality leader, but also "reviewing" the business leader's commitment to appoint someone to the role by a specified date. Even though the recommendation owner was two organizational levels below the business leader, Work-Out forced the business leader to actually report his progress on that commitment to his subordinate.

Action Planning

We said earlier that it is important to make accountability stick (and to seize the energy surrounding the Work-Out) by making an immediate start on work planning. An action plan is important in a number of ways. In the traditional project-planning sense it provides a road map for the achievement of the breakthrough goal, a timetable for completion of action steps, clear accountability for each step, and a method for tracking and reporting progress, thereby avoiding delays.

In the Work-Out context, an action plan also offers a means of managing innovation. It documents the work done so that the team can capture key lessons learned, communicate them to others, and spread the innovation to other parts of the business. The action plan is thus a tool for providing structured leadership for innovation.

Speed Is Better Than Perfection

As mentioned earlier, it is important that the champion start the work-planning process as soon as the Town Meeting is over. If the Work-Out ends at noon, schedule work-planning sessions for a couple of hours in the afternoon. If the Work-Out ends late, schedule time for the following day.

The champion should involve anyone who is available and can contribute to the work-planning effort. This could be all or some of the team members who worked on the issue in the Work-Out, or it could involve others who are asked to join up with the implementation team. The guiding principle is to favor speed over perfection. If some key people are not available, meet anyway. The work plans can be circulated and tested over the coming days with everyone who might be important to their success.

Setting Up an Action Plan

Through the work-planning process, problems, ideas, and the analysis of data are translated into the specific action steps needed to implement the Work-Out recommendation.

Usually at the Work-Out or immediately following, the team members have done some preliminary brainstorming and analysis. They have reviewed the baseline data, and possibly charted the work-flow process and identified some performance barriers. The initial draft of the action plan is based on the experience and information available to the team as the project begins. It will evolve during the course of the project. As the team moves into action, new barriers and opportunities are identified, and in response, the team identifies additional steps for the plan.

A more thorough action plan should be developed by the recommendation owner and (if appropriate) an implementation team within a few days of the Work-Out. We have found that a simple five-step process is most effective for creating a detailed action plan.

1. Brainstorm the full range of action ideas. Use post-it notes to display these on a flip chart or wall. Action ideas should include steps designed to accomplish the following:
   - Collect any additional baseline data that is needed.
   - Get people interested and involved.
   - Coordinate with other groups.
   - Make changes in policies, procedures, and work flow.
   - Measure and communicate progress.
   - Overcome obstacles that could arise.

2. Consolidate related ideas and sequence the steps. Decide which steps to include in your plan and turn these into action-plan steps.
3. Assign accountability for each step. If more than one person will be involved in a step, choose one person to accept prime accountability for getting it done.
4. Decide on a time frame to begin and complete each step.
5. Test the plan for completeness by asking questions such as these:
   - Are any steps missing?
   - What are the chances of success? How can you increase them?
   - Are the sequencing of steps and the due dates realistic . . . given other commitments and priorities?
   - Have you considered key risks and weak spots? Can you build steps into the plan to address these?
   - Who do you need to share the plan with? How will you communicate what you are doing to those affected?
   - How can you build some excitement and energy into the effort?

Steps can be displayed and updated in a simple chart. For an example of an action plan, see Figure 8-4.

Testing the Action Plan with the Champion or Sponsor

Within three to seven days of the Work-Out, the recommendation owner should test the action plan with the champion (or with the Sponsor if there is no champion). This is an opportunity to draw out other steps that might need to be included, and for the champion to reinforce the need for project discipline. Even an early work plan should feature logical steps, clear accountabilities, and specific due dates.

In addition, the action-plan review offers a chance to enlist the champion's help in smoothing the way for implementation. If needed, the champion and Sponsor should discuss the political implications of the work plan and review team membership and allies that may need to be enlisted to get the work done. Early attention to the work plan reinforces the champion's leadership of the Work-Out implementation—and offers the champion a chance to guide the process and offer help to each team.

Action Plan

Date Prepared: March 3

Revised: _____

Goal: Increase systems output by 25 percent during March–April.
(Include *what* will be achieved; *how* it will be *measured;* and the *target date.*)

Prime responsibility of: (Team Leader)

#	STEPS (START EACH WITH ACTION VERB)	PERSON RESPONSIBLE* (INITIALS)	TARGET DATES		STATUS AS OF:
			BEGIN	END	
1.	Announce policy to hold meetings between 10 AM– 12 NOON and 2–4 PM only.	GS	3/2	3/4	
2.	Arrange additional pickups of computer printouts.	BC* AC	3/6	3/13	
3.	Locate and install high-speed printer.	DD	3/2	3/9	
4.	Work with Tech Services to speed up terminal response.	BC	3/9	3/23	
5.	Reduce computer high-priority interrupt (hitting center) by programmers.	DD	3/4	3/11	
6.	Establish common SSR for small, nonfunctional requests.	BC* AC*	3/2	3/7	
7.	Streamline status reporting.	BC	3/9	3/23	
8.	Establish flex-time policies.	AC, DD* GS, BC	3/6	3/13	
9.	Reemphasize use of desk checks and walk-throughs.	BC* AC*	3/6	3/9	
10.	Reduce disruptive "do now" requests from users and managers.	BC, AC, GS	3/4	3/18	
11.	Discuss "real-time" support for DB2 needs with Tech Services.	DD* VL, BC	3/4	3/14	

*If more than one person is responsible, circle who has prime responsibility

Figure 8-4. Sample Action Plan.

Getting to Work on Implementation

Work-Out is about rapid decision making, but the proof of its value to the organization comes during implementation. Just as the Town Meeting process cuts through layers to aid rapid decision making, the follow-up period should help individuals and teams get on with rapidly implementing numerous recommendations. Monitoring progress, keeping the demand for results fresh and at the forefront of the organization, making sure that work on individual recommendations is adding up to the overall result needed from the Work-Out, and communicating at every step of the way: these are things the Sponsor and particularly the champion should be thinking about during the follow-up phase.

There are three aspects to this work. First, it is very important that the Sponsor and champion establish disciplined oversight of the implementation effort. This is necessary to keep progress on track and to reinforce accountability for action. Second, Work-Out provides an excellent window in which senior managers can seize a leadership opportunity, modeling a distinctive way of leading, coaching, and supporting the people who are making change happen in the organization. Third, there is a need for almost constant communication, embedded and adaptive at each point along the way. Let's look at each in turn.

Establishing Disciplined Oversight

Formal follow-up reviews are useful within a few weeks of the Work-Out: once implementation is under way, soon after the overall midpoint, and at the final deadline for delivering on recommendation. The timetable for these reviews will depend on the complexity and overall timetable for implementing the bundle of Work-Out recommendations. Obviously, some recommendations will be easier and quicker to implement than others. However, the review process should draw together progress reports and evaluation of the entire follow-up effort, even those recommendations that were completed early in the cycle.

We have found that reviews at 30, 60, and 90 days usually work well. In this chapter, we use this spacing to illustrate the initial, midpoint, and final reviews. Though your pacing could be faster if the Work-Out recommendations are relatively straightforward, think twice before making it any slower. Even complex recommendations should be carved down to some tangible results that can be delivered in 12 weeks or less—and maintaining the discipline of monthly reviews helps keep even the bigger change efforts on track. However, you can of course set the frequency to suit your own conditions, or even keep the whole review process informal if that fits better with the culture of the organization.

Thirty-Day Review

The aim of the initial review is to bring together the recommendation owners and their teams to report on early progress, plan next steps, and solicit input and help as needed. It offers an opportunity for recommendation owners and teams to hear about each other's progress and plans, learn from each other, and coordinate their action.

The agenda for the meeting should include the following:

- An introduction by the Sponsor, champion, or a Work-Out consultant—to reiterate the goals of the Work-Out and the importance of implementation success.
- A progress report to the Sponsor from each recommendation owner, encompassing the metrics that are being used to track progress, key aspects of the work plan, and any challenges or barriers that have arisen or are anticipated. These progress reports should include time for dialogue—almost like a mini-Town Meeting. The idea here is not to "look good," but to use the combined resources of the group to figure out the best ways to translate the recommendations into results.
- A work session in which recommendation owners and their teams discuss how to address issues or input from the Sponsor, and how the teams will communicate and work together going forward. This is also an opportunity for the recommendation owners and their teams to refine and continue to develop their work plans, especially based on input from the review.

Thirty-day review sessions usually reveal, very quickly, what it is going to take to make real progress and achieve results. Here's a good example: Strix is a company headquartered in the Isle of Man; it is the world's leading manufacturer of heating controls and cordless interfaces for electric kettles. After a Work-Out that focused on reducing persistent quality defects, recommendation owners proceeded to carry out a series of steps aimed at improving quality. At subsequent team meetings and the 30-day review, however, it became clear that the recommendation owners were defining their roles very narrowly. The hierarchical culture had taught them to avoid taking any initiatives beyond the literal agreements at the Town Meeting. For example, one agreement had been to purchase a new guage that would help with calibration of the line. The recommendation owners had given the requisition and request for purchase approval for the equipment to the head of manufacturing, but then had not followed up to see that it was actually approved and ordered—let alone installed, utilized, and making a difference. They were just waiting until someone "higher up" took the next step.

At the review session, this dynamic became apparent in regard to a number of recommendations—and with the help of the Work-Out consultant, was openly discussed. The head of the business, the Sponsor for the Work-Out, and the Work-Out consultant encouraged the recommendation owners to be more proactive, to initiate change, and not to wait for higher approvals. This helped accelerate progress such that defects per million parts were reduced over the next 2 months by over 60 percent. And equally importantly, it began to create a more empowered, change-oriented culture at Strix.

Sixty-Day Review

A midpoint review should be held at about 60 days or soon after the halfway mark. Once again, the meeting is intended to give the Sponsor and champion a chance to review overall progress and probe the specific work being done by each team, and to give recommendation owners a chance to learn from and coordinate with each other.

The agenda for the midpoint review will be similar to the initial review. One key difference is that there should by now be presentation of clear data showing tangible progress on each recommendation.

The agenda for the midpoint review usually includes these two items:

- A formal report to the Sponsor and champion—followed by Town Meeting-type dialogue
- A work session of the recommendation owners and their teams to discuss any issues the Sponsor might raise—and to revise their work plans

Ninety-Day Review

A final review should be held at the conclusion of the scheduled follow-up period or at 90 days, whichever is sooner.

This review will follow a somewhat different agenda, including these activities:

- Presentation by each of the recommendation owners on what they achieved during the implementation period—and what they and their teams learned about making change happen.
- Overall review of Work-Out's progress toward the business goal by the champion.
- Group discussion of how to build on the Work-Out progress to tackle further goals or expand on the current one. This might also include discussion of ideas for future Work-Out sessions.
- Celebration of achievements and the Sponsor's recognition of everyone's hard work. (This part of the agenda often includes a "thank you" dinner or reception.)

One of the key aspects of these final review sessions is to include a full and open discussion of what was learned from the Work-Out experience. As has been stated throughout this book, the value of Work-Out is not just its usefulness as a method for solving organizational problems. It is also a vehicle for building an organization's capacity to change, and become more flexible, boundaryless, and effective. Such change requires a combination of action—through Work-Out implementation—and reflection—through active discussion of what's been learned.

Eagle Star General Insurance in Ireland, a division of Zurich Financial Services, provides a good illustration of how action and learning can be brought to the forefront in the final Work-Out review.

Ian Stuart, the head of Eagle Star (non-Life) Ireland, was the overall Sponsor for introducing the Work-Out methodology. With his support, Alan Grace (the head of the Commercial business) agreed to sponsor a Work-Out aimed at reducing the backlog of premium-account queries from brokers. This backlog was caused by disputes over billing statements to the brokers, leading them to withhold payment until the right information was agreed upon. At the Work-Out, participants had recommended a series of steps both to drive down the existing backlog and to prevent future backlogs. At the 100-day mark, these steps were largely successful, resulting in the collection of 6 million I. pounds in outstanding receivables.

At the closure meeting, after reporting on the overall results and the implementation of specific steps, there was a discussion of the process and what had been learned about managing change at Eagle Star (non-Life) Ireland. Encouraged by the Work-Out consultant, and the internal consultant, Jerry Fitzpatrick, people candidly shared several insights that neither Alan nor others in the room would have realized:

- Much of the success of the backlog-reduction effort came from the persistence of the team leaders and recommendation owners, who felt that they almost had to browbeat others into supporting the projects. They particularly found that other functions had trouble shifting their priorities to provide needed help. In other words, despite Stuart's and Grace's public support for specific goals, not all of their people were on the same page.
- Some of the backlog problem had been caused by people simply not tackling account queries that they didn't want to deal with because they had been outstanding too long, were too difficult to resolve, or would perhaps interfere with meeting other work objectives. Often such queries just went into a drawer, never to emerge again. The Work-Out focus on backlog reduction forced some of these out into the open. Others were found only when people were away—and somebody else looked in the person's files.
- Getting work out of the system (like the premium-collection backlogs) required extra time—and even overtime on the part of some staff members. This surprised many of the managers, who just assumed that Work-Out would somehow magically reduce workloads. However, they did learn that the extra work on the front end to clean up the process seemed now to create less work in the day-to-day running of the business.

A key lesson for Jerry Fitzpatrick was that people learned the importance of careful planning, attention to rigorous implementation disciplines, and the support of the Champion/Sponsor in getting things done to achieve the goal. These insights and others helped reinforce for

Ian Stuart, Alan Grace, and the rest of their team what it would take to make all people in the organization support their goal to make Eagle Star a top performer in the Zurich system.

Seizing the Leadership Opportunity

Immediately after a Work-Out and early in the follow-up phase, team members and recommendation owners will have implicit assumptions about the extent to which they are truly empowered to act. Many team members will be carrying baggage from previous experiences at work, when they have been asked to analyze or make recommendations but not trusted with the responsibility of innovating, influencing, and *acting* to achieve some specific outcome. In one major pharmaceutical company, for example, a veteran senior manager noted that he had never been on a task force that was actually empowered to act—only to study and recommend.

In such cultures, it can be an exciting—and daunting—revelation to those responsible for implementing a Work-Out recommendation that they are actually expected to deliver a real result in a short time frame. Often, the Sponsor and champion must send repeated signals that the demand for results is genuine, progress is being monitored, and final outcomes matter. This is one of the key purposes of the formal review process. It may also need to be emphasized in one-on-one meetings and general communications to the management team.

Communication

Breaking down boundaries by sharing information openly within the organization is an integral part of making Work-Out successful and creating an environment of empowerment and accountability. Information seldom flows by accident, especially across boundaries. It must be communicated systematically and appropriately to the people who need it and who will use it. The Work-Out event itself is a massive communication exercise designed to pull ideas and information up and out of the people who face critical business issues day to day on the front line, and share it across functional and unit lines. Following the Work-Out, communication continues as a parallel stream of work. Some planning is needed to decide what needs to be communicated, how, to whom, and by when.

One additional responsibility of the Work-Out Champion (or Sponsor), often with help from the Work-Out consultant, is to orchestrate a communications process. Following a Work-Out there will be multiple audiences who should be receiving or be tapped for information. There will also be choices about timing and the mode of communication used.

Figure 8-5 offers a guideline for aligning the communication channel with the purpose of the communication—whether it be simply to share information or to shape behavior. Generally speaking, if the aim is to change behavior, you should use more intimate communication methods—you'll find it's much easier to get agreement and action face-to-face than via memos and e-mail. If the aim is to share information, you can use less personal methods of communication to reach large numbers of people efficiently.

HOW TO COMMUNICATE	PURPOSES OF COMMUNICATION	
Channel	Share Information	Shape Behavior
Face-to-face (one-on-one)		
Symbolic (meeting, rally)		
Interactive media (telephone, voice mail, fax, e-mail)		
Static personal media (letter, memo, report)		
Static impersonal media (bulletin, flyer, newsletter, video)		

It is important to align communication tools with the purpose of the communication. If the purpose is to share information (for example, who is doing what), use more impersonal methods. If the purpose of the communication is to change behavior, use more intimate methods (for example, face-to-face).

Source: Ashkenas, R., Jick, T., Ulrich, D., and Paul-Chowdhury, C. (1999). The Boundaryless Organization Field Guide: Practical Tools for Building the New Organization. *San Francisco: Jossey-Bass.*

Figure 8-5. Guidelines for Aligning Communication Channel and Message.

Here are some questions that can be helpful to the champion in laying out a communications plan:

- What message should be communicated?
- Who should receive it?
- What is the appropriate time frame?
- How should the message be communicated?

These thoughts can be structured in a communication plan, as outlined in Figure 8-6. The communication plan can help organize the "work" of communication over the months following the Work-Out. Its main steps, accountabilities, and time frames should be integrated with the overall work plan for implementing a recommendation.

Instructions: Within each cell, note the key message for that audience and the primary modes for conveying it.

	TIME FRAME			
STAKEHOLDERS/AUDIENCE	**MONTH 1**	**MONTH 2**	**MONTH 3**	**MONTH 4**
Senior management				
Middle management				
Line supervisors and employees				
Customers/suppliers/other external stake holders				

Source: Ashkenas, R., Jick, T., Ulrich, D., and Paul-Chowdhury, C. (1999). *The Boundaryless Organization Field Guide: Practical Tools for Building the New Organization.* San Francisco: Jossey-Bass.

Figure 8-6. Outline for a Work-Out Communication Plan.

Conclusion

The follow-up phase of a Work-Out is the key to its success. No matter how exhilarating the experience, no one will want to do another Work-Out if the portfolio of recommendations approved at the Town Meeting doesn't get implemented successfully. For the Work-Out leaders (Sponsor and champion), the main challenge lies in balancing unremitting pressure for results with acting as coach, teacher, chief spokesperson, and prime cheerleader for everyone involved in the Work-Out. For those who are facilitating and supporting the leaders, the challenge is to help coordinate work on multiple fronts and to serve as a bridge between the people doing the work and the Sponsor and champion. For the people who own responsibility for implementing each recommendation and their team colleagues, the challenge is to deliver the expected result on time. This can be a lot of work, but it's a source of strength and empowerment rather than a burden, because it means getting things done that people have developed and chosen for themselves, and that will make an immediate difference to the quality of their own lives. When all three roles are performed well, the organization begins to develop a sense of infinite possibility, and whatever business you're in becomes more capable of realizing its potential.

CHAPTER

IX

Customizing Work-Out for Your Organization

ORGANIZATIONS—AND THEIR PROBLEMS—all differ, and you'll need to adapt your Work-Out plans to suit your own terrain. In the previous chapters, we have given you the full menu of Work-Out. But this menu may be adapted in many ways: What if you can't get people together for three full days? What if you want to involve people scattered around the world and can't afford to haul them all to a central location? What if you want an existing unit to use Work-Out on its own to solve day-to-day problems? What if you want to get the whole organization involved all at once? What if you want to invite customers to participate? What if you want to tackle a problem so deep and complex that nobody could deal with it in three days? What if? What if? The variations are endless.

Happily, Work-Out offers all the flexibility you need. You can customize it to fit your own organization, situation, and problems—it just takes some extra thought if you don't want to use it straight off the showroom floor. This chapter provides several Work-Out variants, to illustrate the program's range and to help stimulate your own thinking, and also includes a number of suggestions for ways to make it work for you when the rubber hits the road.

Time as a Variable: How to Tune the Work-Out Time Frame

Perhaps the first and easiest way to tailor Work-Out to your own needs is to vary the time frame of the Work-Out event. While the Work-Out we described may run three days, it is possible to design Work-Out sessions that can be conducted in a matter of hours, and others that might last for several weeks. See Chapter 4 for an overview of how to lead a typical fast-cycle Work-Out. Here we describe Work-Outs that go beyond three days.

Extended Work-Outs

Some topics do not lend themselves to a three-day Work-Out—let alone a one-day blitz. Instead, they may require research, data collection, and discussion over a period of several weeks. In such cases, you might want to consider designing what we call an "extended" Work-Out.

Some years ago, GE Lighting used this approach to dramatically reduce product breakage. The idea for this Work-Out came from a young member of GE Lighting's finance staff. On her own, she did an analysis of breakage costs across the company's different functions—manufacturing, distribution, and customer service. Prior to this analysis, breakage figures were only collected and acted upon in each subfunction (each plant, ware-house, customer-return center, and so on). And since the numbers were not overly worrisome in any one subfunction or location, there was no impetus for action. When the numbers were aggregated across the company, however, they were staggering, reaching into millions of dollars. As a result, the business leader at the time, John Opie, decided to convene a cross-functional Work-Out aimed at reducing breakage.

The problem with using a standard Work-Out design to address breakage was that nobody really understood the problem or the efficacy of potential solutions. While the overall numbers had been aggregated, they contained no "granularity"—they did not tell the story of where breakage was actually occurring, what caused it, whether some products were more prone to breakage than others, or whether there were patterns over time. Moreover, lighting products were constantly on the move—from plant, to truck, to warehouse, to customer—so the places where broken products were discovered was not necessarily where they broke. And because the lighting products were heavily packaged and shrink-wrapped, often breakage was not even discovered until a customer reached for a bulb or tube.

Given these complexities and gaps in knowledge, the Work-Out was designed in two stages, over a period of weeks. The first stage was a one-day "getting organized" Work-Out. During that day, cross-functional teams, each focused on a product category, met to review the existing data and discuss the possible issues. But the teams' aim for the day was not to come up with recommendations for solving the problems—it was to develop a specific work plan for the next few weeks on how to find out what was really going on. At the end of that day, the teams met with John Opie in a Town Meeting, presented their work plans, and got his approval to proceed. In some cases, those work plans included modest requests for resources, such as a Polaroid camera and some travel funds.

Over the next few weeks, the teams carried out their plans and researched the breakage situation. For example, the team assigned to six-foot fluorescent tubes arranged to have a four-person, cross-functional team physically follow the product from its birth in a lighting plant through its journey to a customer. At each stage along the way, the team asked questions, collected forms and data, and took pictures. During those weeks, others on the team interviewed people in the functions and collected deeper levels of raw data (such as customer-return forms) that could be analyzed.

At the end of the three-week research period, the teams reconvened in a second Work-Out session—this one running two days—at GE Lighting headquarters in Cleveland, Ohio. Using their research, the teams were much more capable of generating solutions to the breakage problem. They had also developed a passion and commitment to the topic—and were determined to save the company money. The team working on six-foot fluorescents, for example, had discovered that even when the trucks were fully loaded, gaps between packages often allowed boxes to shift, cracking their contents. The team recommended using inflatable air bags to fill these gaps and greatly reduce in-transit breakage. The team also discovered that the sizes of pallets and fork lifts in the plants were different from the ones in the warehouses—which was causing breakage in shrink-wrapped pallets when they were off-loaded from factory trucks to warehouses. Relatively simple changes in pallet configurations were recommended to address this issue. In all, millions of dollars worth of savings were identified at the concluding session and then implemented over the next several months.

As this example shows, an extended Work-Out can be extremely effective when the topic requires research and data before robust solutions can be generated. At first glance, it may look similar to appointing a task force and hoping for results, but the difference in practice is astonishing. The added focus and intensity that comes from the widespread participation and the knowledge that the work will produce results within a matter of weeks makes all the difference in the world.

Long-Distance Work-Outs

Sometimes the people who'd be most useful in a Work-Out session cannot be at the same place at the same time. It may cost too much to bring them in; they may have too much work that has to stay within their sight. Yet having everyone participate is crucial. In such cases, technology can help to overcome the limitations of both time and space.

Two examples from SmithKline Beecham Pharmaceuticals (now GlaxoSmithKline) illustrate this variation on the Work-Out theme.

Different Places—Different Times

A number of years ago, SmithKline Beecham's R&D organization consolidated two major units, clinical data operations and information technology services. The leader of the combined unit, Ford Calhoun, decided to use the reorganization to generate ideas and action for reducing the cycle time of clinical trials and the overall costs of his unit—but he wanted to do this in a way that involved all members of his new organization. However, that meant hundreds of people scattered across several locations in the United States and the United Kingdom. To deal with this challenge, Calhoun organized his Work-Out in several stages, with a large dose of technology to enable broad participation.

The first stage of Calhoun's Work-Out was a two-day conference of his extended management team, the top 25 people. At this session, the team examined a number of possible designs for the newly combined organization. After much debate on the pros and cons of each design— weighed against the cycle time and cost goals—the team agreed to an overall organizational structure, which Calhoun approved on the spot.

For the second stage, each unit in the overall structure was given one month to engage people in a "virtual Work-Out," using a Lotus Notes database. During this stage, each unit manager sent a series of questions to people who either had been or might be part of the unit. The questions were aimed at soliciting ideas regarding both organizational design and how the design might lead to reductions in cost and cycle time. Hundreds of people were engaged in this way—with managers actively responding to many of the suggestions and constructing strawman proposals for how the organization might work.

At the end of one month, each manager froze the local Lotus Notes database and developed a set of proposals or recommendations about how to proceed. These were all posted on the database so Calhoun, and the other managers could read them in advance. The management team then reconvened for another Work-Out session to discuss and decide on each of the proposals, making modifications as needed. The result was an organizational structure and a set of recommendations about cycle time and cost reduction that neither Calhoun nor the extended-management team could have conceived of at the beginning of the process. And since hundreds of people had contributed, the implementation proceeded relatively quickly and smoothly—eventually helping SmithKline Beecham take many months out of the clinical-trial process.

Same Time—Different Place

One of the subunits of Calhoun's organization, Clinical Data Management, used an additional variation on Work-Out to address its unique issues. Clinical Data Management is the unit that manages and analyzes very large volumes of clinical data that are generated in the course of clinical drug trials. These trials take place in hospitals and clinics around the world and involve thousands of patients, nurses, and physicians. All this data needs to be validated, formatted, and entered—accurately—before it can be analyzed and used to support submissions to the regulatory authorities.

One of the most significant opportunities for reducing the cycle time of clinical trials was to shrink the time involved in accurately entering this data. Units involved in the process, however, resided in sites both in the United States and the United Kingdom, and it was not realistic to bring them all together for a Work-Out. The solution was to hold a simultaneous Work-Out session on both sides of the ocean. Using video-conferencing, the opening sessions to position the unit's strategy, review the goals of the Work-Out, and introduce the Work-Out process, were done together—though it was early in the morning in the United States and midafternoon in the United Kingdom. U.S. and U.K. teams then worked separately for the next day to develop recommendations for accelerating data entry and improving accuracy. When necessary, people made phone calls "across the pond" to test ideas and coordinate recommendations that might affect both units. At an agreed-upon time on the third day, the videoconference was turned on again for the Town Meeting. The head of the unit was in the United States, but direct reports were in both sites. Facilitators in each site managed the process.

Three Basic Types of Work-Out: Bureaucracy Busting, Process Improvement, Strengthening the Value Chain

Besides time and distance, the third major way to create variations on Work-Out is to "flex the focus"—that is, to shape Work-Outs around three very different kinds of topics and goals. If you have read this far in the book, you already understand that Work-Out is not just a cookie-cutter template into which any topic or issue can be dropped. Considerable thought and effort is needed, up front, to focus the topic, select an appropriate goal, and design the Work-Out process to achieve the goal. In our experience, three very different Work-Out-topic categories can benefit from variations on the Work-Out theme:

- Bureaucracy busting
- Process improvement
- Strengthening the value chain

Bureaucracy-Busting Work-Outs

Since the initial idea of Work-Out was to "get unnecessary work out" of the organization, bureaucracy busting has always been a prime topic. However, a number of variations on the bureaucracy-busting theme are worth noting:

"Dollarizing" Bureaucracy

Although getting rid of unnecessary work seems like a good thing in itself and, logically, should lead to productivity and quality-of-life gains, it is not always clear whether reducing bureaucracy actually has a measurable payoff. Therefore, when attacking bureaucracy, it is often worthwhile to build into the agenda some time to assess the bottom-line impact of work-reduction ideas. This allows you to select ideas that not only sound good but also achieve some threshold of savings.

One way to do this is to "dollarize" each idea—to place a monetary value on the recommendation. At GE Capital, for example, each bureaucracy-busting idea was subjected to questions such as these:

- How many people are involved in this practice? How much time would be saved if the practice were eliminated or streamlined?
- What is the cost of producing this report or document?
- What would be the cost of not doing this?
- If people were not doing this bureaucratic practice, what would they do instead? How would they fill their time with something that is more value-added?
- What will it cost to implement this change?

This process served as a filter, and only ideas that promised returns above a certain dollar amount were presented and selected for implementation. The totals were then added up so that everyone knew the savings the Work-Out had produced.

"Blitzing" Bureaucracy

Since bureaucracy reduction often represents easy wins—the classic low-hanging fruit of the Work-Out process—and does not require deep analysis or subject-matter expertise, it is a topic that is easy to apply on a total-organization basis, sometimes with great fun and energy. Zurich U.K.'s general insurance business, for example, organized a bureaucracy "blitz" that involved several thousand people simultaneously—giving everyone a taste for the Work-Out process.

The blitz began through an e-mail and communications campaign that asked every employee to submit bureaucracy-reduction ideas to an intranet site by a certain date. The campaign featured movie posters using themes from the movies Ghostbusters (renamed "Bureaucracy Busters") and Star Trek ("Boldly Busting the Bureaucracy Frontier"). All the members of Zurich U.K.'s management committee featured prominently in the posters, which encouraged all staff to send in ideas and help change the company.

After the submission deadline, Zurich's Work-Out facilitator team sorted the hundreds of ideas into categories and organized teams of employees to review them, assess savings and impact potential, and select the best ideas for final recommendation. These were then presented, debated, and decided upon at a Town Meeting with the company's management committee, cochaired by the "Transformation Director," Rob Smith, and a frontline employee. Subsequent Management Committee meetings reviewed progress on these actions through to completion. The results of this process, with savings of several hundred thousand pounds, were then communicated back to the entire organization.

Cycling Back on Bureaucracy

Since bureaucracy is a naturally occurring phenomenon that continually grows in every organization, getting rid of it also needs to be a recurring process. It is natural to start the Work-Out process with a focus on bureaucracy and then move on to other business-focused issues, but never forget bureaucracy reduction!

For example, as much as Six Sigma did for GE, it came at a high cost of reintroduced bureaucracy. Elaborate rules were established to govern the earning of different-colored belts (green, black, or master black), that signified different degrees of expertise. Each employee had to be certified as at least a green belt, and this certification required completing projects that were themselves certified only if they possessed certain attributes. Additionally, each project was classified according to stage of completion (define, measure, analyze, improve, or control). As a partial antidote to the bureaucracy that accompanied Six Sigma, and also because so many people had joined GE subsequent to the initial wave of Work-Outs, in 1999 Welch decided that each GE business should undertake a number of Work-Outs during a 90-day period.

Process Improvement Work-Outs

Work-Out is not just about solving problems, but about strengthening the organization's capacity to get results. You can use it to achieve results *and* start to improve the ongoing process that leads to the results. This section describes two common ways to make this happen.

Design the Work-Out Around the Process

In many cases, the idea for a Work-Out springs from a real business problem. *We have too much inventory. Our customer-service response rate is too slow. It's taking us too long to bring new products to market. Our strategic plans take too long to develop and aren't very useful.* During the design phase of Work-Out, any of these business problems can be redefined as part of one or more business processes that need improvement. Figure 9-1 takes each of the three sample problems in this paragraph and lines it up as a symptom in some deeper business processes.

A challenge for the Work-Out designer is to help the presenting manager and the rest of the team define which process is involved, and decide how broad or narrow to make the scope. Once that decision is made, the designer and the team can then sketch out three to five major phases or stages of the process and organize the Work-Out around each of these process elements. Sometimes these stages are sequential; that is, they follow a time line. And sometimes they are process elements that happen in parallel. Here's an example of each.

Designing the Work-Out Around Steps in a Process

Several years ago, the Dole Foods Company, with numerous units around the world, was concerned that its strategic-planning documents took a great deal of time and effort to prepare—and then were shelved and forgotten. To deal with this problem, they used the occasion of a global-management conference to organize a Work-Out to improve the strategic-planning process. The Work-Out consisted of

Stated Problems	Business Processes
"We have too much inventory!"	Production scheduling and inventory management
	Order entry and fulfillment
"Our customer-service response rate is too slow!"	Customer service
	Inquiry resolution
	Order tracking and fulfillment
"It's taking us too long to bring new products to market!"	Product development
	Product commercialization
"Our strategic plans take too long to develop and aren't very useful!"	Strategic planning
	Planning and budgeting

Figure 9-1. Business Problems That Reveal Process-Improvement Opportunities.

four teams, each dealing with a sequential phase of the process, as shown in Figure 9-2.

Each team was asked to quickly sketch out how its phase of the process currently worked, and to then recommend how that phase should work in the planning cycle that was about to start. By organizing the Work-Out in this way, managers from around the world began to appreciate that strategic planning was indeed a process—with a beginning and an end—and not just a set of requirements, forms, and meetings. Most of them had not thought of it in this context or put on a "corporate hat" to understand that many plans had to be balanced, resources allocated, and so on. The managers all came up with ideas for how to make the process work more effectively, most of which were accepted and built into the process going forward.

This table, from a Work-Out at Dole Foods Company, shows how an unwieldy strategic-planning process was broken down into four different parts, each one assigned to a different Work-Out team.

Team	Focus	Question
1.	Preparing for the September Strategic Planning Conference	What happens prior to the official start of the planning process—Assumptions? Guidelines? Templates?
2.	The Divisional Response	What does each division need to do to prepare its plan between September and November?
3.	The Roll-up and Review	How are the divisional plans reviewed, approved, and consolidated for presentation to the Board in December?
4.	Follow-up	How are the plans implemented, monitored, revised, and reviewed during the course of the year?

Figure 9-2. Dividing Parts of a Problem Among Multiple Work-Out Teams.

Designing a Work-Out Around Parallel Processes

GE Lighting bought Hungary's state-owned lighting company, Tungsram, in 1991 and brought in George Varga as the company's new head. Varga initiated a series of Work-Outs to improve Tungsram's core business processes and bring them into line with GE. One of the most crucial of these processes was "new-product introductions"—to ramp up products from prototype into full production. A design team sketched out the key elements of the process, many of which needed to run in parallel, and designed a Work-Out accordingly. Figure 9-3 illustrates how the Work-Out design was portrayed. Note that the design team decided to use an existing product (double-ended metal halide), that was currently being readied for full production, as a live "case study" for each of the Work-Out teams. The goal, then, was not only to improve the overall process but also to accelerate and improve the introduction of this particular product.

Again, one major by-product of organizing Work-Outs in terms of processes is that it helps organizational participants understand that the work they do is indeed part of a process—and that there are interdependencies between functions. Only after internalizing that perspective is it possible for people to improve an entire process jointly. Otherwise, while individual pieces might change, the whole might not get any better. This was indeed the case at Tungsram, where no one had ever looked at end-to-end processes. Through this and other Work-Outs, the Tungsram staff were able to dramatically improve their ability to develop and commercialize new products.

Teach Process Mapping and Process Thinking as Part of Work-Out

Work-Outs also can be designed with time built in explicitly to teach process mapping and process thinking. For example, at Armstrong World Industries, part of the introductory session at the beginning of each Work-Out is devoted to a discussion of "systems thinking," with particular reference to the Toyota Production System.[1] Participants are then given a one-page chart on the "process mindset" (see Figure 9-4), and encouraged to apply this mindset to their Work-Out deliberations. Then, in the Town Meetings, CEO Michael Lockhart reinforces this mind-set by asking "process" questions in regard to the recommendations, such as, How will you know that the process is

Team & Process Element	Team 1 Product Quality	Team 2 Materials and Equipment	Team 3 Workforce	Team 4 Technology Hand-Off	Team 5 Product Launch	Team 6 Design-Process Assessment
Questions	How do we agree on quality standards? What is the process for assuring quality in production? How do we measure quality? How do we monitor and make corrections?	What's the process for obtaining needed supplies and equipment? How do we make sure we have everything needed for production? How do we deal with shortages?	How do we best prepare the workforce for production? • Training • Scheduling • Assignments • Transfer process What other people are affected?	How do we plan the transition from prototype to production? What are the roles of technology and production at different stages? How do we ensure that production is ready?	What's the process for product launch? How do we plan product availability?	Looking back, how effective was the design process? What were the steps? Could anything have been done faster? Were the right people involved at the right times?
Participating Functions	Technology Quality Product Management Finance Production	Purchasing Technology Production Finance Systems	HR Production	Technology Production	Product Management Sales Finance Production Distribution	Technology Production Product Management

Figure 9-3. Improving a Parallel Process: A GE Tungsram Work-Out On Streamlining New-Product Introductions.

- All work activities are part of a process.
- Steps within processes should be highly specified (content, sequence, timing, outcome) to reduce variance.
- Connections between activities should be simple and direct—with standard senders, receivers, service levels, and responses.
- Performance against "spec" should be clear and easy to monitor.
- Improvements in process should be made with "scientific method" at the working level.

Figure 9-4.   The Process-Improvement Mind-Set.

working? What performance specifications can be monitored? Who is the process champion?

A more intensive way of teaching process thinking and mapping is to design a process-mapping tutorial into the Work-Out agenda. When GE began to shift its Work-Out efforts from bureaucracy reduction to process improvement, many people in the businesses did not understand what process improvement meant. To remedy this, Richard Hilbart from the corporate business-planning staff put together a simple tutorial. In it, he walked participants through a number of common, everyday processes, such as ordering food at a restaurant or buying a car. (See Figure 9-5.) He than gave people time to construct a process map of a common process of their own choosing.

With this foundation, Hilbart found that most participants could then start to map more complicated business processes in their Work-Out sessions, such as customer service, order fulfillment, production planning, product development, and the like—at least at a high level. Over time, facilitators were able to add more sophisticated tools to the process-mapping arsenal. These included cycle-time analysis, rework assessments, value- and nonvalue-added analysis, volume analysis, and more. (See Figure 9-6.)

This approach to Work-Out often requires a different type of agenda. Much of the first day is spent going through the process-mapping tutorial—both in the large group and in small groups. On the second day, the focus shifts to the subject of the Work-Out. However, the process that is being improved is not carved up into chunks or phases ahead of time, as

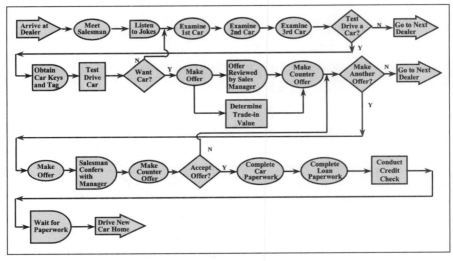

Figure 9-5. Process Map Example: Buying a Car.

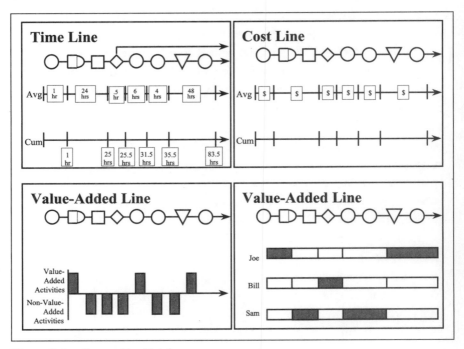

Figure 9-6. Process-Map Variations.

in the earlier examples. Instead, one or two teams create as-is process maps of the current operation—and then identify incremental improvements that can be made right away to eliminate bottlenecks, reduce cycle time, and take out cost. Simultaneously, one or two other Work-Out teams create a blank-sheet process map and identify what it might take to create the ideal process. At the Town Meeting, both the as-is and the blank-sheet maps and ideas are presented, and the business leader helps the group think through the trade-offs and sequencing of both short-term and longer-term improvements. (See Figure 9-7.)

Value-Chain Work-Outs

As process thinking becomes embedded in your organization, the natural next step is to consider the overall context in which processes occur—the value chain of suppliers and customers of which the organization is a part. Just as "no man is an island," so too no organization stands alone. Every firm depends on suppliers who provide raw materials, services, systems, credit, or information. And every firm has customers or clients who use what it produces.

Unfortunately, most western organizations live in a world where customers and suppliers have traditionally dealt with each other at arm's length, using negotiation, haggling, and pressure tactics as much as collaboration, cooperation, and partnership. And despite all the platitudes about "customer focus," "preferred suppliers," and "partnering," most

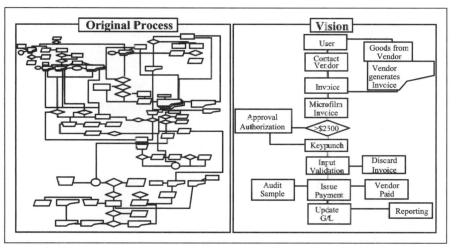

Figure 9-7. A Process Map "Before" and "After" a Work-Out: From GE Capital Purchasing.

companies revert to their old, familiar modes when the heat is on. For example, when Daimler-Chrysler faced mounting losses in the United States, it tossed years of development of preferred suppliers out the window, along with all existing contracts. It forced every supplier to accept a price cut without discussion or negotiation.

In this traditional value-chain environment, Work-Out can have a major positive impact on the relationship between the organization and its customers and suppliers. The key is to focus the Work-Out process on achieving a tangible business result that will be a win for both parties. There is no better way to build trust and collaboration than to work on something together and experience a success. And while this will not by itself change the traditional customer-supplier paradigm, it will lead to a relationship that can be more profitable and rewarding for both parties over time.

One ground rule to consider in designing Work-Outs with your suppliers or customers is to wall off subjects that could be acrimonious and lead to win-lose discussions or negotiations. The most obvious topic to avoid is pricing. Work-Out is generally not the forum for negotiation of terms, conditions, or prices. It's usually best to keep data on internal costing and profit margins out of customer-supplier discussions as well.

A second ground rule is that success depends on putting yourself in your customer's or supplier's shoes. You need to think about issues from their perspectives, not just your own. What is it that they are trying to accomplish? What pressures are they under? What forces them to do things that might not be as productive as possible? What help might they need? How can you measure results from their perspectives and not just yours? One thing GE found useful when a supplier or customer showed up for a Work-Out without a priority issue to deal with, was to toss out a catch-all topic that was so evocative that it never failed to stimulate many good ideas: "If we were one business instead of two, what would you do differently?"

Work-Outs and the Value Chain

An example from GE Medical Systems shows why this is so powerful. In the early 1990s, GEMS—which manufactures and sells CAT scanners and other large diagnostic equipment to hospitals—was proud of its order-fulfillment performance. By its measures, its people were delivering equipment to their customers on the promised dates over

95 percent of the time. Unfortunately, the customers were not satisfied . . . and it showed in their dismal rate of on-time payment. When managers from GEMS asked customers about performance from *their* perspectives, they learned that the GE equipment was arriving on time, but ancillary equipment from other manufacturers—pieces required to make the whole system work—was not. In other words, GE's products were multimillion-dollar doorstops without the right table, the right kinds of electrical connectors, and other parts of the scanning system— more frustrating sitting in their boxes than if they weren't there at all. Armed with this insight, GEMS management organized Work-Outs with other suppliers in the value chain so as to improve system delivery. And they made their key measurement truly customer focused—shifting from "on-time delivery" to "system up and running."

If you look around, you'll probably discover a myriad of topics that can benefit from joint problem solving between parties in the value chain—from reducing transportation and distribution costs to sharing product development so as to maximize returns all down the line. In fact, just having a preliminary discussion with a customer or supplier about Work-Out possibilities can be productive. It will force dialogue about what each party can do to help the other, thereby making the overall value chain stronger. And it will often dispel myths about what the other party is willing or not willing to do, or at least consider.

To give you a flavor for a customer-supplier Work-Out, here is a description of GE's very first experience with doing this—a Work-Out between GE Appliances and Sears. It is told by our colleague, Todd Jick, who was the Work-Out facilitator for the session:

> **The pioneering, and most visible, Customer Work-Out effort in GE was undertaken between GE Appliances (GEA) and Sears. Its origins dated to early 1989 discussions between Sears Marketing and Sales managers and GEA counterparts. This effort was followed and reinforced in November 1989 when Jack Welch met with a number of top Sears managers. In a conversation with Sears' National Merchandising Manager, Dick Lieberman, Welch described Work-Out and enthusiastically suggested that it would provide a natural opportunity for Sears and GEA to seek ways to improve their relationship. This willingness to experiment was extraordinary given the stakes for GE and the fact that although**

Sears had become GEA's largest customer, the two had been competitive rivals for decades . . . [and] the legacy born of years of distance and hostility was still palpable.

The goal was to use Work-Out to accelerate the creation of a fruitful partnership between a key customer and a new supplier. The actual effort began by holding separate meetings with the Sears senior merchandising management and with GEA's senior managers responsible for Sears Marketing and Sales to clarify the Work-Out concept, to determine who should be involved at the outset and what a design of the off-site might look like. It was decided to hold a three-day off-site at GE's management development facility (Crotonville) with 25 Sears and 16 GEA senior managers.

A [GEA] HR professional assisted by an external consultant, coordinated and spearheaded the Work-Out off-site design and execution. He set up and led a steering committee with three people from each organization to identify Work-Out "issues" which would be preselected for the workshop. These had to be: under joint control, important, resolvable, and visible.

Five issues were ultimately identified by the steering committee, in consultation with senior management from both organizations. The committee also organized and preassigned the names of participants into cross-company teams to work on these issues at the workshop.

Participants were very positive about the initial Work-Out off-site, which took place in February 1990. Not only had a comfort level between the organizations been fostered, but a variety of tangible action steps were agreed to that would resolve some critical issues in the relationship. As Sears' National Merchandising Manager recalled: "The actual Work-Out sessions [were] some of the most encouraging ones we've ever spent with a supplier. We questioned procedures that had outlived their usefulness, examined ways to remove redundancy, and tried to reduce the business equation to its bare essentials."

Nonetheless, optimism was cautious because the next steps were fraught with fragility, and each organization felt some healthy skepticism that the other could really change.

Most of the first joint projects were followed up and concluded. Progress was reviewed at each of the respective staff meetings, reinforcing the importance and commitment to action. Sears itself then had two internal Work-Out sessions, and GE Appliances had its own internal Work-Out meeting.

Remarkably, Sears people began to use the expression "in the spirit of Work-Out" as part of their common parlance. And the GEA people continued to search for ways to make it still easier for Sears to do business with them. Thus, tangible actions and a shared vocabulary were created and served as the foundation for future efforts to strengthen the relationship.

A second joint meeting occurred in July 1990 for one day. The spirit between the two groups was very positive, as were the results of the joint projects. A decision was reached to prepare for a set of new projects heading into 1991, one of which involved production, sales, and inventory, and new participants were selected to join some of the "old timers."

This new Work-Out partnership had thus been both widened and deepened—and was expected to continue for the foreseeable future. . . . The continuing goal was restated as "GE and its customers—one system, not two systems."[2]

After GE's initial experience with the Sears Work-Out, customer and supplier participation in Work-Outs became an accepted and regular occurrence. GE Lighting, for example, went on from its breakage extended Work-Out (described earlier in this chapter), which was done internally, to work with its packaging suppliers to develop stronger yet less-expensive packaging that would reduce breakage of light bulbs. Four GE businesses—Lighting, Motors, Electrical Distribution and Controls, and GE Supply—jointly organized a Work-Out with General Motors that led to a reduction in energy usage in GM factories (and more business for GE). GE Plastics had Work-Out sessions with Ford and Canon. GE Aerospace used Work-Out to strengthen its business relationships with the U.S. Department of Defense. And GE Capital's Fleet Leasing business had a Work-Out with 10 of its largest customers simultaneously to reduce paperwork and reporting.

All this experience eventually led GE to internalization of the notion that it's easier and better to do business with successful suppliers and customers. And GE therefore had an interest in helping its business partners succeed, and in not exploiting them on terms and conditions. This did not mean that GE didn't continue to drive hard bargains and look for supplier consolidations and high margins. But it led GE down the path of always looking for ways to help its customers and suppliers, even beyond joint efforts. For example, GE provided the budget to support one of its external consultants to introduce the Work-Out process to Wal-Mart, and to train Wal-Mart's internal people in it. Similarly, from the mid-1990s on, a large percentage of participants in Crotonville programs were not GE employees—they came from supplier or customer organizations.

Organizing a Value-Chain Work-Out

If you want to organize Work-Outs with your suppliers or customers to strengthen your value chain, these steps will get you there:

1. Sketch out the key constituents in your value chain. Who are your crucial suppliers and most significant customer (or categories of customers)? Where might some joint efforts leverage success for you and your partners?
2. Select a few partners (customers or suppliers) with whom you can begin some dialogue about doing a joint Work-Out. Identify in advance who you might talk with. What are the possible issues? What will be in it for them?
3. Begin the dialogue. Listen to their perspectives. Agree on a few issues or opportunities where everyone can achieve more by working together.
4. Create a joint design team with a few people from each company to shape the Work-Out process. Ask the team to sharpen the focus of the issues, select participants from both sides, and arrange the logistics. Agree on who will make the decisions at the

Town Meeting (a senior person from each company). Send out invitations that come from both of those senior managers.

5. Hold the Work-Out event and start the process. Make sure that some of the outcomes require joint effort, so people on both sides have an opportunity to work together over time. Also make sure that any commitments on your side of the fence are fulfilled in the required time frame so your partner knows you are serious and committed.

6. Review the initial efforts jointly—and keep the process going. If you are successful, this will be just the beginning of an ongoing process, both with this partner and with others.

Work-Out: Do It Your Way

What all these various vehicles for the Work-Out road add up to is that Work-Out needs to be done your way. It is not a cookie-cutter formula. It needs to fit into your situation and reality. You can even give it your own name. For example, New York Life Insurance Company called its process "Work-Wise." Armstrong World Industries refers to Work-Out as "Trailblazing." Aetna used "Out-of-the-Box." General Motors utilizes "Go-Fast." Call it what you wish. Do it your own way. Make Work-Out work for you.

Work-Out at Work

How Zurich Financial Services U.K. Used Work-Out to Transform the Company

W HEN PATRICK O'SULLIVAN took over at U.K.-based insurer Eagle Star in September of 1997, he was its sixth CEO in as many years. The company, a division of British American Tobacco and the third-largest general insurance firm in the United Kingdom, had lost more than $2 billion in mortgage-underwriting products in the past 10 years, and was still on a downward trend. Its fundamental business processes were in disarray. Its marketing strategy was focused on gaining share no matter what the cost, and its continuing losses were enormous. But even worse was the total lack of receptivity to change. As O'Sullivan put it, "Almost no one had any idea how bad the situation was. As the losses mounted, so did the benefits and perks. Everybody thought it was a great place to work. Moreover, some senior managers, whom I called the 'permafrost,' were quietly resistant, sensing a threat to their positions and to a system they didn't want to change."

No Time to Lose

In this situation, O'Sullivan realized that he had to move quickly. He knew he had to transform both the company's financial performance and its corporate culture. To start, he hired McKinsey, a strategic consulting firm with considerable insurance experience, to conduct a top-to-bottom strategic review. In addition, O'Sullivan himself went out and talked to employees—visiting 40 facilities and thousands of people in just a few months. At these meetings, O'Sullivan explained in detail that the company was in the midst of a very real crisis, and that major change was mandatory.

It was as a result of these meetings that O'Sullivan came to the conclusion that something like Work-Out was necessary. Everywhere he went, he found people who were working hard and were committed to the success of the company. They had ideas and they had talent. But they had no urgent need to change, and no support from their managers to do so, mostly because none of them had a clue about how bad things had become. They were living in what he called "Happy Valley," a state of ignorant bliss.

From his previous exposure at GE, O'Sullivan thought that Work-Out could be used to tap into the talent and ideas of the workforce—while forcing managers to move into action quickly, with a sense of urgency. He also thought that Work-Out could help in the implementation of the strategic initiatives that were starting to emerge from the consulting study. He was worried that the study was already coming up with ideas for changes in pricing, products, cost structure, brand, and systems—in short, for radical change—that would have to be implemented in a company that had demonstrated very little capacity to execute such change. Thus, even if the strategic insights were on target, they would be valueless because no one would be able to act on them.

In essence, then, O'Sullivan thought that the Work-Out process he'd participated in as a General Electric executive might help break the logjam. He believed the approach could generate some urgently needed cost reductions and revenue enhancements. At the same time, it could help develop the organization's fundamental capacity to implement change. Little did he know at the time that Work-Out would end up doing much more.

Getting Started

Two months into his tenure, O'Sullivan and his boss Sandy Leitch (chair of British American Tobacco's financial services arm) sat down and explained the situation to Charles Rosner, a U.S. marketing-communications consultant that he had known from his earlier days at GE Capital, along with Ron Ashkenas. They talked about what they needed to achieve financially, and about the daunting cultural shifts that were needed as well. And then together they began to shape a pilot Work-Out session that could get started before the end of the year to test the applicability of the process and to jump-start the company's performance. O'Sullivan thought that the selection of the first people to participate would be crucial—to make sure that the process was embraced with enthusiasm and had a chance of early success. To make this happen, he chose a group of mostly young sales and customer-service people from the Newcastle and Cheltenham call centers of Eagle Star Direct—people who were innovative, lively, and customer oriented. And he decided to ask them to focus on how to deliver on the company's "brand promise" with customers.

Within a week, one of Ron's colleagues, Matthew McCreight, was in the United Kingdom planning the Work-Out session, which was then held two weeks later, in early December. The business issue was that Eagle Star was promising its customers that it could deliver excellent customer service—fast telephone answering, fast credit approval on new policies, and fast claims resolution. Yet the company did not have the capacity to deliver on any of these promises. And there was no plan in place to make any improvements. The promises were nothing more than marketing hype.

At the start of the Work-Out, attended by 40 employees working in 3 teams, O'Sullivan again shared his view of the crisis the company was facing. In his words, "they had to confront the stark reality that unless we remade the company together, no one would be employed." But with that said, he also told them that the solution to the crisis was in their hands. They could raise issues and present proposals. And he would accept or reject them—as long as they were willing to dig in immediately and implement the ideas that he accepted.

With that introduction, the employees got to work and, as in any Work-Out, quickly generated dozens of ideas, many with significant financial implications. For example, one team focused on the fact that auto and home-policy renewals were a key to profitability. People whose policy terms were ending were already customers, and their credit records had already been examined and only needed updating. So it was much less costly to win their business for another term than to go after cold calls. Yet Eagle Star had not focused on renewals as a sales opportunity. As a result, the renewal rate was in the 70-percent range—and there were no attempts to cross-sell to these customers. Armed with these insights, one team developed an organized, proactive early-renewal program aimed at locking in renewals, increasing the hit ratio to over 85 percent, and expanding the business of these existing customers. Much to the team's amazement, the idea was approved, and others like it, in a heartbeat. The process was off and running.

And Now Let's Have a Merger

Within days after the first Work-Out session in Newcastle, even before the glow began to fade, another bit of news jolted Eagle Star. The company, along with all of BAT's financial services businesses, was being purchased by the Zurich Insurance Company. Eagle Star would be merged with Zurich's existing general-insurance business in the UK, and would be run by O'Sullivan. Sandy Leitch would become the chairman of all of Zurich's financial-services operations in the United Kingdom, Ireland, and South Africa. So now, in addition to a major turnaround, O'Sullivan was faced with the challenges of a merger and the integration of corporate cultures. As he said, "I don't think I've ever been in a tougher environment."

Since the merger would not be consummated until well into the new year (it turned out to be September), O'Sullivan decided to use the first half or more of 1998 to accelerate Eagle Star's turnaround efforts. He wanted the company to be on the best footing possible by the time the deal closed. To do this, he focused Work-Out on three priorities that had emerged from the strategic review:

- Reducing overpayments on claims
- Reducing costs in general
- Simplifying (and speeding up) certain core customer processes

In business after business, Work-Outs were organized on these and related subjects.

For example, in the personal-lines area, claims representatives in 12 branches used a Work-Out to launch a series of short-term projects targeted at reducing the cost of auto claims by over $10 million in the first year. Separately, in an effort to improve productivity and answer more incoming calls while also improving sales, call-center staff cut the average length of a sales call by over 25 percent in two months.

These rapid-cycle successes had the additional aim of helping the senior-management team learn how to provide overall sponsorship for results-focused change, while breaking up the middle-management permafrost. O'Sullivan realized that he could not get middle managers to change and to open themselves to the Work-Out process just through rhetoric and speech making. Instead, he had to give them the experience. So in that first year, over 100 managers were asked to play leadership roles in over 30 separate Work-Outs—to be on the front line and make decisions on the spot.

These early Work-Out sessions were by no means perfect. As O'Sullivan later reflected, "Some of the managers agreed to proposals at Town Meetings and then had second thoughts on implementation. Some were openly hostile to the whole idea. But the beauty of the Work-Out process is that it made this heretofore 'underground behavior' quite apparent."

The early Work-Outs also helped the leadership team learn how to tailor the GE process to the unique culture of Eagle Star, and then Zurich. For example, many managers and staff had never managed change projects before, so training and development in short-cycle breakthrough projects were included as part of the Work-Out process. And since the merger put increased scrutiny on the numbers, a rigorous tracking and follow-up process was added—including an actuarial audit to confirm financial results.

On with the Zurich Show

By April of 1998, merger planning was in full swing, and Patrick O'Sullivan held the first meeting of what would become his new, combined management team. Sensing that Work-Out would be a useful merger-integration tool as well as a turnaround vehicle, he used that session not only to introduce himself and the team, but also to introduce the Work-Out process to the Zurich people who were joining him.

When Eagle Star officially became part of Zurich in September of 1998, Work-Out was used extensively to bring new teams together—with a focus on achieving results. But this was no easy task, since the companies had quite different cultures and histories. Zurich, for example, brought underwriting and financial disciplines to the merger, but also a great deal of institutional bureaucracy. Eagle Star brought a more relaxed culture with great U.K. brand recognition—but little management discipline and accountability. But by keeping the focus on results—results that everyone knew had to be achieved—the groups gradually learned how to work together, and became one.

For example, after the merger, Information Technology, which had been a shambles at Eagle Star, ran a three-day Work-Out focused on cost savings. In the process, according to team members, IT people from both sides also did a lot of bridge building. As a result, by the end of the next year, the newly combined IT function came in at more than $3 million under budget, while providing better service. But perhaps the most important result was the feeling that many participants in those merger-related Work-Outs expressed: "We came in as two companies, but we're leaving a few days later feeling as though we're all working for the same company."

From "O'Sullivan's Work-Out" to "The Way We Work"

With the merger completed and the leadership team finally able to select the management teams to run the company, the major goal in 1999 was to return to profitability—no easy feat given the extent of losses in Eagle Star's underwriting portfolio. Tough monthly operating reviews with each of the company's SBUs and SSUs (such as HR, Finance, IT), major reductions in staff (over 2000 in all), reorganizations of business units and closures of locations, and dramatic changes in the composition of the business—as unprofitable business was dropped by the armload or priced for real profitability—all meant the business was in the midst of unprecedented change and uncertainty. In the words of O'Sullivan, "We were literally fighting for our right to exist as a company—we knew that if we did not show substantial improvement in results in 1999, we would not be in business in 2000."

In the midst of this turmoil, Work-Out became a central vehicle for improving performance at the new Zurich U.K. To emphasize this point, O'Sullivan ran his first management conference in January of 1999 as a Work-Out. The company's top 150 managers spent 2 days identifying opportunities to reduce costs and improve profitability—ending up targeting over $10 million worth of savings. Subsequent management conferences that year continued the focus on using Work-Out to engage all staff in the "do or die" effort to achieve quantum leaps in performance.

To support this burgeoning effort, O'Sullivan asked his then-HR Director, Rob Smith, to expand the Work-Out support team that had been started during the previous year. This team, led by Mohinder (Mo) Kang, eventually grew to a full-time "Work-Out Office" of four to eight people (at various times) with the goal of championing the use of Work-Out across the company. Working with Matthew McCreight and two colleagues from Robert H. Schaffer & Associates, by the end of 1999 the team trained over 40 Work-Out "designers" who could help managers identify topics and shape Work-Outs. The team also trained and certified over 130 facilitators who could be called upon during the sessions and the follow-up periods. In addition, it supported the financial analysts who tracked results. The team also orchestrated a comprehensive communications campaign to publicize Work-Out and highlight the many heroes that were following through on Work-Out commitments.

The push to use Work-Out to improve performance accelerated in 2000 and 2001 as the company achieved its financial turnaround and began to think ambitiously about moving to the front ranks of its competitors. Throughout this period, one aim was to embed Work-Out throughout the company—so it became part and parcel of the way managers led and how people worked. To this end, the number of people trained in specific Work-Out roles doubled, to over 100 designers and more than 300 facilitators—so that each part of the business had people who could play these special roles. The core Work-Out team trained all top managers in how to sponsor and lead Work-Out sessions. And Schaffer consultants developed a Web-based version of the Work-Out process for use on the company's intranet—a combination self-directed work space and resource guide for all staff to use.

By the end of 2001, hundreds of Work-Outs (large and small) had been held involving over 3000 employees, or 50 percent of the workforce. Verified savings over the preceding four years totaled over $100 million, and came from every part of the company. In addition, business after business reported additional gains in customer service, product development, and process improvement. For example:

- Finance improved cash flow by tens of millions of pounds, resulting in millions in bottom-line benefits to the company.
- Claims introduced innovative, proactive methods for handling whiplash injuries that saved the company millions while improv-

ing the care received by customers—and received an industry award for "claims team of the year" for this work.

- Zurich International held Work-Outs with key global customers and brokers—streamlining effort, achieving service gains and cost savings for their clients, and strengthening their business relationships in the process.

Just as importantly, during this period Work-Out did become the natural way that improvement happened at Zurich U.K. As Mo Kang reported in one of his annual reviews of Work-Out, "Our frontline staff are being empowered to work on real business solutions in a programme that is fast-moving, innovative, relentlessly customer-focused, and results-driven. People learn how to behave differently and, as Work-Out has gained momentum across the business, apply these changes in their day-to-day jobs."

A Challenge That Never Ends

No Work-Out process, and no change process, can ever be complete in any company. And Patrick O'Sullivan would be the first to admit that even after almost four years of Work-Out at Zurich U.K., there is still a long way to go. But by sustaining the process and making it part of the fabric of the company, O'Sullivan was able to take an organization that had chronically underperformed and, even with the distraction of a merger, transform it into one of the highest-performing units of Zurich Financial Services.

Of course, Work-Out alone did not change the company by itself. O'Sullivan and his leadership team also reengineered the strategy, product mix, and cost structure. But these changes would probably not have been possible if Work-Out had not captured the imagination of Zurich U.K. employees at all levels. Picture this, especially at a staid British insurer: a woman stands up at a Work-Out session clad in black garbage liners. Clutching 75 balloons—symbolizing the £75 it costs every time a customer is lost—she marches onto the podium and invites the audience to burst them, one at a time. She then outlines a series of proposals from telesales staff to improve customer retention.

That is Work-Out at Zurich U.K. That—and audited savings of over $100 million.[1]

PART
III

Work-Out's Long-Term Payoff

Using Work-Out to Create GE-Style Organizational Leaders

IN THE FIRST two parts of this book, we described Work-Out as an approach for engaging employees and solving organizational problems. But Work-Out is more than that. By opening up dialogue across boundaries and by insisting on rapid, on-the-spot decision making, Work-Out also transforms how leaders think and act. In fact, for Work-Out to really make a difference, ultimately it requires leaders who can challenge and stretch people, mobilize resources, make rapid decisions, encourage innovation, drive for speed, challenge assumptions, insist on results, and much more. These Work-Out leaders must exist at all levels of the firm and in all organizational units.

But this kind of leadership doesn't just happen by itself, or even evolve naturally over time through the use of Work-Out. It needs to be explicitly encouraged and developed. This chapter explores the kind of leadership that Work-Out both requires and helps to create, and then provides explicit guidance about how to accelerate its development.

It's Always About Leadership

Transforming an organization—to make it more competitive, productive, innovative, or better in any way—always requires leadership. Tools and methods alone are not sufficient. Nor are strategies, assets, and resources. Ultimately, human beings who have leadership roles need to step up to create change—and start a chain reaction that gets more and more people to change as well.

Leaders create the transformation and sustain it; leaders model new behaviors and engage others in new behaviors; leaders make decisions and empower others by letting them make decisions; leaders deliver results.

Sometimes this process starts at the very top of the organization with a CEO like Jack Welch, someone who has a vision about a different kind of organization and a different kind of leader. But sometimes the process starts at other levels, with unit managers who have the foresight, energy, and courage to model a new kind of leadership and prove that it can lead to superior results. Ultimately, however, leadership change needs both to cascade down and to bubble up—so that effective "new" leadership exists at all levels of the organization.

The starting point for accelerating the development of Work-Out leaders is to describe what Work-Out leadership actually means—to create what we call the Work-Out "leadership brand."[1] These are the expectations of *what* leaders should achieve (results), and *how* leaders should do it (behaviors). Clarity about these "brand characteristics" gives managers at all levels a picture of what it takes to succeed, provides a direction for development, and helps to make decisions about the kinds of leaders that come into the firm and move up in it.

The Work-Out Leadership Brand

When Work-Out began in late 1988, its leadership brand was fuzzy at best. Clearly, GE leaders were expected to produce superior business results as measured by the standard financial numbers—revenue, margin, net income, expense, and so on. They were also expected to "reduce bureaucracy," whatever that meant. How they were to achieve these results was less clear. Somehow, GE leaders were supposed to "liberate" their people, engage in direct dialogue—unfiltered by staff—and make decisions "on the spot." Not surprisingly, the model was Jack Welch's own give-and-take style in the Crotonville "Pit." But it was far from clear how this would play out on the job, in the face of day-to-day routine and emergencies.

Given this lack of clarity about the leadership brand that was expected, it is not surprising that many GE leaders reacted to Work-Out with a mixture of skepticism and confusion. They knew that Welch wanted them to do something differently, but they weren't sure what that was. Others had a sense of what Welch was expecting but didn't necessarily agree, especially since they had been successful up until then without these kinds of behaviors. Others saw where Welch was heading but were incapable of moving in that direction. And still others—as noted earlier—were skeptical about how sincere "Neutron Jack" could be about engaging and empowering the workforce he'd just pruned so enthusiastically.

No matter the reaction, the one thing that was clear beyond a doubt in the early days of Work-Out was that the GE leadership brand was changing. Through the use of Work-Out, GE leaders would be forced to achieve business results in new ways. In fact, in early meetings with the external Work-Out faculty, Welch made it clear that his intention in hiring the faculty was not just to develop and implement the Work-Out process but also to coach his senior leaders. Somehow they had to change or be changed—although it wasn't yet clear what they had to do differently or how they would learn to do it.

Speed, Simplicity, and Self-Confidence

In the early months of 1989, as the GE businesses experimented with Work-Out, Welch—with the help of the Crotonville staff and the external faculty—began to clarify and sharpen his notion of the GE leadership brand. In April of that year, at the Annual Share Owners meeting, Welch talked about "speed, simplicity, and self-confidence" as the "keys to leading in the '90s." And with these three simple words, he began to demystify the behaviors that were central to the Work-Out way of managing. As he said in that speech:

> **We found in the '80s that speed increases in an organization as control decreases. . . . When we [decreased control] we began to see people who for years had spent half their time serving the system and the other half fighting it, suddenly come to life, making decisions in minutes, face to face, on matters that once would have produced months of staff gyrations and forests of paper. But this transformation, this rebirth, was largely confined to upper**

management. In the '90s we want to see it engulf and galvanize the entire company.

We found in the '80s that becoming faster is tied to becoming simpler. Our businesses, most with tens of thousands of employees, will not respond to visions that have sub-paragraphs and footnotes.

If we're not simple we can't be fast . . . and if we're not fast we can't win. . . .

But just as surely as speed flows from simplicity, simplicity is grounded in self-confidence. Self-confidence does not grow in someone who is just another appendage on the bureaucracy . . . whose authority rests on little more than a title. Bureaucracy is terrified by speed and hates simplicity. It fosters defensiveness, intrigue, sometimes meanness. Those who are trapped in it are afraid to share, can't be passionate and—in the '90s— won't win.

But people who are freed from the confines of their box on the organization chart, whose status rests on real-world achievement . . . those are the people who develop the self-confidence to be simple, to share every bit of information available to them, to listen to those above, below and around them and then move boldly.

But a company can't distribute self-confidence. What it can do . . . is give each of our people an opportunity to win, to contribute, and hence earn self-confidence themselves. . . . That is what our Work-out program is designed to create.[2]

Translating Aspiration into Reality

By the middle of 1989, then, the leadership brand that Work-Out was meant to foster had started to take shape. Throughout most of the company, however, it was still an aspiration rather than a reality. Hundreds of managers were indeed leading Work-Out sessions and getting real-time coaching about how to behave effectively. But this was a slow process of change, requiring high levels of coaching sophistication and lots of one-on-one discussions. And the definitions of appropriate Work-Out behavior were still ad hoc, often depending on interpretation.

To give the leadership brand further definition, and to dramatically accelerate the process by which GE leaders could turn the words into actions, many of the faculty members in 1990 and 1991 designed leadership-assessment and development programs for senior managers and their teams. The program at GE Capital, designed by Ron Ashkenas and consultant Richard Korn, and ultimately rolled out to management teams in over 20 GE Capital businesses, is a good illustration of how this was done.

The GE Capital program, called the "Leadership Challenge Workshop," was based on a simple 360-degree assessment instrument that translated "speed, simplicity, and self-confidence" into 20 specific leadership behaviors. The instrument asked people to assess the extent to which a particular manager exhibited those behaviors (never, rarely, occasionally, frequently, always). (See Figure 11-1 for the specific questions.)

Prior to the workshop, each participating manager would ask peers, subordinates, and the boss to complete the assessment, and would also do a self-assessment. All of these were sent (anonymously) to the consultants for scoring and analysis.

The one-day workshop, held for management teams, began with some group discussion about leadership concepts and differences in leadership styles. A Harvard Business School case study was used to stimulate discussion—and in particular to generate dialogue about the kind of leadership needed at GE Capital to win in the global competitive environment. Managers also used this forum to talk about their experiences with Work-Out and their own roles either as leaders of the Town Meetings or as participants.

Following this discussion, one of the consultants presented the team's aggregate results from the assessment survey—the average scores given by subordinates and by the team itself. This included some group discussion of overall patterns, including particularly high or low scores on clusters of items as well as differences in perceptions between subordinates and the team itself. The managers were each then given their own scores, along with some time to identify questions or issues—for example, key differences between self-ratings and the ratings of others. Managers then met in small groups to discuss their scores and

Business Unit: _____   Participant: _____

GE Capital Corporation   Date: _____
Leadership Challenge Workshop

		Rating					
	Not Rated	Never	Rarely	Occasionally	Frequently	Always	Total Valid Responses	Average
Dimension: *Speed*								
1. Is quick and flexible in making decisions.								
2. Anticipates changes in business and work conditions.								
3. Passionately strives to put the customer first.								
4. Articulates a customer-oriented purpose.								
5. Articulates and delivers a clear vision.								
Total:								
Dimension: *Simplicity*								
1. Openly and completely shares information.								
2. Is not confined by the "usual way."								
3. Encourages creative problem solving, innovation.								
4. Gets to the basics of getting the job done.								
5. Runs a streamlined organization.								
Total:								

Figure 11-1. 360-Degree Assessment Questionnaire for a Leadership-Challenge Workshop.

Dimension: Self-Confidence							
1. Encourages me to positively confront and challenge.							
2. Treats me with respect, values my talent.							
3. Trusts me to respond to change.							
4. Respects individual and business integrity.							
5. Demonstrates sound business ethics.							
6. Inspires me and my peers to excel.							
7. Deals directly with uncomfortable situations.							
8. Faces the reality of a situation.							
9. Accurately ties incentive rewards to performance.							
10. Uses positive feedback, recognition, and challenge.							
Total:							

Figure 11-1. (Continued.)

create individual development plans, that is, targeted actions that they could take either to build on some key strengths or to work on some weaknesses. At the end of the workshop, the development plans were shared with the entire team, and the team discussed its collective development needs and how its members could help support each other.

The process by which the Leadership Challenge Workshop was conducted also mirrored and modeled the emerging GE leadership brand. The session was fast moving. The instrument was simple. And the information was openly shared and discussed, with the assumption that self-confident managers could reveal their weaknesses as well as their strengths. Naturally, this process was anxiety producing for some and exhilarating for others, which provided further data about people's ability to actualize the new leadership brand.

Following each workshop with a senior team, members of the team were asked to replicate the process with their direct reports at the next one or two levels, which provided additional learning. By running these workshops over the course of a year, all of the senior GE Capital leaders gained a sharper picture of the new leadership brand and what they needed to do to make it their own.

In 1990 and 1991, similar developmental processes occurred throughout all the GE businesses—and hundreds of managers deepened their understanding of the new leadership brand and what it would take to provide leadership in the "Work-Out way."

Putting Teeth into the Leadership Brand

By the end of 1991, it was clear that behaving according to the new leadership brand was expected at GE. And hundreds of managers were coming face to face with the realities of that new brand, both through their experiences with Work-Out and through a variety of self-assessment and training experiences. But the demand for shifting from the old style of GE leadership to the new style was still somewhat soft—conveyed mostly through exhortation, speeches, Crotonville courses, and discussions with consultants. Thus, many senior leaders still questioned the need to change: How serious was Welch about the new leadership? Did it really make a difference in terms of pay and promotion? Could you be successful at GE without changing to the new brand?

These, of course, are questions that would be raised in any organization undergoing change. They were especially important at GE because the authenticity of the entire Work-Out process in some ways depended on their answers. Thousands of employees at GE were aware that Welch was trying to change the leadership brand. Yet, for the most part, the very same senior leaders who were in place in 1988 were still running the major businesses of GE. And many of them, despite talking a good game about Work-Out and employee involvement, still operated in traditional ways—through control, intimidation, and reliance on a small circle of staff.

The real dilemma that GE faced was that the traditional, old-style leaders were still achieving superior business results, regardless of their leadership behaviors. From their perspectives, they were still playing the same game as always—produce the numbers—and winning, and this gave them immunity from having to make deeper behavioral or stylistic changes. Unless they stumbled, and nobody wanted that to happen either, there was no cause to make a change.

Perhaps with this dilemma in mind, Welch and the GE HR community began to make it clear, throughout 1991, that GE leaders were expected not just to make their numbers but to exhibit the values inherent in Work-Out at the same time. These values were further crystallized and defined, as shown in Figure 11-2. And they were considered during the yearly discussions of promotions and executive staffing.

GE Leaders . . . Always with Unyielding Integrity:

- Have a passion for excellence and hate bureaucracy
- Are open to ideas from anywhere . . . and committed to Work-Out
- Live quality . . . and drive cost and speed for competitive advantage
- Have the self-confidence to involve everyone and behave in a boundaryless fashion
- Create a clear, simple, reality-based vision . . . and communicate it to all constituents
- Have enormous energy and the ability to energize others
- Stretch . . . set aggressive goals . . . reward progress . . . yet understand accountability and commitment
- See change as opportunity . . . not threat
- Have global brains . . . and build diverse and global teams

---

Figure 11-2.   GE Values.

Through the end of 1991 it was still an open question whether achieving results—without living the values—would be tolerated at GE. Then, at the annual GE officers' meeting at Boca Raton in January of 1992, Welch answered this question in a dramatic fashion. In front of all the senior leaders of GE, Welch announced several major changes in senior leadership—including heads of GE businesses. And among those changes was the removal of leaders who had achieved their numbers without exhibiting the GE values.

Welch described the decision-making process for these shifts through the use of a simple two-by-two matrix, as shown in Figure 11-3.

	Results	
	TYPE I MANAGER: **Delivers Results and** **Exhibits the Values**	**TYPE III MANAGER:** **Does Not Deliver Results but** **Does Exhibit the Values**
Values		
	TYPE IV MANAGER: **Delivers Results but** **Does Not Exhibit the Values**	**TYPE II MANAGER:** **Does Not Deliver Results and** **Does Not Exhibit the Values**

Figure 11-3. GE Leadership Decision Matrix.

Later, Welch summarized this matrix in the 1995 Annual Report, as follows:

It was at Work-Out sessions that it became clear that some of the rhetoric heard at the corporate level—about involvement and excitement and turning people loose—did not match the reality of life in the businesses. The problem was that some of our leaders were unwilling, or unable, to abandon big-company, big-shot autocracy and embrace the values we were trying to grow. So we defined our management styles, or "types," and how they furthered or blocked our values. And then we acted.

Type I not only delivers on performance commitments, but believes in and furthers GE's small-company values. The trajectory of this group is "onward and upward," and the men and women who comprise it will represent the core of our senior leadership into the next century.

Type II does not meet commitments, nor share our values—nor last long at GE.

Type III believes in the values but sometimes misses commitments. We encourage taking swings, and Type III is typically given another chance.

Type IV. The "calls" on the first two types are easy. Type III takes some judgment; but Type IV is the most difficult. One is always tempted to avoid taking action, because Type IV's deliver short-term results. But Type IV's do so without regard to values and, in fact, often diminish them by grinding people down, squeezing them, stifling them. Some of these learned to change; most couldn't. The decision to begin removing Type IV's was a watershed—the ultimate test of our ability to "walk the talk," but it had to be done if we wanted GE people to be open, to speak up, to share, and to act boldly outside traditional "lines of authority" and "functional boxes" in this new learning, sharing, environment."[3]

The Boca meeting in January of 1992 was indeed a watershed event, gaining widespread news coverage in publications like the *Wall Street Journal*. But its main reverberations were within GE, where it became clear that the GE values—leadership the Work-Out way—had real teeth. It was no longer enough just to make the numbers. The numbers had to be achieved through utilization of the GE leadership brand.

For a company that had always placed a premium on achieving business results—over and above anything else—this was a stunning development. One of the Type IV business leaders who had been fired and made an example of at the Boca meeting later reflected on the importance of this move:

Just after Christmas, I got a call from Welch asking me to meet him in Fairfield. Our business had just wrapped up the numbers for the year, and they were outstanding. We had come in well over our tar-

gets and had achieved a real turnaround. I was sure that Welch wanted to congratulate me and tell me about my bonus. You can imagine how shocked I was when he told me that I was being fired. I couldn't believe it. Once he explained it to me, I certainly could see his perspective. I know that I can be pretty rough on people. So what he did was probably the right thing. But I sure didn't see it coming.

In other words, despite several years of emphasis on the Work-Out way, and countless discussions of the type of leadership needed in GE, this exceptionally bright and talented business leader still had not gotten the word. And thus, if Welch had not acted, there would have been a strong double message in the GE system—that the Work-Out leadership brand was important, but was not as important as achieving business results. By putting teeth into the leadership brand, Welch shifted the leadership model from an either-or debate to a clear requirement to achieve both results *and* live the values.

Learning from GE: Four Steps for Developing Work-Out Leaders

Based on the GE experience and our work with other firms, we see four major steps involved in developing Work-Out leaders. To the extent that you want to use Work-Out as more than just one more problem-solving tool, and instead position it as a vehicle for transforming your organization and its leadership, you can employ these four steps:

1. Define, clarify, and communicate your leadership brand.
2. Assess managers against the leadership brand.
3. Invest in development processes to help managers learn how to live the brand.
4. Reinforce the leadership brand.

Step 1: Define, Clarify, and Communicate Your Leadership Brand

As noted earlier, the leadership brand is your firm's theory of leadership—the attributes that you expect leaders to have and the results that you expect them to achieve. Work-Out has a number of such characteristics already embedded, based on the process itself—the encouragement of cross-boundary involvement, rapid decision-making, intolerance for bureaucracy, focus on short-term results, and more. For your firm's version of Work-Out, you might want to emphasize and articulate other elements of your own leadership brand. For example, Aetna's "Out-of-the-Box" process put a premium on innovative thinking and challenging of prevailing assumptions. Armstrong's "Trailblazing" process encourages systems thinking, among other things. The State of West Virginia, under the leadership of Governor Caperton, called its program "Inspire," emphasizing the empowerment aspects of Work-Out in support of constituent service. And General Motors' "GoFast" process singles out "speed" as the crucial leadership and organizational characteristic.

However, as you define your leadership brand, we encourage you to keep it simple. Long lists of management competencies and multicell matrices make most managers' eyes glaze over. Instead, focus on the few key attributes that will distinguish your organization from others. What results should your managers achieve? What should they know? What kind of people should they be? How should they behave?

As you define your leadership brand, also think about the extent to which the leadership brand can pervade all levels of your organization. A fundamental mistake that many firms make is to think about leadership brand as being most applicable at the senior levels. For example, it is common for organizations to emphasize "strategic thinking" as a senior management skill, without worrying about whether first-level supervisors or even employees can think strategically or understand the firm's strategy. But if first-level managers are not thinking strategically then the decisions they make—and they make many on a day-to-day basis—will not have the right context, and may take the firm in the wrong direction, one small step at a time. In contrast, at GE, virtually every training program or meeting, including Work-Outs, usually includes some discussion of strategy so that all decisions, even very tactical ones, are made in the same context.

Finally, as you clarify the leadership brand, communicate it to managers and to employees within the firm. Make it clear what the expectations are—even if they are aspirations that are not yet achieved. Change will not occur unless there is a gap between today's reality and tomorrow's vision, and that gap needs to be articulated and discussed. In addition, by sharing the leadership brand with employees, you can make it clear what they should expect from their leaders. This will put additional pressure on managers to live up to expectations both from above and from below.

Step 2: Assess Managers Against the Leadership Brand

Once you have articulated your firm's leadership brand, the second step is to put in place a process of assessment—to illuminate the gap between current performance and living the brand. Work-Out, of course, is itself both an assessment and development vehicle. When managers lead Work-Out sessions, and particularly Town Meetings, the gap between desired and actual behavior often hits them (and others) right between the eyes. No longer can they hide behind staff or behind positional authority. In Town Meetings, managers are exposed for who they are, for better or worse. Thus, requiring managers to lead Work-Out sessions can itself be a powerful way to assess progress toward the leadership brand. At Armstrong, for example, CEO Mike Lockhart required all of his business and functional leaders to run Trailblazing (Work-Out) sessions personally within six months of starting the effort, and to get feedback on how well they did it.

In addition to the Work-Outs themselves, however, you can either initiate or use other assessment processes. The Leadership Challenge Workshop that GE Capital employed was a good example of a 360-degree feedback process that can be very effective. Building the leadership-brand criteria into the assessment processes that already exist in your organization—such as performance management, career planning, and job selection—is another way to proceed.

Step 3: Invest in Development Processes to Help Managers Learn How to Live the Brand

As managers get a better sense of the gap between their current realization of the leadership brand and the desired level, you then have an obligation to support their development. Some small number of managers can change their behavior and effectiveness based purely on an understanding of their own "gap;" most need some amount of support. The investment that you and your organization make in this learning process is itself a signal about how seriously you are driving the organization toward the new leadership brand.

A number of development vehicles can be used to help your leaders step up to the new leadership brand and become Work-Out leaders. You might want to create an overall plan for what vehicles to use, at what pace, and with which managers. Figure 11-4 provides a tool for creating this kind of plan.

DEVELOPMENT VEHICLES	Q1	Q2	Q3	Q4
In-house training				
External training (for example, at a university)				
Special job assignments				
Coaching				
Mentoring				
Assignment to project teams				
Structured development planning				
Participation in learning networks				
Performance management				
Participation in external groups (such as boards, associations)				
And so on. . . .				

Figure 11-4.   Leadership Development Worksheet.

The extent to which you can lay out a plan like this on a departmental or organizationwide basis will help you turn development from a catch-as-catch-can process into a well-organized investment. In fact, in most organizations that we have seen, many activities already are taking place—but not within an overall framework. Thus, senior leaders and HR heads have little sense of how much investment really is being made and where it is being targeted. Nor do managers and employees see or understand the level of commitment that the organization has toward development of the leadership brand.

Step 4: Reinforce the Leadership Brand

Once you have articulated what you mean by Work-Out leadership and have started to make investments in closing the gap between today's reality and tomorrow's needs, the fourth step is to reinforce the brand through clear rewards and clear consequences. As the GE experience shows, even the most passionate articulation of "new leadership" means nothing unless it is followed up with serious actions—such as promoting people who demonstrate the brand and firing people who do not.

Naturally, you have a number of options for reinforcing the Work-Out brand besides just promoting and firing. The leadership brand characteristics can be criteria for compensation and bonus decisions. People who get results and demonstrate the leadership brand can be recognized through nonmonetary rewards and can be publicized as heroes of the firm as well. Managers who do not make enough progress toward the leadership brand can be passed over for special assignments.

While at GE, Steve Kerr developed a powerful tool for making sure that desired leadership behaviors are truly aligned with rewards and recognition. This tool lists the desired leadership behaviors, along with some that are not desired, in a questionnaire format. For each behavior, people can rate the extent to which the behavior is:

- Rewarded
- Punished or discouraged
- Sometimes rewarded and sometimes punished
- Neither rewarded nor punished

The questionnaire that results is then filled out by people in a business unit or across an entire organization. The statistics that emerge show the extent to which the leadership brand is in alignment with rewards and consequences. For example, this process was used at a large Town Meeting at the World Bank during a time when the bank was trying to develop professional networks for the sharing of technical knowledge and resources across regions of the bank. The questionnaire showed that the desired leadership value of knowledge-sharing was just as often punished as it was rewarded in the bank—which led to extensive work to recalibrate both rewards and leadership behavior.

Supporting the Work-Out Process—While Building Leadership

The four steps described here represent an iterative, ongoing process and not a linear, one-time event. As the Work-Out program evolves, and as your organization's environment changes, definitions of the leadership brand will continue to sharpen and shift. At GE, for example, the focus on being global, the emphasis on quality, and "digitization" all emerged over time. Thus, the leadership brand for your firm must, in some ways, continually be rewritten—driving a continuing iteration of assessment, development, and reinforcement.

At the same time, while you are always sharpening the leadership brand, you are also sponsoring, designing, conducting, and following up on Work-Outs. These Work-Outs are, as we have described throughout the book, the engines of real change—the catalysts that help the organization solve problems and open up new opportunities. But they also have an additional benefit: They are real-time training sites, not only for senior managers, but also for the next generation of leaders, the people who are designated as Work-Out facilitators. Thus, in a positive cycle of action, reaction, and growth, while you are sponsoring, designing, conducting, and following up on Work-Outs, you also are developing leaders with the skills to facilitate both small-group and large-group sessions.

Fostering the growth of such skills within an organization is a key leadership-development initiative in and of itself. In the context of the Work-Out leadership brand, as discussed earlier in this chapter, effective leaders are also good facilitators. They know how to create a team and manage its dynamics. They know how to lead working sessions and meetings that have the right blend of participation, brainstorming, and action focus. And they know how to keep a group on track and get it to an outcome. So training facilitators for Work-Out is the equivalent of killing two birds with one stone—it provides support for the Work-Out process, and it develops future leaders. Because of this dual-action effect, most organizations that have employed Work-Out over time have focused on building facilitation capacity through both the *selection* and the *training and development* of Work-Out facilitators.

Selecting Work-Out Facilitators

In organizations that want to encourage the Work-Out leadership brand, facilitators are usually drawn from the ranks of people who have been identified as "high potentials." For such people, Work-Out represents a wonderful opportunity for additional training, skill development, exposure to other parts of the organization, and visibility with senior leaders. In some organizations, there is a tendency to draw facilitators exclusively from Human Resources, Quality, or Training functions, where facilitation skills have already been developed. While this is often expedient, it may also be short-sighted. In the longer term, developing facilitation capability in line-management people may have greater impact on the organization's ability to compete and thrive.

Internal facilitators should be high-potential, individual-contributor employees who have the chance to move into managerial jobs within the next year or two. They should be able to dedicate 20–25 percent of their time to facilitation for four to six months—and be willing to learn the skills needed for the role.

Although Work-Out facilitators can certainly be developed, some degree of innate skill and ability is required as a starting point. It is unfair to ask someone who is very uncomfortable or anxious in small-group settings to try to become a facilitator. The chances of success are not high. Therefore, a starting point for facilitator selection is to develop a set of characteristics or criteria that describe the type of person you are looking for. Of course, no one will ever meet all the criteria, but the list provides a useful starting point—and a description that people can use to see if they want to apply for the role.

Here are some criteria that might be included:

- Effective presentation skills
- Good listening, speaking, and interpersonal skills
- Ability to relate well and command respect when standing in front of a group, and to provide effective leadership even if not completely familiar with the subject
- High degree of confidence and comfort level in briefing and dealing with senior managers
- Excellent skills in proactive facilitation of group sessions (intervention to resolve conflict, stopping inappropriate or unproductive discussion, keeping the pace moving, and the like)
- Ability to relate to a cross section of staff from all levels and roles
- Ability and willingness to observe and provide constructive feedback to a team leader

- Versatility, flexibility, and creativity in running team sessions (able to make changes on the fly in timings and methods used to brainstorm or reach group consensus and the like)
- Ability to facilitate team sessions and to simultaneously capture key issues, questions, and decisions on a flip chart
- Ability to manage a group agenda within the overall timetable
- Ability to deal sensitively but assertively with resistance or dysfunctional behavior

Based on criteria such as these, companies have used different approaches for selecting facilitators. In many GE businesses, Human Resources managers used the high-potential lists to identify possible facilitators, and then just asked them directly to participate. At Armstrong, each business-unit leader and the heads of the corporate functions nominated several candidates that they thought would meet the criteria. After some amount of sorting out with the corporate head of HR, these candidates were asked to attend a facilitator-training session. At Zurich U.K., the criteria were posted electronically, and anyone in the company was given an opportunity to apply. Because of the large number of candidates, a one-day facilitator-training session was then used to screen candidates and select those most likely to succeed in the role.

Training and Developing Work-Out Facilitators

Once potential facilitators have been identified, you need a process to develop them so they can effectively support Work-Out in the short term and strengthen their managerial skills over time. As with any human-development process, this is not a one-time event or program. There are at least several steps along the way, all of which can be deepened or continued over time. Again, the degree of structure or formality required for these steps might differ, depending on your organization and its needs. For example, we have seen some organizations identify facilitators and then just throw them in the water at real Work-Out sessions, with minimal or no preparation. At the other extreme, some organizations have created extensive facilitator training, complete with manuals and certification.

Whether formal or informal, we suggest that facilitator training might include these three ingredients:

An orientation to the Work-Out process and its intent in the organization. Even in the least-formal training processes, it is useful to help the facilitators stay one step ahead of the participants. This can be accomplished through a formal couple of hours, or a short briefing in advance of a Work-Out.

Hands-on, real-time facilitation experience. The only way to really train people in facilitation is through giving them the experience of facilitation. If the process is totally informal, the sink-or-swim method at a real Work-Out session can be applied. A somewhat less risky alternative is to pair the new facilitator with a more experienced internal facilitator or an external facilitator. At Armstrong and in many of the GE businesses, this "shadow facilitation" approach was used to build a small cadre of experienced internal facilitators quickly, with minimal formal training.

A more structured and even less risky approach is to conduct a formal training session for facilitators—with lots of real facilitation practice built into the agenda. Most of the GE businesses eventually took this route and created a standard course that was offered periodically for potential facilitators—but was also part of the business-management-development curriculum. All these courses included exercises, role plays, and experiential sessions where participants could facilitate simulated Work-Outs and then get immediate feedback on their performance, sometimes on videotape. The sessions also included discussions and practice about difficult situations and other possible scenarios that might come up. Figure 11-5 provides a suggested agenda for facilitator training. A Work-Out simulation exercise called "The United Bank of London" can also be found in Appendix B.

Ongoing feedback and development. Once facilitators have some experience under their belts, you should put mechanisms in place to continue the learning process. For example, the Work-Out program manager or a senior HR person might actively solicit feedback from Work-Out team leaders and participants about the facilitators, and provide anonymous and helpful feedback. Facilitators can also be asked to assess themselves after each Work-Out to identify things they might have done differently, or areas to strengthen in future sessions. You can also organize "clinic" sessions for facilitators, where they can share their experiences, talk through difficult situations and how to handle them,

---

A Work-Out Facilitation Skills Training Agenda

1. Introductions and Workshop Overview
2. Facilitator Assignment #1: Workshop Expectations
   - Facilitators use brainstorming and nominal group technique to help teams develop a prioritized list of their workshop learning expectations.
3. Background to Work-Out
4. Facilitator Roles and Skills
5. Facilitator Assignment #2: Great Meetings and Terrible Meetings
   - Facilitators examine what makes meetings successful (and what causes them to fail) while practicing warm-up techniques, brainstorming, group discussion, and checklist development.
6. Facilitator Assignment #3: Group Norms
   - Facilitators use role play to practice how to develop group consensus and summarize group work.
7. Facilitation Assignment #4: United Bank of London Simulation
   - Facilitators move beyond brainstorming to help groups organize and prioritize ideas using the Payoff Matrix.
8. Review Session—Summary and Adjourn

Figure 11-5.

and reinforce learning with each other. The key in all of these mechanisms is to encourage constant self-reflection and learning—which are habits of good Work-Out leaders in any case.

We Have Met the Leadership and It Is Us

This chapter has discussed how Work-Out can transform the leadership of your organization, and has suggested a number of specific steps by which you can accelerate this transformation. Supporting a full-scale Work-Out process across an organization—and transforming leadership—are, however, big, daunting subjects. Maybe an organization such as GE can do it with all its resources and the drive of a charismatic, powerful CEO. But how can other organizations, often without the assets of GE, make this kind of progress? In the next chapter, we will discuss how to start Work-Out on a small scale, no matter where you may be in your organization, and use initial success to build a larger-scale effort. Just remember that whether starting big or starting small—from the top or from the bottom—the key is still leadership. And Work-Out can help to strengthen it, no matter where you start.

Embedding the Process in Your Organization

ORK-OUT OFTEN begins with a pilot, an experiment where managers can observe how employees respond to opportunities to make recommendations and implement decisions on the spot. But pilots and experiments do not create sustained transformation. For Work-Out to have a lasting impact, it must move on from the experimental stage and become embedded in company programs and activities.

Moving Work-Out from pilot to program requires 12 key decisions. We like to refer to them as a "12-step process" for Work-Out, capitalizing on the concept of the many 12-step programs that help people try to change various behaviors. Here they are:

1. Approach Work-Out as an adjective rather than a noun.
2. Stack the deck for success.
3. Use facilitators to show the way.
4. Build in enough support.
5. Help managers get ready to deploy Work-Out.
6. Set specific Work-Out delivery goals.
7. Publicize the successes.
8. Align your actions with your commitment.

9. Reach the tipping point.
10. Resource your Work-Outs.
11. Follow up and share knowledge.
12. Apply Work-Out to other programs.

No 12-step program is magical, but the decisions and activities of each step ensure progress toward an overall goal. This one is no exception!

Step 1: Approach Work-Out as an Adjective Rather Than a Noun

Work-Out moves from pilot to program when it enables business outcomes. If the business outcomes are the nouns—the things you're looking for—then Work-Out has to be an adjective. Adjectives modify nouns in ways that add meaning (*tall* man, *gifted* teacher, *demanding* executive). As an adjective, the Work-Out experience informs and enables business goals. For example, if customer share (revenue from targeted customers) is a business goal, Work-Out becomes a means of accomplishing that goal better and faster. Work-Out removes bureaucracy, engages employees, generates ideas, and leads to actions that accomplish business goals. Work-Out pilot tests that are not linked to business results will not be sustained.

Integrating Work-Out into the business begins with the clear definition of business goals, followed by the institutionalization of Work-Out as a means to accomplish those goals. We have seen some leaders attempt to apply Work-Out as a tool in the absence of a business goal. These sessions become abstract at times and episodic at best. Because the outcomes of Work-Out are not linked to clear business results, leaders are not inclined to sustain Work-Out. When Work-Out activities help accomplish business goals, leaders have clear reasons to participate in and sustain the activities.

Step 2: Stack the Deck for Success

Pilot tests serve a valuable purpose. They allow leaders to experiment, learn, and adapt ideas so the ideas can be improved over time. In adopting Work-Out, leaders have two extreme options: roll out the effort simultaneously throughout an entire organization, or select pilot sites to begin the initiative. While Work-Out should affect an entire organization over time, we advocate beginning Work-Out in a pilot site where trial and error can lead to rapid learning. Desirable pilot sites tend to share several features:

First and most basic, you want to try Work-Out at a pilot site where it is likely to succeed. Preconditions for success include a leader who likes the Work-Out idea, an organization rife with bureaucracy and full of those low-hanging fruit that provide the quickest hits for Work-Out, and an organization that already recognizes the need for change (for example, because new market conditions clearly require new ways of doing business).

Second, pick a visible unit as a pilot site. That generally means avoiding the corporate-staff groups, even though those groups are often burdened with bureaucracy and have leaders predisposed to welcoming change. Staff groups tend to be relatively invisible to line management. To make a strong impression, Work-Out needs to make a difference to a unit that is central to the business-value proposition. When Work-Out adds value in a key profit-generating unit, managers of other such units are more likely to sit up and take notice.

Third, pick a pilot site that is *bounded*—that is, a plant, site, function, process, or whatever, that is relatively isolated, rather than one in the middle of a matrix. Doing Work-Out within boundaries will increase your chances of success. Units embedded in a complex matrix tend to have unclear accountability for who makes decisions, why bureaucracy exists, and how employees can control their work environment. Selecting bounded units increases the probability that leaders will have the authority to enact employee recommendations in real time.

Finally, select a site where you can get started right away, with a minimum of preparation, fuss, and persuasion. Time is an enemy. The longer the interval between announcement and action, the more frustration people will feel and the more unrealistic their expectations will become. We advocate starting Work-Out by doing rather than preparing, experimenting rather than studying, and practicing rather than preaching.

Step 3: Use Facilitators to Show the Way

Ultimately, Work-Out becomes a way managers manage . . . by engaging employees, taking action, and making real-time decisions. However, this outcome is tough to achieve on your own, and much easier with a group of facilitators. Facilitators offer unbiased views on how to make Work-Out happen. They can coach you on demonstrating Work-Out behaviors, and they help make Work-Out sessions run smoothly. In our work with a number of companies, we've found that facilitation tends to run through four phases.

Phase 1: External Facilitators

When your organization is new to the Work-Out approach, it's a really good idea to bring in someone with a strong track record from a consulting firm or from academia to assist as an external facilitator, bringing potentially invaluable experiences from other firms that can help you tailor the concept to your own conditions. In addition, coming from outside the firm makes such facilitators relatively immune to its internal political pressures. They find it much easier to deflect executives other than the Sponsor when they demand progress reports and predictions of possible recommendations, and to provide the Sponsor with blunt, honest feedback. Many times in Work-Out sessions, for example, we found senior managers calling internal people ahead of time wanting to know what was being discussed so that they could prepare their responses prior to the Town Meeting. The internal people, in most cases, found it difficult to deal with those requests—while external consultants could much more easily say, "you'll find out when you get there," or "the value of the process is for you to be spontaneous, and perhaps we should talk about how that makes you feel."

External facilitators may work as coaches or process architects. As coaches, they help business leaders change. They do this by defining expected behaviors, offering feedback on the extent to which leaders exhibit useful or counterproductive behaviors, and providing motivation to behave in the right way.

As process architects, external facilitators help design the first Work-Out sessions overall and facilitate teams in which everyone is new to the process. Designing a Work-Out session requires setting the agenda, inviting the right people, and managing the logistics to ensure success—all of which are areas where experience makes it much easier to get the desired results without wasted effort and ruffled feathers. The same applies to helping teams during the Work-Out session—keeping people focused on their purpose, ensuring open and full participation from all team members, and making sure that the team meets its goals are things that come much easier with practice.

Phase 2: Cross-Unit Facilitators

External facilitators may be politically immune, offer candid feedback, and draw on experiences from other companies, but they are still rented experts. At some point, integrating Work-Out means leasing to own, not renting. Renting knowledge does not have sustainability when the external facilitators leave. Leasing to own means that the knowledge and experience of facilitation becomes embedded in long-term employees, not just outside consultants.

But that doesn't mean you have to jump straight from external facilitators for the pilot test to an every-unit-for-itself cycle of Work-Outs. That first successful pilot test will give you a group of people who know Work-Out from the inside. Some of these individuals may well have the interpersonal skills, the understanding of the process, and the interest to serve as facilitators in other units. They can then coach the new sponsors and help with process architecture and session management, assisting or even replacing external facilitators for the next round.

Although cross-unit facilitators lack the external facilitators' perfect immunity to internal pressure, they tend to be quite willing to confront executives outside their own lines of authority if necessary—especially when they are sure of backing from their own unit. Besides saving the cost of hiring outside experts, bringing in facilitators from sister functions helps to reinforce the idea of the whole organization as an entity with shared interests. This opens up internal boundaries and makes them more permeable to useful ideas in ways that can reach far beyond the Work-Out process.

Phase 3: Internal Facilitators

Eventually, an organization develops a sizeable cadre of people who can act as internal facilitators—that is, who can serve as process consultants for running Work-Outs, team facilitators who make sure that teams solve problems well, and business coaches who help managers change behaviors. Shifting facilitation from external to internal ensures a repository of internal coaches who have the ability to lead the firm in the future. As noted in Chapter 11, the benefits of this can extend far beyond the Work-Out process—the skills involved are neither highly technical nor heavily specialized, so Work-Out facilitators can apply their skills to the conduct of tense or sensitive meetings that have nothing to do with Work-Out itself. This makes Work-Out facilitation a good training ground for future leaders. As trained internal facilitators move to other jobs, they take their new facilitation skills into these assignments.

Internal facilitators often form a community of practice, meeting frequently to share experiences, receive training, and learn from one another. Internal facilitation is often managed through the overall Work-Out coordinator. Business leaders nominate individuals who would be qualified to fulfill these roles and ensure that the internal facilitators are freed up from some other duties to accomplish the facilitation role.

Phase 4: Leaders Themselves

Work-Out makes its final move to integration into the life of the organization when individual leaders begin to practice Work-Out behaviors in their day-to-day actions. Involving people who have information to make decisions, making decisions on the spot, focusing on action and not analysis, and other Work-Out tenets take hold when managers apply these ideas on the job. That is, as we've said on many occasions, when they become natural acts in natural places—simply the way work gets done within a company—rather than unnatural oddities that can only be attempted in the protected isolation of a Work-Out session.

Leaders who act in a Work-Out way do so because it helps them reach their goals. Over time, a firm's incentive system needs to reinforce leaders who behave in a Work-Out way and punish leaders who do not. But even without formal incentives as inducements, leaders' day-to-day actions become the clarion call for Work-Out—specific incentives for Work-Out-style behavior may bring it on more quickly, but leaders get paid for results anyway, and what these behaviors do best is enhance results.

Step 4: Build In Enough Support

Work-Out does not just happen. It requires careful attention, and many organizations find it useful to set up an infrastructure to support Work-Out. The trick is to provide enough support to make Work-Out effective, without inventing duties or making it all unnecessarily burdensome. With a corporate program named "Work-Out," it takes very little frustration for some wag in the workforce to start calling it "Work-In" instead—and the last thing you want is to provide grounds for that to catch on.

In most organizations that we have seen, such an infrastructure consists of external consultants, Work-Out program managers, and Work-Out facilitators. Depending on the scope and formality of your organization's Work-Out effort, these elements can be either highly structured or largely ad hoc.

External Consultants

As noted in the preceding section, it is very difficult to launch a Work-Out process without some amount of external support. The sessions themselves may be possible to organize internally, but identifying, promoting, and supporting changes in leadership style and culture are hard to do from within. It is very difficult for an internal person, whose life and career depends on being viewed favorably by powerful senior managers, to actively confront, push back, coach, and counsel those same managers.

External consultants thus do more than provide expert advice about the process itself and the transfer of best practices from other organizations. They can help an organization see the bigger picture of Work-Out and how the pieces (sessions, leadership, culture, rewards, and so on) are connected into an overall architecture of change. They also serve as coaches to leaders, both in specific Work-Out sessions and across a longer continuum of development. And they can serve as facilitators for Work-Out sessions and teams.

Over time, the role of the external consultant should diminish and shift. In the early stages, the external consultant takes much of the lead, working with client managers. During this period, the external consultant might pair up with one or more internal people who will become the internal consultants or program managers. Gradually, the internal consultant should take the lead, with occasional support and back up from the external consultant. And over time, the external consultant should disappear completely, as the client managers themselves take the lead on the process, and the internal consultants become their supporters.

Work-Out Program Managers

In almost all of the GE businesses, and in many other organizations that have used Work-Out more than once, one or more full-time people have been designated as Work-Out program managers. In essence, these people become the internal Work-Out consultants, at first working in close collaboration with the external consultant, and then gradually taking on the external consultant's responsibilities.

Work-Out program managers, however, play a number of other roles that are crucial for supporting the evolution of Work-Out within an organization:

- Marketing Work-Out
- Prioritizing Work-Outs
- Providing administrative support
- Coordinating Work-Out follow-up and tracking
- Communicating and reinforcing Work-Out

Marketing Work-Out

The Work-Out program manager often develops a presentation about Work-Out and conducts working sessions with business-unit and functional managers and their teams to explore their participation. For example, in the early stages at Armstrong, Jo Tyler, the Trailblazing (Work-Out) program manager, organized formal sessions with the Office of the Chair (the senior team), each of the business unit teams, and each functional team. The program manager might also organize quasimarketing materials and events throughout the organization to acquaint employees at all levels with the process. Often this involves using existing forums, such as employee meetings and company newsletters, to spread the word so people know that Work-Out is coming. In some organizations, this work might also involve "branding" Work-Out by creating a logo, a name, key marketing messages, and various branded "take-aways" (T-shirts, coffee mugs, and other mementos).

Prioritizing Work-Outs

Even after a successful pilot test, it's often useful to prioritize and sequence Work-Outs across the rest of the organization. Particularly in a setting where there might be skepticism or resistance, it is important that sponsoring managers receive appropriate coaching, that good facilitators are used, that the topics allow for some low-hanging fruit to be picked, and that the overall experience is viewed as worthwhile. If everyone gets started at once, it is difficult to make sure that all of these elements are in place. At the same time, most organizations have limits as to the amount of Work-Out activity that can be absorbed at any one time—especially when Work-Out follow-up might involve making changes in lots of processes at once, often involving the same people. Again using Armstrong's Jo Tyler as an example, based on her meetings with business-unit and functional managers, she compiled a list of possible Trailblazing sessions to discuss with the senior management team. The senior team then established a schedule of Trailblazing events for the following six months.

Providing Administrative Support

Administrative support includes making logistical arrangements (conference rooms, breakout rooms, projectors, markers, food, name cards) for particular sessions. It can also involve writing invitation letters, sending letter and e-mail reminders, helping with out-of-town travel, writing up notes from sessions, putting together presession information packets, and more. If Work-Out is being done once, in one business unit, the senior manager's administrative support can usually handle these activities. When Work-Out expands across an organization, it may be useful for the program manager to coordinate this support to ensure consistency and efficiency.

Coordinating Work-Out Follow-Up and Tracking

Though sponsoring managers are accountable for organizing follow-up reviews for their own sessions and for tracking progress, they often ask the program manager to help them with this process. In addition, across the organization, the program manager should also be keeping an eye on Work-Out progress at a higher level, making sure that reviews are taking place and that sponsoring managers are holding their people accountable. Some organizations also want the program manager to look at aggregated results across Work-Outs to help determine the overall impact of the program. Such measurement processes are sometimes difficult, but whatever data is available may be worth capturing and using as part of the reinforcement of the Work-Out change process. For example, Mo Kang, the head of Zurich U.K.'s Work-Out Program Office, aggregates Work-Out results every year, in collaboration with the internal audit staff, to determine an overall return on the Work-Out investment.

Communicating and Reinforcing Work-Out

The Work-Out program manager has a major role in the activities described for Step 7 ("Publicize the Successes"). It's always important to find Work-Out heroes, tell Work-Out stories, and make sure everyone knows how Work-Out is working and what is being accomplished. Again, this does not need to be a major bureaucratic production. For the most part, the program manager can use existing communication mechanisms and channels, and call upon whatever communications professionals the organization may have on staff. GE Capital, for example, had an extremely effective corporate communications function that, in the first couple years of Work-Out, was applied to publicizing Work-Out success. The internal program manager, Cathy Kaczmarski, worked with the head of the communications function to identify appropriate Work-Out stories and settings. The communications people wrote up these stories for newsletters, video "documentaries," and other presentations. They organized companywide videoconferences and incorporated Work-Out stories and reports into senior leaders' speeches and almost every facet of corporate communications. Mo Kang at Zurich U.K., on the other hand, not only uses existing communications mechanisms but also publishes an "annual report" on Work-Out that is distributed to all employees.

Work-Out Facilitators

As we've noted repeatedly, one of the key features of Work-Out is that the small-group sessions are facilitated. Most companies usually start Work-Out with external facilitators—drawn at minimum from outside the business unit or function, so they can maintain objectivity and not get sucked into the dynamics and politics of the organizational unit. As soon as possible, internal facilitators can be paired up with externals to get real-time experience, and then replace the external facilitators altogether. In organizations that have used Work-Out for years, managers or other organization members can facilitate within their own units, as long as everyone involved knows that those people have been designated as facilitators.

Step 5: Help Managers Get Ready to Deploy Work-Out

Work-Out requires that business leaders learn how to coach, engage, and listen to employees. It also requires that leaders make decisions on the spot with focused data. These new leadership skills may be difficult to adopt, and they may require that leaders first recognize some gap between current and future leadership skills.

Here is where the factors discussed in Chapter 11 come into play. Once you have a list of specific leadership Work-Out skills, you can begin to identify, train, coach, and motivate leaders for Work-Out. Employees observe what leaders do more than what they say. Ensuring that leaders consistently behave congruently with Work-Out principles offers employees assurance that Work-Out is real. Some leaders have a natural predisposition for the Work-Out style, belief system, and approach. These leaders are the ones most likely to be promoted into visible positions of authority. Leaders not so predisposed may be trained and coached to demonstrate Work-Out behaviors over time. Leaders who do not engage in Work-Out behaviors and who cannot acquire those behaviors will be more likely to exit the firm over time.

But you have to stick with the new patterns. When the business environment turns hostile and competition increases, leaders with recently acquired skills often abandon their new behaviors for a more traditionally autocratic and dictatorial style. Employees invariably respond to this shift by becoming very cynical of the espoused behaviors—and their productivity drops sharply.

The leader behaviors prescribed by Work-Out apply equally in good times and bad—or maybe even more in bad times than in good. In one division of GE Aerospace, the traditional dependence on government contracts had to shift to a more commercial set of customers. Leaders used Work-Out to convene a group of the employees most affected by the change. Rather than prescribe a response to new market conditions, these leaders shared the information with the group. In what is now popularly called "open book management," they reported the decline in government contracts and the requirements of commercial bids, and then asked employees what changes would be required to compete in the new market. Employees responded with innovative solutions to the business problems. And, in Work-Out style, decisions were made quickly to shift to a commercial focus. Work-Out, in this case, became a way managers managed, particularly in tough economic times.

Step 6: Set Specific Work-Out Delivery Goals

Some firms try to introduce Work-Out by allowing leaders throughout the organization to choose to deploy or not to deploy Work-Out principles. These firms generally get very poor results. Work-Out moves most quickly when the CEO lays down a number or a goal for it: "You will run this many workshops in this period of time," or "You will spend 10 percent of your time in Work-Out activities," or "Your bonus this year will be tied to your implementing Work-Out."

The challenge of specific Work-Out goals is not to get caught up in the numbers of Work-Outs as much as the impact Work-Outs have on the company. At GE, Welch prescribed that managers should "spend 20 percent of their time on Work-Out," but he did not mandate numbers of events or participants. A GE Work-Out coordinator used to keep a consolidated list of Work-Outs and numbers of participants in his desk drawer, assuming that one day Welch would ask for it. After a couple of years, he threw it out and stopped keeping track, since Welch never asked. He was more interested in results and personal commitment than just numbers of events.

Another key to monitoring the success of Work-Out is to focus on the end and not the means. For example, if a Work-Out session is designed to cut cycle time for product commercialization, then the measure of success is speed to market with new products, not how many Work-Out sessions were run or how many people attended them. And when GE held some customer-focused Work-Outs designed to build better relationships with key customers, the measure of success was whether GE received a higher customer share over time, not how many sessions were run.

Step 7: Publicize the Successes

Work-Out shifts most smoothly from pilot to program when successes are visible and shared. Every 12-step program for sustained change requires public disclosure. When an alcoholic, drug addict, or smoker stands and publicly declares, "I am an addict and I need to change,"

change is more likely to occur. Going public brings enormous personal pressure to live up to expectations, not to disappoint significant others, and to risk personal shame for failure.

Likewise, Work-Out successes need to be publicized. Talk about the importance, the tools, and the personal results achieved with Work-Out—such public expressions communicate commitment to others. Employees often listen for signs of leaders' commitment. Consistently shared messages in many public forums create clear calls for change. In almost every public statement (annual-report letter to shareholders, all-employee videos, media interviews, and so on), Jack Welch alluded to his commitment to Work-Out. When Work-Out began, some seasoned GE employees shrugged and said, "This too shall pass." About a year later, these same employees realized that they had better sign on to the effort—Welch's clear and consistent message finally persuaded them it wasn't going to disappear, it was going to pass them by and leave them behind if they didn't climb on board.

And you'll find that making such public expressions of support will also enhance the speaker's own commitment to the process. Compelling leaders to support Work-Out ideas and practices publicly in fact commits these leaders to them. Such public-leader support for the ideas in a Work-Out session is the conceptual foundation for the leader panel at the end of a Work-Out described in Chapter 6. In one GE business, some of the most cynical employees were made owners of the ideas generated in a Work-Out session. As owners, they were responsible for following up and reporting on the Work-Out recommendations—and this public advocacy turned their cynicism into commitment.

Finally, public presentation of success stories creates heroes and models that others can identify and use as a base for their own behavior. At GE Capital, Gary Wendt held quarterly teleconferences that were broadcast live from business sites to all the other major sites in GE Capital, and videotape was distributed elsewhere. At one of these, he interviewed several Work-Out participants, talked about Work-Out, and interviewed one of the authors as a way of giving it weight. Capital also created and distributed a video Work-Out documentary with great music, along with regular Work-Out reports and newsletters. And at the Cerromar annual meeting, Work-Out was heavily publicized and reported on by business after business. It was impossible, after the first year or two, to be in GE Capital and not to have heard about Work-Out and its manifold successes.

Leaders who integrate Work-Out into their businesses go public frequently with their commitment to Work-Out and with stories about Work-Out successes.

Step 8: Align Your Actions with Your Commitment

Sometimes a leader's public rhetoric is congruent with private behavior; at other times it is not. In one company where we worked a number of years ago, the CEO selected "quality" as a dominant theme and spoke about it frequently with great passion. Six months into the year, however, in examining his calendar, we found that he was only spending about 3–5 percent of his time on activities even loosely related to quality. Employees heard the rhetoric, but those closest to him—the ones who were his centurions in his quality program—observed his behavior. Behavior won. Confronted with this information, the CEO literally blocked out time on his calendar for "quality" and then asked those charged with quality to fill in the blocks of time, which they gladly did.

Senior leaders who espouse Work-Out ideas must live them. This might mean senior leaders' attending Work-Out sessions as participants, sponsoring sessions, and participating in the panel at the end of sessions. It might mean having a Work-Out conversation in every staff meeting. It might mean attending facilitator training. It might mean adjusting compensation to favor others who make progress on Work-Out.

Even more than these relatively public acts, private conversations about Work-Out become crucial as signals of leader support. In one company, the senior leader sponsoring Work-Out hesitated to push one of his direct reports to engage more because the second-level leader was producing such good results, despite using a more traditional management style. The direct report listened to the public rhetoric about Work-Out ideas, but felt he could ignore the program because of his long service with the company and his results. The senior leader finally said (in a private conversation), "It is time you got on board with this initiative. I expect you to fully engage—which means sponsoring and attending programs and putting key resources (people and budget) into the Work-Out program. And a sizeable portion of your compensation and a high predictor of your future promotion opportunities will be tied to your being a Work-Out sponsor." After this, the hold-out's behavior began to change. He started participating in sessions and working with a coach to examine his own behavior.

Step 9: Reach the Tipping Point

People often ask us, "What percent of a workforce should experience Work-Out before we reach critical mass?" *Critical mass* occurs when a large enough number of employees have experienced Work-Out so that the ideas are embedded in the organization, not just because a given leader sponsors the idea, but because a large number of employees have internalized it. In recent research, scholars have found that early, small changes may not have sustainable impact, but the cumulative effect of little changes eventually reaches a "tipping point," where significant and lasting change occurs.[1] For example, early adopters of a new fashion (thick-soled, square-toed shoes, for example) may get a lot of grief for their choice, but after a while, a critical mass builds up and the style becomes fashionable—at which point many of the people who laughed hardest at the early adopters take it up for themselves.

In Work-Out, reaching critical mass is important so that the impetus for Work-Out shifts from the personal values of the leader who sponsors Work-Out to the value added for each organization member. We estimate that critical mass occurs when about three to five percent of employees are exposed to Work-Out. This means that smaller organization units might be more likely to experience Work-Out's programmatic impact than large organizational units. In GE, the nuclear business, with less than 3000 employees, was quicker to reach critical mass than GE Aircraft Engine, which had 35,000 employees.

One way to reach critical mass is to continually winnow the organization unit affected by Work-Out. This means subdividing larger organizational units into component parts and then focusing Work-Out on those parts. GE's Aircraft Engine business, for example, focused Work-Out on subunits of the overall business and worked to reach critical mass within those units. This also means that if a business has 10 sites with 1000 people per site (10,000 employees total) and has the capacity to run 4 Work-Outs (with 50 people per session) in a time period, it would be better to run 2 Work-Outs in 2 of the 10 units than to run 1 Work-Out apiece in 4 units. The 4 units would barely be noticed, but the chances of reaching critical mass in 2 units would be good.

Step 10: Resource Your Work-Outs

Work-Out saves money, but it is not a free good. Resources for Work-Out include the external and internal facilitators, participant time away from other work projects, and logistical support (travel, meals, facilities). Ultimately, Work-Out saves you money through increased productivity and better problem solving, but it takes some initial investment—though it can start small. As it develops, it's apt to take more—for ongoing training of facilitators, internal management, and whatnot—but the payoff should always be impressive. The 10× expected return noted in Chapter 3 is actually on the modest side.

At GE, Welch established resource streams for Work-Out in three phases. First, he made it a corporate-sponsored and funded activity. This meant that hard costs (facilitators, logistics) would be paid through a corporate account. Essentially, it was a discretionary account controlled by the chairman's office. Businesses could draw on this account to get started with Work-Out.

In phase 2, he instituted a joint-venture or 50-50 funding. He had the corporation pay 50 percent of the costs and the business pay 50 percent of the costs. This ensured that a transition period occurred when businesses could feel supported by the corporate level, but still have obligation to help fund the effort.

In phase 3, the businesses became self-sufficient in funding. At this point, the view was that if Work-Out ideas were not adding value to the business, they should be abandoned. And if they added value, costs would be offset by value created within the business.

Step 11: Follow Up and Share Knowledge

After every Work-Out session, it's essential to follow up on the ideas that are approved. The people who accept ownership of the individual Work-Out recommendations can't be left to struggle with the forces of inertia on their own. They're in charge of getting action—but their chances of success are greatly enhanced when everyone knows that the management committee is keeping tabs on their progress and the support they are receiving (or not receiving, as the case may be).

It's also useful to provide a showcase for solutions that can apply to parts of the company beyond the ones that participated in the Work-Out session that came up with the idea. Creating communities of interest where people who experience common problems share their solutions to those problems allows for knowledge to be shared. A global financial-service organization created "practice boards" where people from different businesses could share experiences in different countries with similar products. These practice boards facilitated sharing of knowledge without infringing on the autonomy of the local units to generate ways to solve their problems. Another firm created a Web site organized around common processes. Anyone anticipating a Work-Out on a process could find what others had done and adapt accordingly. After the Work-Out, they could add their experience to the Web site for others. Such knowledge-sharing mechanisms begin to cumulate the value of different Work-Outs on similar issues.

Step 12: Apply Work-Out to Other Programs

One of the frequent (and often apt) criticisms of management programs is that they are fads, driven by the latest whims of business fashion. Eager management devotees want to attire themselves in the latest fashion to be popular and current. But as the fashion fades, the new management idea goes to the back of the closet only to be looked at by subsequent generations of managers with horrified amusement. (Think of the leisure suits and the quality circles of yesteryear. Where are they now?)

To take full advantage of Work-Out, an organization needs to make sure the principles and practices are instilled in subsequent management initiatives. Work-Out often begins as an attention-grabbing initiative of senior management; then, as the ideas become a way of doing business within the company, management needs to move to other key initiatives. Thinking of these initiatives as an evolution rather than a revolution helps. Each initiative builds on its predecessors and offers grounding for subsequent initiatives. In technology, the 386 chip gave way to the 486, then the Pentium, then the Pentium II, and so forth. Each subsequent generation of chips was not a fad destined for the closet, but an evolutionary stage toward faster processing.

Likewise, Work-Out as a management initiative can and should be seen as an evolutionary stage toward better management. As Work-Out principles permeate a company, it is appropriate at times to shift to other initiatives. Knowing when to shift management attention to other initiatives without discarding previous ideas becomes tricky. Moving too soon to new initiatives creates havoc and cynicism, and new ideas are never installed before abandoned. Moving too slowly to new initiatives loses the vitality and freshness of trying new ideas.

At GE, early stages of Work-Out required extensive senior-management attention—in speeches, exhortations, budgets, and conversations. Over time, the Work-Out means of engaging employees became a pipeline for making other changes happen. When Six Sigma became the major management initiative, the tools and disciplines for Six Sigma were implemented quicker because employees had been sensitized through Work-Out to having productive conversations and making timely decisions. Other programs—Web-based business, customer-focused investments, and globalization—were more quickly implemented because of Work-Out exposure and mastery of Work-Out principles.

Jack Welch sees the lineage of Work-Out as it facilitated the implementation of subsequent GE initiatives: "Our leaders are changing the very DNA of the GE culture. In the 1980s [with Work-Out] we opened our culture up to ideas from everyone, everywhere. We stopped NIH [not invented here] thinking, decimated the bureaucracy, and made boundaryless behavior a reflexive and natural part of our culture, thus creating the learning culture that led to Six Sigma. . . . Work-Out defined how we behave. Today, Six Sigma defines how we work."

Leaders who integrate Work-Out into their organizations create a story line that shifts from focused attention on Work-Out to embedded Work-Out as a way to do daily work. In many ways, Work-Out is fully integrated when it is invisible. As a visible initiative, specific events run with wide publicity under the Work-Out label. As an invisible program, Work-Out is assimilated into the way things are done without fanfare or formal events.

Embedded Work-Out

Established behavior is always hard to change. Most 12-step programs offer some hope but still require enormous effort. As Work-Out becomes embedded into a company and moves from a pilot experience to a true program, the choices and decisions around these 12 items increase the probability of success. Eventually, the whole culture of the organization will be reinvigorated and tuned to the pace of modern business—but that's a matter for the next chapter.

CHAPTER

Work-Out as
Culture Change

THE IMPETUS FOR trying Work-Out in your organization may be the kind of quick, dramatic change that everyone can recognize easily—a competitor's moves, a new technology to use or sell, the arrival of a new CEO. Or it may be the quieter, more insidious change of declining performance and increasing bureaucracy that can strangle an organization in its sleep.

Work-Out can bring quick, targeted, clear, and high-impact change. Unfortunately, changes generated through Work-Out may be short-lived if the basic approach and assumptions that support Work-Out do not become more fundamental to your organization's DNA, its identity, its culture. In the short term, Work-Out generates immediate improvement, but in the long term, its more profound agenda is to alter an organization's culture.

Much has been written about the significance of a culture. With varying definitions, *culture* and *culture change* may refer to:

- Sustained transformation—not just a turnaround—as when Sears leaders worked to transform their culture rather than just cut costs in their 1990s transformation.

- A new identity, reputation, or firm brand—like the one Nordstrom leaders have created around service, which has become their reputation in the retail industry.
- An articulated set of norms, beliefs, or values—as with Hewlett-Packard and Johnson & Johnson, which are well known for value statements and credos that define what they stand for and influence business decisions.
- An organization's DNA—like Dell, which proclaims its genetic code is to have low inventories, fast service over the Internet, and demanding profitability goals.
- A firm's personality—as when Southwest Airlines adopted the personality of its founder and decade-long CEO Herb Kelleher.

Each definition implies that culture is more than random or isolated activities. Your organization begins to have a culture, a unique identity, when its array of management approaches outlive any one executive and involve more than any single management practice, fad, or era.

Cultures matter because they affect employees, customers, and investors. Employees self-select into companies because they fit the existing company culture. Employee commitments, productivity, and behaviors both shape and are shaped by the culture of the firm. Employees who choose to work for Nordstrom must realize up front that they will be expected to provide exceptional customer service. Once hired, they find that management practices reinforce the customer-service mantra—and employees who don't fit are likely to leave. Cultures change employee thinking and action.

Customers show that they value cultures through the firm's identity. When a firm develops a reputation for quality, service, or economy, customers begin to rely on this identity and do business with the firm based on the reputation or identity. This identity of the firm in the mind of its best customers becomes a firm brand and demonstrates the impact of culture on customer value. Recent research shows that firms with strong and visible brands, such as McDonald's, American Express, Harley Davidson, Herman Miller, and so forth, create higher shareholder value.

Investors have recently recognized the importance of intangibles that reflect the market value of a firm above or beyond its expected market value given cash flow or earnings. Culture and its derivatives (employee commitment and competence) become intangibles when they lead to investor confidence in the firm's future growth. Cultures can also become negative intangibles when the investor perception shifts—as when Lucent's intellectual capital (embodied in Bell Labs) became seen as lost in bureaucracy and the market's confidence in Lucent's ability to innovate began to fail, along with the company's market value.

Managers trying to create sustained transformation or change may find that an embedded culture—"That's the way we've always done it!"—is nearly impossible to overcome as employees continually return the firm to old ways and extinguish the new ones. For example, IBM's success in the 1960s through 1980s in the mainframe business was almost unparalleled in business history. The firm set the standard, defined the industry, and established products and services customers craved. But as technology changed into the 1990s, as distributed networks replaced mainframes, as the Internet became the technology driver, and as software replaced hardware, IBM's old culture became a liability. Many of the employees and managers who created the old culture and its management practices were captives to it. They could not adjust quickly enough to changing business realities. IBM leaders had to change not only management practices (things like its dress code), but the underlying culture, for IBM to compete in the Internet economy.

In many cases, strong cultures eventually become liabilities. A strong culture implies that employees have been hired, trained, and compensated to think and behave in a certain way, that targeted customers have become dependent on a particular set of products or services, and that the organization has little need to adapt to the future. When the future changes in ways that invalidate those habits and products, the stability goes from advantage to disadvantage—sometimes overnight.

Changing cultures is difficult at best, and often only accomplished through some demanding external event. Indeed, it's almost impossible to find examples of companies that changed their underlying culture without a crisis. AT&T began a cultural transformation when the divestiture forced a breakup into parts, but even then the cultures embedded at Lucent and the remaining AT&T units persisted, and AT&T as a firm did not adapt to new conditions. Harley Davidson almost went broke as it emerged from the AMF umbrella, and that led to a service-culture revolution. Sears was being beaten badly by Wal-Mart, and revenue per store was falling behind industry average. IBM had more market value as parts than the whole, and investors demanded more from their investment. And both Sears and IBM had outside leaders who came into their firms with a strong endorsement for change from their boards.

It's seductive but dangerous to wait for an external crisis—often called a "burning platform"—to drive culture change. By the time an external change is big enough to focus attention and energy, competitors who anticipated the change will already have reacted. In fact, learning to create culture change in the midst of business success becomes one of the most important benefits of Work-Out.

GE's Old Culture

In the mid-1980s, Jack Welch was on the horns of a dilemma. He had changed GE's business mix by buying over 200 businesses and selling over 200 others with the strategic mantra "fix, close, or sell." Being able to change the portfolio, while not easy, was in many ways less complex than changing the culture that pervaded how GE's decisions were made, how people were treated, how information was shared, and how things got done.

For example, GE had essentially invented strategic-management-portfolio planning in the 1960s. Strategic planning was ingrained in its culture and hugely important to all its operations. Its business units relied on disciplined processes for doing strategic plans that assessed market opportunities and aligned resources with these opportunities. In a business environment where markets could be predicted and plans implemented, strategic planning became the mechanism for governing the business. However, as the business environment changed, plans were out of date before they were implemented. In one case, Welch pointed out to the top 500 managers at Boca Raton that 6 weeks of rigorous planning reviews had produced a perfect plan for 1990–91—except that the world they were planning for disappeared when Sadam Hussein invaded Kuwait. Much of the plan was suddenly irrelevant, and the time spent planning did not help the business succeed. What it needed then was the ability to adapt quickly to new opportunities and challenges.

The GE planning culture relied on market conditions that stayed stable or changed steadily and in predictable ways. GE people chuckled over the old joke about the two guys being chased by a bear. (One turns to the other and says, "We can't outrun that bear." The other says, "I'm not trying to outrun the bear; I'm trying to outrun you.") That strategy works well when you know you're only dealing with a bear and can be sure that running faster than your competitor will get the other guy eaten, but it doesn't prime you to look around and see what else may be out there ready to eat you. When market conditions vary rapidly, you're not just running away from a bear, you're running across a melting glacier inhabited by a whole range of other hungry creatures. You can't just plan out a route and run; you have to stay wide awake and respond instantly as things change around you.

Transforming GE

Using Work-Out to change GE's culture was challenging and problematic. As noted earlier, culture change is easiest to present as a way to avert a recent or pending crisis—which GE did not have. There was no external bogeyman or crisis to rally the troops. GE had sustained earnings, an outstanding reputation, and great regard among all stakeholders. It did not face a viable, legitimate external threat that would have forced it to transform. It did not have an internal threat with new leaders from the outside who could do what insiders had not done. Instead, GE tried to change a culture from the inside out while adding value from the outside in.

Of course, Work-Out did not start as a set of practices for culture change. It started as a way to remove bureaucracy and get rid of silly and useless work so those who stayed at GE could focus on the right things. But the reports, approvals, and meetings that were eliminated in the early Work-Out sessions tended to reappear because "that is the way things are done."

Work-Out as "culture change" shifted the focus from a simple workshop to a more fundamental exploration of how work is done, from a set of management activities (for example, no more than five layers of management from CEO to any first-line employee) to a different way of doing work, from rhetoric in reports and speeches to realities in management behavior.

Eventually, Work-Out redefined the culture of GE, creating a new set of work norms that affected how employees thought and acted. It helped the company shape a new identity that customers would relate to, and allowed it to create a story that boosted investor confidence in future GE earnings, thus enhancing its market value.

Work-Out as Culture Change

Work-Out began as a series of events, as workshops where employees and managers could solve problems, share ideas, and engage in dialogue about bureaucracy and how the business could be better run. Dozens if not hundreds of companies have done similar forums under many labels: quality circles, problem-solving teams, corrective action teams, participative management, and so on. What distinguishes Work-Out is the way the events and behaviors became new patterns. Here's one example:

> **A young woman once stood up in a Town Meeting to present her team's ideas to an engineering director with a long history within GE. He had a reputation for being a rather autocratic leader, for not being open to new ideas. He focused on goals and outcomes more than processes for reaching outcomes. The selected presenter—a junior engineer—had been nervous about offering him the group's list of bureaucracy-changing recommendations, but had gained confidence with the support of her group. Within minutes, however, the engineering director (2 levels above her in the hierarchy and 20 years her senior) responded abruptly, "That's a crazy idea. We already tried that and it failed. What else do you have to show me?" When he responded with a similar outburst on the next idea, the presenter was clearly intimidated and unsure.**
>
> **At this point, the facilitator intervened and called a time out. He took the director aside and asked, "What did you think you were doing?" The director said that his intent was to push, probe, and demand rigor of thinking in all ideas to ensure that engineering standards were maintained, that this was the way to do things. The facilitator coached the director in some alternative behaviors—holding back the initial scorn, being courteous and thankful for ideas, exploring alternatives.**

> When the director returned to the room, a different type of dialogue occurred. Rather than respond with immediate criticism, the director did explore options and try to figure out why the group (not just the presenter) made the recommendations and what ideas might be readily and quickly implemented. In this forum, the director changed his behavior and discovered a new way to deal with issues.

It was a real accomplishment for the director to change his response pattern in this manner, but it was also very much "an unnatural act in an unnatural place"—and like many people, he found it much less difficult to be open to new behavior in an off-site setting like a Work-Out session than to do so on the job. For long-term benefits, beginning with effective and enduring implementation of the Work-Out ideas, an organization needs such openness to become "a natural act in a natural place"—the existing work environment. Culture change may begin with events like this workshop where new behaviors emerge, but culture change does not occur unless those events and behaviors become patterns that sustain themselves without external influence.

In this case, the engineering director returned to work after the workshop well aware that his traditional behavior did not accomplish what he intended, and that engineering excellence could be better achieved with a different set of behaviors. Like other managers in that position, he had three choices:

- Learn the new behaviors and begin to change the culture in the department. This path comes with coaching, feedback, training, ongoing dialogue, experimenting with new behaviors, failure, and learning.
- Try to hide and continue the old behaviors and management style, hoping that no one would notice. Old patterns can be hard to change, particularly when a crisis hits and tried-and-true ways to solve problems reemerge. Often managers who hide behaviors are clever and may exhibit public support but private antipathy for a corporate initiative.
- Recognize that the new behaviors and culture no longer aligned with his style, and leave the firm. At times the exit may be by the leader's choice and at times by the firm's choice.

In GE, the majority of the managers who experienced Work-Out followed the first path; they worked to implement new ways to get work done, thus changing the embedded culture. GE's top management made sincere efforts to find and expose those who tried hiding along the second path. This required performance-management disciplines that focused not only on results but on how results were produced. GE made the process stick by enforcing the third path—leaders producing results but not doing so in the right way were identified and given a choice to change behaviors or change companies.

The engineering director in the case described here was one of those who tried to take the second path. He expressed public loyalty to the Work-Out initiative, sponsored and attended workshops, and seemed committed to the new culture. But his private demeanor and predispositions did not change. After about 18 months, he realized that Work-Out was more than a series of workshops where he could pledge loyalty to a new future; it was in fact a culture change where he would have to manage in ways that were not comfortable to him. With mutual agreement, he left GE. Few tied his leaving to any one workshop or event, but many realized that this senior person's exiting the firm indicated a new way of doing business.

Culture change also shifts the identify of the firm in the mind of key customers. Some of the most important Work-Out experiences occurred when GE invited customers (or suppliers) to a Work-Out. In these sessions, GE employees and customers would work jointly to solve problems to their mutual benefit.

The GE unit that services railroad cars learned that customer participation in Work-Out enlarged their vision and improved their performance. The GE people learned that they spent an average of 20 days servicing each railroad car. Through process reengineering, they changed their processes and were delighted to spend only 10 days servicing railroad cars, which felt like a 50-percent improvement in service quality. They were somewhat surprised that customers were not as ecstatic as they were. When they invited customers to a Work-Out session, they learned that customers' measures were not GE measures. Customers tracked the total time that the railroad car was out of service, not the time that GE had the railroad car in its care. This total time was 40 days, not the original 20 days that GE took to service the car. So, while

GE people felt they had removed 50 percent of the service time, from the customers' perspective, they had only removed 25 percent.

At a Work-Out session, this obvious difference of how to measure service quality arose, and GE and the customers focused aggressively on cutting time from the total 40 days, not just the 20 days that GE had the car. Through joint problem solving, they were able to take over 50 percent of the total time out of the customer definition of service. Through this process, GE changed its image of customer responsiveness.

Guiding Principles

While Work-Out did not begin as a linear culture-change initiative, it morphed into one. Out of the many trials that were attempted and errors made, we've learned several lessons that could be applied to other settings to facilitate culture change more rapidly:

- Articulate an intellectual agenda.
- Establish a behavioral agenda.
- Institutionalize an organizational agenda.
- Work simultaneously on all three agendas.

Articulate an Intellectual Agenda

A culture change must have a clear, simple message that is repeated redundantly throughout the organization. This is the top-down agenda for senior management. At times, culture-change messages might be too complex, too transient, or too elegant. Finding a simple, clear message that resonates with employees and captures the intellectual agenda for the new culture is critical. Here are some characteristics of the message that help assure it will have impact:

- Simplicity
- Redundancy
- Commitment
- Publicity
- Continuous growth
- Firm roots in business results
- Customer focus

Simplicity

The message needs to be simple and clear while still capturing a broader perspective. One firm trying to transform had six elements of a mission, seven strategies, five operating principles, seven superordinate goals, six values, and a vision. Proponents of this behemoth felt that the fact they could put it on one page made it simple. Not so. Few in the firm could remember the 30-plus items crammed into that one page. Simple means memorable. Simple, memorable phrases give direction to the new culture.

At GE, Welch brilliantly crafted simple phrases that captured cultural transformation:

- Having too many layers is like wearing layers of clothing. When you go outside, you don't know if it is cold or not.
- We need managers who wear their face to the customer and backsides to the company.
- Bureaucracy is the Dracula of institutional behavior and will rise again and again, requiring everyone in the organization to reflexively pound stakes through its reappearances.

Redundancy

The message needs to be shared continually. In research on communication, it's shown up over and over again that people don't fully grasp a message until they have heard it 10 times. When simple and similar messages are shared through multiple media (video, speeches, forums, meetings, phone calls, and so on), they are both better understood and more likely to have a lasting impact. In particular, it is crucial for leaders to share the messages in private and not to back off the implications of a new culture in private conversations. Clever managers can always find excuses for not behaving in congruence with a new culture. Strong leaders see through the haze and share both public and private commitment to change.

At GE, Welch believed in the new culture and expressed his belief with passion and energy. He saw it as a long-term agenda for transforming GE. In his public meetings (annual letters to shareholders, videos, officer-meeting speeches, and so on) he updated the culture journey and kept showing how the journey was evolving. In his private conversations with business leaders and employees, he reinforced his deep-felt belief in the new culture and challenged leaders to align their behavior with it.

Commitment

Culture change rarely works with a lifeboat. Leaders often like to have escape clauses in change—it's comforting to be able to say, "If this change does not work, I can go back to the old way!" But when times are difficult, the tendency to fall back is high. A strong intellectual agenda publicly commits the leader to new ways of doing work with no escape clauses. Good leaders know that in difficult times the new culture will be the means to compete, not something to be set aside.

Publicity

Leaders who go public with their intellectual agendas are more likely to maintain commitment to them. Going public to employees means sharing the agenda in written, personal, and verbal communications. To customers, going public means making promises to the customers about how the firm will interact with them in the future. Going public also means sharing ideas with investors and encouraging investors to see beyond the financials to have confidence in the processes used to generate the financials.

Because Welch went so public with Work-Out, he could not go back on the culture change. Employees who believed Work-Out was a short-term quick fix—something that they could pledge allegiance to, but not believe—watched Welch's consistent public commitments and finally realized that they had to get on board or get out of GE.

Continuous Growth

Culture change is not one-stop shopping; it's an evolving process. Knowing when to shift an intellectual agenda is challenging—shifting too soon means that your agenda is unlikely to be embedded in the system; shifting too late means the agenda has become stale. An evolving intellectual agenda often has two elements: a theme that moves the item forward, and specific menu items that can be enacted to accomplish the theme.

At GE, the Work-Out agenda began with a bureaucracy-busting theme that had many tools and action items that business leaders could select to remove bureaucracy. As Work-Out evolved, a second theme of boundaryless development emerged, with its own sets of tools and action items. This theme then evolved into Six Sigma and Web-based business—then bureaucracy-busting returned to the limelight. Knowing how to evolve an agenda becomes part of keeping the culture change fresh.

Firm Roots in Business Results

Culture deals with how work is accomplished. It becomes an adjective rather than a noun. As noted in Chapter 12, the "nouns" are the outcomes or results of work. Culture talks about how that work will be accomplished. If culture becomes the end or goal ("we want a culture change"), attention is misfocused. The goal is to deliver investor and customer value. Culture is an enabler to that process, not the end game.

At GE, it was clear that the new culture (speed, simplicity, self-confidence) had to lead to financial results, or it would not survive. Culture does not endure as a hazing activity that must be tolerated to get into the club. Culture enables and allows long-term results to happen.

Customer Focus

An intellectual agenda that focuses inside may last as long as the internal champion remains at the company. When a culture becomes a firm brand, customer expectations create an enduring demand for the new culture, and it persists beyond any one leader or sponsor. Culture as firm brand or identity becomes a key part of the intellectual agenda. What would our best customers want us to be known for? This query takes the intellectual agenda outside and moves culture from a latent set of desired values to a firm brand that creates lasting value.

As a leader wanting to create a new culture, you must craft an intellectual agenda that characterizes what you want to be known for by employees, customers, and investors. This identity may exist at local levels (plants, sites, business units, or divisions) or on a broader, corporate-wide level. Defining this identity or intellectual agenda becomes a primary responsibility for senior leaders.

Establish a Behavioral Agenda

A culture change occurs if and only if it changes the behavior of employees throughout the firm. Whereas the intellectual agenda is primarily top-down, the behavioral agenda is bottom-up and shaped by employees.

Words, phrases, and concepts that resonate but don't change behavior create cynicism. Generally, employees who experience day-to-day business problems know what to do to turn cultural concepts into actions. By developing mechanisms to engage employees and to enable them to figure out what behaviors to change, organizations create enduring culture.

A behavioral agenda occurs when employees are involved in shaping how they will enact the new culture. When people are involved in an activity, they are more likely to feel ownership. Agents seldom feel the same intensity as owners. Creating ownership may occur through some of the following activities:

- Firsthand experience
- Local ownership
- Small beginnings
- Links to culture

Firsthand Experience

The people who actually do the work know best how to change it. When given direction about principles for the new regime, they soon see ways to adapt their behaviors for the new principles. To make the new culture real to employees at all levels of the firm, you need to trust people to figure this out. That means making sure they have the skills to do the new behaviors and trusting them to see the link between their behaviors and the new culture.

The Town Meetings at GE were designed to make the new culture real to employees. Across very different businesses (from NBC, to Nuclear, to Engineering, to Financial Services) three simple principles were proposed: speed, simplicity, self-confidence. Employees in each business were then charged to identify the actions they could own and take to make these principles real to them. Allowing employees to participate in defining new actions created a behavioral agenda and made the culture real.

Local Ownership

You want to get ownership by local line managers, as they're the ones who build long-term relationships and embody the values of the corporate leaders. When local leaders change their behavior, employees believe in the new culture.

Local ownership comes when local managers are invited to present publicly and engage in the new culture. Over time, GE's local Town Meetings were not run by external facilitators or by corporate leaders. Local leaders with local credibility and respect ensured that changes approved in the meetings would last.

Small Beginnings

It helps to change small things. As noted in Chapter 11, in recent research on change, sociologists have found that when small things continue to occur, large things may happen.[1] When you take this approach, it often seems as though the little things you're doing don't have much impact either in themselves or together—but then you reach a "tipping point," when a few more little things are added, and then things begin to change fast. Crime in New York City began to fall rapidly after a lot of relatively little crimes were attended to (graffiti tagging, uninvited windshield washing, panhandling, and the like). The whole system of social relations began to change.

Work-Out started with lots of little things: revamped and removed reports, approvals, measures, meetings, policies, practices, and other bits of bureaucracy. No one of these little changes would be seen as a culture change, but their cumulative effect added up to a new culture. At Sears, town-hall meetings generated over five million ideas in a two-year period—mostly small changes that could be enacted at the local-store level. The accumulation of these little things added up to a large transformation.

Links to Culture

Make change real to employees by tying their little changes to the larger culture change you intend. One of the things that happened at GE was that many things managers were already doing came under the Work-Out umbrella. Training programs that were going on already were tweaked to fit the Work-Out and culture-change agenda. This clear line of sight between the little things employees did and the broader culture change helped assure the reality of the culture change.

Leaders of culture change create a behavioral agenda when they turn their ideas into employee actions. Work-Out Town Meetings are an excellent tool for taking an abstract idea like *speed* and allowing employees to determine how their behavior impacts the idea. When employees have a line of sight between what they do day to day and the identity of the firm in the mind of the customer, employees are more committed to changing the culture.

Institutionalize an Organizational Agenda

A culture change occurs when the principles of the new culture become embedded in the organization's systems and processes. We call this the side-to-side agenda for change. Organizations are often characterized by ways of doing things that endure beyond any one leader or event the leader may plan. Figuring out how to adapt these processes to the new culture ensures that it will endure:

- Talent flow
- Performance management
- Training and development
- Communication
- Budgeting
- Leadership brand
- Organization processes

Talent Flow

Moving talent into, up, through, and out of the organization sends messages about the new culture. Hiring new people who embody the new culture—and promoting employees who live the new culture and removing those who don't—become critical tools for embedding culture. Those who are not hired, promoted, or removed observe what is happening and adapt their behaviors accordingly. In addition, focusing the culture on talent flow requires a behavioral rigor in the culture. The abstract idea of *speed* becomes real, for example, when employees can identify people who do and do not deliver with speed.

GE culture change became real when the players who "got it" stayed and moved up and those who did not "get it" left. It did not take a mass exodus of officers for the remaining employees to realize that the way work was accomplished had career implications. As Work-Out behaviors became part of the hiring and promotion process, employees throughout GE knew it would last. More importantly, future leaders not only believed in Work-Out, but did it, which helped make Work-Out more than a single leader's agenda.

Performance Management

Incentives work both to change and to reinforce behavior. A primary challenge of any performance-management system is to operationalize and measure what is expected of employees. Then, when employees behave in positive ways, the next challenge is to reinforce those behaviors with both financial and nonfinancial rewards.

Under Steve Kerr's direction, the principles of Work-Out became a part of the managerial performance-management system. Work-Out behaviors were tied to performance goals. Managers who did not behave in ways consistent with Work-Out principles did not get positive reinforcement and in some cases were encouraged to leave the firm. Managers who did behave according to Work-Out principles received rewards and recognition.

Training and Development

Designing and delivering training courses sends messages about what matters. At the same time, it offers leaders skills and tools to act on those messages.

GE, through its curriculum at Crotonville, wove Work-Out concepts and principles into all training activities. Employees, suppliers, and customers who attended GE workshops learned about Work-Out both as a concept and as a set of tools. Cases of success and failure, action plans, and worksheets for doing Work-Out became part of many training programs.

Communication

Information is shared in many ways with employees, customers, and investors. The GE culture change was central to all of these audiences. In annual reports and investor-relations meetings, Welch and other officers shared their agenda with Work-Out. In employee communications (newsletters, videos, meetings, and so on) messages about Work-Out as culture change became a common theme and agenda.

Budgeting

Allocating resources to the culture change is not trivial. At GE, some of the budget went to external resources; more went to organizing and delivering Work-Out events. At times, the budget for culture change may come from the corporate level to sponsor and support the new culture. At other times, the culture change might be embedded in the local business budget. Regardless of the source, providing resources to the culture change is essential.

Leadership Brand

Culture must ultimately be embedded in how leaders behave throughout the organization. A leadership brand exists when leaders throughout an organization deliver results in the right ways. At GE, the leadership brand became a way to describe GE leaders, what they produced, and how they produced it. The GE leadership brand was evident to employees, who knew what to expect from their leaders; to customers, who knew how GE would likely respond to a given situation; and to investors, who would sometimes even follow GE leaders to other firms anticipating that these new leaders would instill some of the same GE leadership brand in those firms. As you plan the culture-change process, give some thought to what your organization needs leaders to be and do, and build that message into your efforts.

Organization Processes

Many organization processes (order to remittance, supplier management, customer interface, productivity, globalization, and so on) can be adapted to communicate to employees a new way of doing business. Organizations may be seen as bundles of processes of how work is done. When these processes are done in line with your desired culture, the culture will be sustained. At GE, key management processes were identified and examined through Work-Out. By allowing employees to figure out how to improve the process, GE made sure its employees could see that the Work-Out culture would endure over time.

Leaders who want to create sustained culture must embed that culture in organization systems and practices. The organization agenda becomes a way to ensure that culture is maintained over time, even without a specific leader championing it.

Work Simultaneously on All Three Agendas

Figure 13-1 sketches the three agendas. Organizations are more likely to make culture change endure when leaders work all three of these agendas (intellectual, behavioral, and organizational) at the same time.

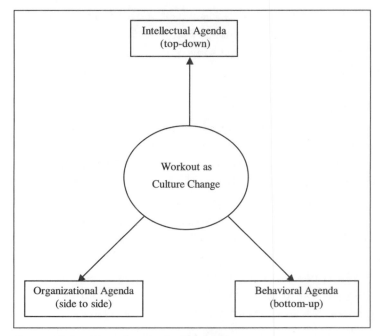

Figure 13-1. Three Agendas for Culture Change.

Working only one agenda will fail. Intellectual agendas give ideas, but they may not be seen as real or sustainable. Behavioral agendas may be excellent events, but they are not sustained or integrated. Organizational agendas may be innovative programs, but they lack coherence unless backed up at the intellectual and behavioral levels.

We often use mosquito control as an example to illustrate the importance of applying all three agendas. Intellectual, top-down change means that government agencies allocate money for mosquito abatement. They write policies, draft statements, and enact legislation to get rid of mosquitoes. Organizational, side-to-side change means changing the processes that cause mosquitoes—draining swamps, spraying fields, getting rid of cast-off tires, and the like. And behavioral, bottom-up change means that when a mosquito lands on you, you should kill it. Doing any one of the three without the other two will not lead to eradication of mosquitoes.

The three agendas may be cyclical over time. As new behaviors are enacted, new organization systems emerge and the intellectual agenda changes. Cycling through these three agendas makes culture change an outcome of the otherwise isolated activities.

Are You Ready for Culture Change?

Work-Out is often conceived as an event where people come together and solve problems. But if you want to get full value from Work-Out, the events need to lead to a new pattern of how employees behave. The pattern of behaviors that emerges from the separate workshops begins to redefine your organization's culture or DNA.

Culture is found in employee behaviors and actions, but it also represents the identity of your organization in the mind of your best customers. When your employees behave in ways that customers would like them to behave, both employees and customers are well served. Work-Out ultimately succeeds when employees, customers, and investors develop a strong and positive identity of your firm, and when that identity is clearly embedded in work patterns.

When you change your culture, it is less dependent on one person. After Welch left GE, the success of Work-Out revealed itself in the extent to which employees continued the behaviors Work-Out encouraged. Where they do so, the culture has changed; if there are places where they do not, Work-Out was only a management event. To embed the culture, you need to pay attention to three things: a clear intellectual agenda that lays out what you want to be known for by your customers and employees; a behavioral agenda whereby employees translate this identity into their day-to-day behavior (Work-Out events over time can shape these new behavioral patterns); and an organizational agenda whereby your organization practices reinforce and sustain the new behaviors. When you have managed all these agendas, Work-Out moves from engaging events to sustaining culture.

Making Work-Out
Work for You

At the end, it all comes back to how simple Work-Out really is. The background and the theory help explain the idea's force. The ways others have used it help with new implementations. But you can strip away all the trimmings. Just bring people together to work on a common problem. Allow them to recommend specific changes that make their jobs easier. Share the ideas with a manager who makes decisions on the spot and appoints owners who volunteer to follow up and make sure the decisions get put into effect. That's the real Work-Out. It's that simple. But it's not necessarily easy.

Throughout the book, we have given you background information, tools, templates, and actions to make Work-Out work for you. We have primarily used GE as the case study, since many of these ideas came together at GE. The GE story might seem overwhelming—the powerful and committed CEO, the immense resources invested in the massive Work-Out effort, and the widespread ability to innovate throughout the effort aren't forces many companies can bring to bear so extensively.

It turns out that although Work-Out does require leadership commitment, it needn't come from a powerful CEO. Work-Out tools can be adapted and applied within a division, business, function, plant, or establishment by local leaders. CEO support helps, but it isn't essential for Work-Out to work. Any leader at any level in an organization can use Work-Out ideas and tools to better engage employees and solve problems. You can change your corner of the world—and if enough corners change, the territory starts to look different.

Work-Out requires more resolve than resources. In Chapter 2 and throughout the book, we have suggested a continuum of Work-Out efforts from simple to complex. Much of our experience emphasizes a simple, straightforward forum where employees and managers meet to discuss and solve problems with minimal planning or advance preparation. Sometimes, adding rules, processes, and requirements for a formal Work-Out actually detracts from a manager's ability to listen and act on employee suggestions. Resources for fancy facilities, workbooks, and facilitators are less important than leaders who believe in and engage their employees—and employees who are willing to improve their work settings.

Work-Out requires risk taking and willingness to experiment. At Hallmark, they used the mantra, *Think big, Act small, Fail fast, and Learn rapidly* to describe their philosophy for innovation. These principles apply to Work-Out and may be applied in firms of almost any size:

- *Think big:* Employees need to understand industry trends, grasp strategy, relate to customers, and see the big issues facing their firm. Leaders need to articulate agendas that position their units to win, and capture employee imagination, energy, and action. Everyone in the firm needs a shared mindset about what it takes to succeed.

- *Act small:* Employees need to see how their daily experiences reflect their units' strategies. Work-Out focuses on small things that employees see as relevant: reports, approvals, meetings, measures, policies, and daily procedures. When liberated to eliminate these things, partially eliminate them, modify them, do them less frequently, or do them in different ways, employees experience and become committed to change. As the Chinese proverb states, a journey of a thousand miles really does begin with a single step. Let someone get rid of only one minor irritation and keep it from cropping back up on the job, and suddenly improvement begins to look possible instead of impossible.

- *Fail fast:* Not all ideas work. Too often managers stick with ideas that fail to deliver value. Learning to end a program or initiative is often just as crucial as initiating one. Without endings, new beginnings cannot occur. Work-Out enables employees to audit ideas and quickly decide what works and what does not. Then, decisions can be made to stop doing things that don't work. Learning does not occur without letting go. It is often easier to learn than to forget, yet forgetting enables learning.
- *Learn rapidly:* Learning occurs when ideas are transferred from one time or setting to another. Through Work-Outs, employees share insights with leaders; over time, insights from one Work-Out group may be shared with another group in the company. Work-Out also enables rapid learning, as decisions that might have taken weeks or months are made instantly. Work-Out creates the forum for dialogue where people hear what happens in the different corners of the building.

With these principles in mind, in this last chapter, we want to talk about how you might get started and succeed in doing your own version of Work-Out. The version that will work for you. Now. Whether you are a CEO yourself, or a unit manager—with or without strong CEO support. Whether you have extensive resources or not. Whether you are a line manager or a staff professional. It is important to adapt and not simply adopt what GE and other companies have done. *Adapt* means to learn from, not to copy or replicate. With the information and insight in this book, we hope you will be able to create your own Work-Out masterpiece.

The View from the Top

If you are CEO or head of a division, Work-Out can be a means to help you achieve your goals. Start by understanding the new business realities facing your business that might arise from customer expectations, competitive threats, technology changes, and market opportunities. To deal with these new realities, craft a strategy that offers your unique point of view about how you will win in your market. Based on this strategy statement (which might be in the form of a vision, a mission, or objectives), articulate a leadership that defines both the attributes and the results you expect of your leaders to help you win.

These steps help you figure out where you are going and the leadership requirements needed to get you there. You might then decide to create specific programs or work projects that will enable you to make your strategy happen. These programs become topics for your Work-Out sessions. In one company, programs designed to accomplish strategy were framed as "90-day projects," and represented specific investments with resources and outcomes, most of which could be accomplished in 90 days. This effort chunks or breaks up big things into little things. You have now identified the topics for some of your Work-Out sessions.

Give It a Name

Find a name for your Work-Out effort that works for you. We have seen versions of Work-Out efforts called transformation/town-hall meetings (Sears), GoFast (General Motors), Cleanout (Unilever), centurion program (Phillips), Work-Wise (New York Life), Out-of-the-Box (Aetna), Trailblazing (Armstrong), and one small step (Rolls Royce). Select a name that reflects what matters most to you and captures your goals for Work-Out. Find a way to state your goals for Work-Out in simple, concrete terms and metaphors, and use them redundantly so employees throughout your organization understand what you intend.

Give It a Framework

It is important to establish a small but focused Work-Out office to help build and facilitate the process. The job of this unit is to design the Work-Out agenda in your company by laying out a blueprint for what will be done and when. Its staff members interact with business leaders, ensuring that they are aware of and committed to the Work-Out agenda. They contract with external consultants and help select and train internal facilitators. They manage the implementation of Work-Out and offer continual reports about what is working and not working.

These assignments might be a fertile ground for your leaders of the future. You might consider funding this staff with resources from your own level to signal your support for the effort.

Start the Game

Now you are ready for Work-Out forums where people come together who have information about and/or ability to impact work projects.

Help ensure that the first forums have clear focus (tied to the work projects that embody your strategy) and ensure that these initial Work-Outs have a high probability of success (by your attending, encouraging, and staging the event).

When you attend the initial events, make sure you listen carefully, especially to people who do not always have opportunities to express their views. Find in the early workshops specific recommendations these people have made to support and implement on the spot.

As Work-Outs begin, hold managers who report to you accountable for sponsoring, attending, and leading Work-Outs of their own. Set specific goals for each manager and track their successes in holding Work-Outs and in engaging employees. Periodically call employees who attended a Work-Out session who might be three or four levels below you and ask them how it went. Affirm and encourage them to keep making Work-Out ideas work for them. Talk frequently in public forums (investor and customer groups, employee meetings, media, and other talks) about Work-Out and provide specific examples of successes, always framed as a way for you and your leaders to reach business goals through culture change. You might start some Work-Out awards that your office sponsors to employees who have unique or good experiences with Work-Out. Use your office as a bully pulpit to gain visibility and attention.

Keep It in Play

Keep the pressure on for continued Work-Out efforts. In your staff meetings, have Work-Out progress reports. Invite owners of Work-Out recommendations to report to the staff about their progress. In private conversations with your direct reports, reinforce your commitment to Work-Out. If business becomes more difficult, don't stop the Work-Out initiative. Persist.

Evolve Work-Out without abandoning it. Don't leave Work-Out for new initiatives. When new initiatives come, see Work-Out as the pipeline through which those initiatives will be implemented. Keep finding new ways to talk about Work-Out . . . as a change program, a way to reduce bureaucracy, a way to engage employees, a way to build a new culture, a new way of leading. Keep new metaphors alive and fresh so employees see your commitment to the Work-Out principles.

Work-Out leadership at the top sends clear signals throughout the organization about what you intend in your Work-Out program.

The Rest of the Angles

Though much of this book is framed in terms that assume you've got wide authority over an entire organization or a large segment of one, you can recast it to fit the authority you do have and the resources you can command. As long as you've got responsibility for a group of people doing a variety of tasks—or the ear of someone who does—you can begin to convert this advice into reality.

At the Corporate-Staff Level

If you are the head of a functional area, you can use Work-Out to ensure that your function adds value to the corporation. Once you have stated your function's goals and objectives, you can identify work processes that are central to its success (for example, the Finance function takes the lead on auditing, reporting, and resource allocation; the HR function takes the lead on staffing, compensation, training, and communication).

For each of these processes, you can organize a Work-Out session. This session should include individuals from your corporate staff, functional experts in the businesses who apply the processes, and some managers or users who experience the processes. These participants can examine through the Work-Out lens how the processes work for them, and then recommend changes that will streamline and improve the processes. They can help you figure out what processes should be standardized and shared across your enterprise and what ones should be customized and tailored to local business needs. They can help you simplify these processes to make sure they are understood and used in the right ways.

As the functional head, you need to be both the Sponsor and champion of early functional Work-Outs. You need to find an early success of a process you control and make changes in it. Advertise and communicate those changes so that people inside and outside your function see what you are doing to improve how your function works. Build in a scorecard for your function that includes Work-Out indicators. Talk about Work-Out in functional reviews and show how it helps fulfill your function's purpose.

Be willing to support Work-Out efforts with talent, money, and expertise from your function. Let some of your rising stars become internal facilitators, champions, or owners of Work-Out issues. Allocate some of your function's budget to designing, delivering, or supporting Work-Out. Apply your expertise to sustain Work-Out. For example, if you are in Communications, use your expertise to share the Work-Out story; if you are in Information Systems, use your expertise to build a Work-Out knowledge database. Collaborate with other functional leaders on problems that might cut across functions by sending top talent to issue-oriented Work-Out sessions, and by being a responsive panelist at the conclusion of these Work-Out events.

In the Middle

If you are a middle manager, you can also be a Work-Out leader. Recognize that Work-Out processes and actions will help you reach your goals. Examine the goals that you have to accomplish through your company's goal- or objective-setting process. Define the goals that are within your control or the control of your work unit, and accept that certain goals are outside your control. For those goals within your control, you can organize Work-Out forums where employees recommend changes that will help you reach your goals.

Analyze your leadership style against the type of behavior that helps promote Work-Out (see assessment in Figure 11-1). Identify where you are more or less inclined to lead in a Work-Out way: Are you open to employee ideas? Are you able to make decisions quickly? Are you able to learn from successes and failures? Are you able to craft a new culture within your unit that meets your goals? Find a coach who can work privately with you to help you see how your intended behaviors come across to others. Invite this coach to observe you in multiple settings and to help you examine and improve your behavior.

Hold Work-Out sessions that you can sponsor and implement within your unit. Select topics for early sessions that will be under your control and are likely to provide you with some early wins. Don't wait for the corporate level to mandate your Work-Out—experience Work-Out on your own. Dedicate resources to sustain your Work-Out effort. This might mean having a Work-Out coordinator within your business who regularly updates you on what sessions are being held, what results are being achieved, and which managers are being most supportive. Make sure that at staff meetings, you talk about Work-Out and reinforce your commitment to it.

Find allies among your peers who are trying to do what you are doing. Seek ways to share your successes and failures with them so you come to be seen as a cohort of Work-Out leaders. Offer to attend your peers' sessions to learn from them, and invite them to attend your sessions. See if there are issues that cut across your boundary with a peer, and hold a Work-Out session across groups to resolve those issues.

Be consistent and persistent in making sure Work-Out ideas are implemented in day-to-day actions. Have someone—perhaps a secretary or administrative assistant who observes you frequently—offer you 10 to 15 minutes of feedback a week on how you are doing on your new behaviors. Create a language in your unit that enables employees to resonate with Work-Out. Hanneke Frese from Zuirch Financial Services legitimated candor by encouraging employees to "talk Dutch;" she would preface her candid, and at times challenging, remarks to her employees as a "Dutch conversation."

Share your experiences with corporate leaders so they can learn from you. Be willing to report both what works and what does not work so your lessons can be generalized to others. Don't use Work-Out as a political ploy. ("I am doing it because it will get me promoted.") Use Work-Out as a way for you to reach your goals. ("I am doing it because it will get this essential thing done.") Hold those who report to you accountable for doing Work-Out as well. In your formal and informal reviews, make sure that your direct reports know you are serious. If you are an internal consultant or HR professional, you can use Work-Out to build your credibility and impact. The distinction between line and staff is continuing to blur, but staff personnel still deliver value when they help leaders accomplish results. If you become an expert at Work-Out, you can help your leaders deploy Work-Out and reach their business goals.

Helping leaders with Work-Out might mean educating your leadership team about what Work-Out is. Promote Work-Out. Stimulate ideas about Work-Out topics. Suggest issues that would easily be dealt with in a Work-Out session. Make sure that Work-Out is on your leaders' staff agendas. Gather and display resources to support the Work-Out effort.

Gain personal expertise in furthering Work-Out. Learn how to facilitate a Work-Out session. Become an owner of a Work-Out idea for follow-up. Learn to draft a work plan for delivering Work-Out in your business that includes questions like these: What topics will be covered in workshops? Who will attend? Where will the workshop be held? What logistics are required for the workshop? Who will facilitate? Review this plan with your business leaders so they feel ownership of it.

Prepare yourself to be a coach for your business leaders. Build a relationship of trust with them so you can offer honest feedback. Learn how to give your leaders feedback in ways that are helpful. Become a trusted advisor to whom your leaders turn for personal counsel.

Align your HR systems with Work-Out goals. Make sure that hiring criteria include assessment of the extent to which potential candidates behave in a Work-Out way. Ensure that Work-Out ideas and tools are taught in training events. Create rewards that are built on the standards of Work-Out behavior. Confirm that communications about the business include discussion of Work-Out as a means to accomplish goals.

Become a center of expertise for Work-Out. Do Work-Out first within your own function so you can learn how it applies to your organization, and so others believe in your commitment to it. Develop a cadre of facilitators by offering train-the-trainer workshops. Make sure that once trained, trainers have the opportunity to learn by doing. Derive measures to track progress on Work-Out, and keep and publicize those indicators.

Share your Work-Out experience with individuals with similar jobs in other units. Establish mechanisms to collaborate—a Work-Out buddy system where two people team up to support each other, a knowledge base through which technology ideas are shared, a community of practice where people within similar roles meet to share experiences, or an informal alliance where you can casually share your insights.

Keep seeing Work-Outs as an ongoing culture change, not just discrete events. Try to find and highlight connections between workshops so lessons from one setting transfer to another. Describe the longer-term outcomes of Work-Out as an identity of your work unit in the mind of your users. Keep reminding people that new identity is what each discrete event is intended to accomplish collectively. Never let people lose sight of the longer-term goal or become frustrated with day-to-day delays. If they keep doing the extra work to think things through and propose change after change that makes no difference to the underlying system, they're going to start feeling like old Sisyphus, endlessly pushing the same rock up the same hill—the original "Work-In" program.

From the Outside Looking In

If you are an external consultant, Work-Out may become a product or service you can offer to a client. As you acquire competence in conceiving and delivering Work-Out, you can contract with your clients for Work-Out goals. Help your clients assess if they are ready for Work-Out. Identify the types of Work-Out that would work best in their unique settings. Orchestrate early successes in your Work-Out effort. Working with your clients, assure that early Work-Outs succeed. Keep the clients in front of the group. Be an active but behind-the-scenes consultant who makes sure that the program is owned by the client, not the consultant. Don't let the Work-Out program attach itself to your name as "the XYZ consulting-firm project"—that will kill it as soon as the consulting arrangement ends, if not before. Instead, make sure it is credited to your client's senior leaders. Aggressively coach leaders who don't follow Work-Out behaviors. Part of the credibility of external consultants is their ability and willingness to raise sensitive issues that internal facilitators tend to avoid with senior leaders.

Assign excellent talent to the client's Work-Out, but ensure that your consultants transfer their knowledge to internal talent. Hold train-the-trainer events, coach and mentor internal facilitators, and build their confidence in facilitating Work-Out. Become an ally of the internal resources by being accessible to them and letting them know you have their interests in mind.

Bring other experiences to your clients. Some of this will come as you share what has worked or not worked for other clients. Be willing to continually adapt what you have done previously with each new client. Facilitate your clients as they visit other clients to gain face-to-face contact with leaders in other companies who have experienced Work-Out.

On the Front Lines

Finally, if you are an employee and you have ideas and energy and believe that Work-Out might be a means of voicing your ideas and unleashing your energy, you can encourage your business leaders to adapt Work-Out to their business. Teach your leaders about Work-Out by having them read and learn about Work-Out. Provide them with information from legitimate and credible sources. Find the organizations that your leaders admire and help them see that some of these organizations might have achieved success through Work-Out. Share this information with your leaders so they develop the desire to experiment with Work-Out.

Find a leader in your organization who is predisposed to Work-Out. Propose that you might help facilitate a Work-Out as a pilot or experiment. Find ways that some of the Work-Out ideas or tools might be used in your business. Seek simple, quick, and high-payoff successes.

Now What?

Some final thoughts about implementing Work-Out: Do it. Get started without lots of planning and structure. Find a place to experiment and try something. Stay focused on business goals, ensuring that Work-Out is a means to those goals, not the end in itself. Expect resistance. No change occurs without resistance. Be persistent. Don't do what GE did; adapt it for you. Make Work-Out yours.

A little more than a decade after GE instituted Work-Out, it's clear that Work-Out is neither a panacea nor a business fad. It is a set of principles, tools, and actions that helps managers reach their goals faster through engaging employees. It can be the foundation of some of the most exciting and positive experiences employees will have in their companies. Yes . . . Work-Out can work for you!

Appendix A: The Work-Out Leader's Tool Kit

This appendix summarizes the Work-Out implementation tools and worksheets contained throughout the book. (The first number in each figure number indicates the chapter in which the tool can be found.)

The "Plan" Stage

Overview of the Work-Out Process

- Figure 4-4, A Work-Out Reference Guide
  An important "master document" outlining the key steps in planning, conducting, and implementing a Work-Out.

- Figure 5-5, Sample Time Line for a Full-Length Work-Out
  Shows a four-month time Line from planning to the Work-Out session itself, to implementation of the Work-Out recommendations. (Simple Work-Outs can be completed much faster than this.)

- Figure 11-2, GE Values
  An official statement of the GE values that Work-Out helps make real.

- Figure 4-2, Agenda for an Express Work-Out at GE Plant
  A typical agenda for a one-day Work-Out.

- Figure 7-7, A Sample Three-Day Work-Out Agenda

- Figure 5-4, Work-Out Roles: Who Does What?
  Shows the three main types of roles in a Work-Out: leaders, facilitators, and participants.

- Figure 8-1, Key Players in Implementing a Work-Out
- Figure 6-2, Sample Work-Out Design Goals and Starter Questions for Problem-Solving Teams
  Examples from Armstrong, Allied Signal, Wal-Mart, and GE Capital.

Preparation for the Work-Out Event

- Figure 9-1, Business Problems That Reveal Process-Improvement Opportunities
  This table shows typical business problems and the related business processes that probably need improvement.
- Figure 9-2, Dividing Parts of a Problem Among Multiple Work-Out Teams
  This table, from a Work-Out at Dole Foods Company, shows how an unwieldy strategic-planning process was broken down into four different parts, each one assigned to a different Work-Out team.
- Figure 9-3, Improving a Parallel Process: From a GE Tungsram Work-Out on Streamlining New-Product Introductions
  This table shows how parallel processes were divided among Work-Out teams at a GE Work-Out on speeding up new-product production.
- Figure 9-5, Process-Map Example—Buying a Car
- Figure 9-6, Process-Map Variations
- Figure 9-7, A Process Map "Before" and "After" a Work-Out: From GE Capital Purchasing
  Work-Out design teams typically create a high-level process map as part of organizing the Work-Out event. These maps show the various steps, processes, and subprocesses that make it easier to identify which steps to shorten, combine, or omit.

The "Conduct" Stage

Introduction and Warm Up

- Figure 7-2, Collage Exercise Instructions

- Figure 7-3, Tennis Ball Exercise Instructions
  These exercises are good warm-ups for teams at the beginning of a Work-Out session because they teach the principles of process improvement.

Gallery of Ideas: Brainstorming What Could Be Improved

- Figure 2-3, The RAMMPP Matrix
  Helps identify reports, approvals, meetings, measures, policies, and practices that could be improved or omitted.

- Figure 4-1, Wasteful Work Practices: A Subjective Survey
  Simple questions for identifying parts of the daily work routine that don't make sense.

- Figure 9-4, The Process-Improvement Mind-Set
  A list of principles for improving processes that team members should apply to their Work-Out deliberations.

Prioritization: Winnowing Down Ideas

- Figure 2-4, The Payoff Matrix
  Useful for weighing the potential value of an improvement idea against the difficulty of implementing it.

Making Recommendations for the Best Ideas

- Figure 7-5, Town Meeting Presentation Worksheet
  Helps teams organize a presentation on Work-Out improvement recommendations for a Town Meeting.

- Figure 7-6, Worksheet: Strengthening Action Plans
  These hard-nosed questions will help a team improve an action plan before presenting it for approval at a Town Meeting.

- Figure 8-4, Sample Action Plan
  A sample plan developed by the recommendation owner and implementation team after a Work-Out.

The "Implement" Stage

Implementing the Approved Recommendations

- Figure 8-3, Dynamics of Team Performance
  This diagram illustrates the different levels of team energy and
  enthusiasm at the Work-Out and in the weeks following.

- Figure 8-6, Outline for a Work-Out Communication Plan
  Helps organize the work of communication over the months following a Work-Out.

Appendix B: A Work-Out Simulation Exercise: The United Bank of London[1]

Part of any Work-Out is devoted to brainstorming improvement ideas—and then prioritizing these into those ideas that the team feels will help to achieve the team's goal. In this exercise, facilitators practice the skills needed to help teams prioritize their ideas using the Payoff Matrix (Figure 2-4).

Facilitator Instructions

1. Ask one person to assume the role of team leader. Ask other people to assume the other roles on the team.
2. Lead a warm-up exercise with the group in which members introduce themselves and say what their favorite magazine is, and why.
3. Review the group's goal, as stated in the Bank of London background information and the memo (below).
4. Ask the group to take a few minutes to review individually their background information on the case—and write as many ideas as possible for reducing ATM downtime.
5. Facilitate a brainstorming discussion to list on flip-chart pages as many ideas as possible for reducing ATM downtime. Assign each idea a different letter—for future reference by the group.
6. Review the Payoff Matrix with the group—noting the attributes of each quadrant of the Matrix.

7. Ask participants to work individually for a few minutes to place each brainstormed idea in one of the quadrants of the Payoff Matrix (on their own worksheets).
8. Then have each person pick the top five ideas—from among those ideas they have placed in the two left-hand quadrants in the Payoff Matrix (Quick Hit and Bonus Opportunity).
9. Write each person's top five ideas on a flip chart. Use the nominal group technique to get the group to select its top five ideas from among those listed.

Help the group select someone to present its top ideas in a meeting of all the groups that have been working on this case.

ASSIGNMENT:

Develop a list of five priority ideas for making major progress toward achieving the goal of the United Bank of London team.

United Bank of London

Background

Dana Hagarty is vice president for data services at the United Bank of London. One of Dana's major responsibilities is maintaining the performance of the Bank's network of Automated Teller Machines (ATMs).

Despite previous efforts to improve the network's performance record, the average availability (able to conduct transactions) of machines across the network still stands at 85 percent, far below the overall performance target of 98-percent availability. This means that, on average, each machine is out of service 3.5 hours each day, versus the goal of .5 hours.

It is vitally important that availability be improved since, in the words of United's president, "The ATMs are our face to the public—and a competitive advantage if managed well. People place their accounts at banks with convenient and dependable ATMs."

There are over 200 ATMs at over 150 United branch locations throughout the city. They are linked through telecommunications lines to United's central data-processing facility. From there, the ATMs are connected to various interbank services that enable United's customers to gain access to their accounts at non-United ATMs, and for customers of other banks to use United's ATMs to access their accounts.

Though Dana is ultimately responsible for assuring a high level of performance from the ATM network, Dana directly manages only the people who work in the central Data Center—responsible for the computer software, hardware, and the telecommunications network that supports the machines. Regular and emergency maintenance is done by a separate maintenance group. Each branch supplies its ATMs with cash, with paper for receipts, and with tape for internal audit purposes.

The Improvement Goal

Senior management is looking for rapid improvement in ATM availability. In fact, Dana Hagarty recently received several calls from United's President when ATMs in the Bank's main office were out of service. As Dana sees it, the overall issue is bringing ATM systemwide availability up to the 98-percent performance target and beyond. The first challenge, however, is to decide where to begin and how.

According to the information already available to Dana, there are many different sources of ATM downtime:

- Some ATM failures are caused by the way the machines are supplied with money, receipt paper, and audit tape in the branches.
- Some failures are caused by the errors customers make when they use the machines.
- Other failures are caused by mechanical problems, notably cash-dispenser malfunctions.
- Some branches have very high availability levels, while others are far too low. ATM use also varies, with some machines in high-profile areas conducting twice as many transactions a week as others.
- Once an ATM is down and a fix cannot be made by branch personnel, getting it back in service can take far too long. The average response time for maintenance personnel to arrive at an ATM is over 2.5 hours. In 10 percent of the service calls, additional parts have to be secured before the machine can be returned to service.

Considering all these issues, Dana decides to refine the improvement opportunity prior to presenting it to a team to focus on the performance of the machines in the branches. Dana will leave the broader network-performance issues as a second stage. Dana asks Lee Smith, one of the Data Center managers, to act as the team leader. Together they select an interfunctional team for the project, consisting of representatives from the Data Center, ATM maintenance, and the Bank's branches.

Assignment Memo to the Team Leader

TO: Lee Smith
FROM: Dana Hagarty
SUBJECT: Improving ATM Availability

As you know, the Data Services group has been charged with upgrading ATM performance to the 98-percent availability target across our network of 200+ ATMs—a level that would place us head and shoulders above our competition. The reason for this ambitious goal is clear. Many customers now "talk" more frequently with an ATM than with a teller in our branches. As a result, superior availability is the key to keeping these people as United customers and to attracting new customers.

We have already made some changes that have improved availability to current levels of approximately 85 percent. However, there is still much that can be done to improve even further. The purpose of this memo is to ask you to lead a cross-functional effort to take a significant step toward the 98-percent performance target in the next two months. Your team's specific goal is to improve performance by 5 percent over the next two months—to a 90-percent performance level.

Initially, I would like you to focus on reducing failures of the ATMs themselves. Progress in this area will have immediate, tangible payoffs for our customers and the Bank. Once we have had some success, we can move on to network issues that also affect the availability numbers.

Your team should include representatives from all the groups involved in ATM performance. This includes ATM maintenance and the branches as well as your area, Data Services.

This is an exciting chance to build the best ATM network in the region, while also building closer working ties among groups throughout the Bank. I look forward to working with you on it.

The Project Structure

The Improvement Goal

"Improve the performance record of the ATMs located in United's branches by 5 percent in the next two months."

The Team Leader

Lee Smith, Manager, Data Services

The Team Members

Data Services technician
ATM Maintenance mechanic
Branch representative

The Facilitator

Internal consultant

Appendix C:
Work-Out—The
Foundations of a
Cultural Revolution

(A speech given to General Electric officers in January, 1990)
By Dave Ulrich

For a piece of wood to catch fire, it must first be heated to a tempera-ture at which it ignites, then it burns by itself. The initial heating requires energy from outside. When the wood is ignited, it becomes self-sustaining and gives off light and heat.

There is a more intense fire than that of burning wood. It is produced from a mixture of aluminum powder and metal oxide. By itself, the mix-ture is cold and lifeless, but when heated to the ignition temperature, it becomes a self-sustaining source of brilliant light and intense heat.

Once it ignites it cannot be put out by ordinary means. It will burn under water or in other environments that extinguish an ordinary flame. When it burns, it does not depend on its surroundings for sup-port. It is self-sustaining.[1]

In the last year, the General Electric Company has initiated one of the largest corporate cultural revolutions in the history of American industry. The goal is to ignite a fire, within each of 277,000 General Electric employees, that will be self-sustaining and provide intense energy to meet the requirements of employees, customers, and investors.

My remarks today will review the progress of that effort, suggest some of the challenges that lie ahead, and offer an external perspective on the importance and magnitude of the Work-Out agenda. Hopefully, this review will give you a glimpse of the fire we are trying to ignite and a feel for the commitment and intensity required to fuel the fire.

The beginning of any cultural revolution requires that imaginative ideas translate to specific actions. The Work-Out concept has been evolving over the last decade, but it gained form about one year ago this month. In the first six months of Work-Out, a flurry of activities occurred. Perhaps the most miraculous of all has been the dedication and competence demonstrated by Jim Baughman and his team. They seized the Work-Out initiative and translated it to a specific set of managerial actions. Their behind-the-scenes work included refining the concept, designing a flexible structure to deliver Work-Out across 23 GE businesses, coordinating one of the largest and most diverse groups of facilitators ever assembled, and matching these facilitators to each business's needs.

Since April, 160 Work-Out workshops have been run. This means that approximately 8000 individuals across General Electric have been directly involved in a Work-Out workshop by the end of 1989. In addition, over 5000 participants in Crotonville and corporate programs have been exposed to the Work-Out philosophy. Over the next year, we project that about 1200 participants per month will continue to participate in Work-Out Town Meetings, where dialogue between employees and managers occurs.

To deliver Work-Out, each General Electric business has adapted the fundamental premises of speed, simplicity, and self-confidence and applied them to their business requirements. These unique applications illustrate the range, diversity, and intensity of activity that have kindled a cultural revolution within each GE business. Tomorrow, you will hear more about the details of these unique approaches.

My progress report is straightforward: To date, an enormous amount of movement has occurred, more than we anticipated a year ago. The external energy for igniting the cultural revolution has been supplied, received, and had impact.

One of the most common questions we are asked is how we will know if Work-Out works. Internal fires are sometimes difficult to detect. Let me suggest, we can report some early indicators of progress to both employees and the business.

First, employees have seen the value of Work-Out. We have heard for years the cynicism of employees who feel that with the demise of corporate loyalty, they are left holding an empty contract. Work-Out is beginning to help employees see that corporate loyalty can be replaced with opportunity, and that as employees take advantage of the chance to dialogue with senior managers, they learn that their corporate citizenship can make a difference. About half the way through one workshop, an engineer who had been with the company for a long time stopped a dialogue that could quickly have turned into an "ain't it awful" discussion, and said:

> **Let's give this program a whirl. I have been in the company 28 years and seen a lot of attempts to try to change things. At least this one starts by asking me what I think, not just telling me what to do.**

This manager realized that Work-Out was not another top-down initiative, but one that focused on meeting employee needs.

In addition to employees seeing the value of Work-Out, managers and officers like yourselves have been responding favorably. This quote from a manager

> **As a manager for 10 years, it was a little hard to open myself up and ask for feedback on what I can do to improve. But, by doing so, I have more respect for the commitment and quality of our employees.**

is from someone who confided in me that he was worried about revealing himself in the Work-Out session, about acknowledging his inadequacies in front of his subordinates. He left Work-Out with more self-confidence about his management style and the quality of the employees who worked for him.

Second, we have seen business value out of the 100 workshops. Employees are recognizing work activities that get in the way of meeting customer needs, and they are beginning to remove those barriers. Hundreds and thousands of little changes are occurring, whose cumulative sparks will kindle a cultural revolution.

Some examples include:

What:	Reduce paperwork.
How:	Call all recipients of reports and find out which are being used.
Progress:	Cut number of reports sent out by 50 percent.

What:	Reduce or eliminate time spent doing monthly B&P expenditures by hand.
How:	Write a computer program to automatically provide the data to people who need it.
Progress:	100 percent completed. Saves two to three days of work per month.

What:	Bill customers sooner.
How:	Consolidate the unfocused efforts of eight people into one person.
Progress:	Data now collected more swiftly and accurately, resulting in more-timely client billing and a $300,000 reduction in costs.

What:	Cut time spent on the procurement cycle by 50 percent.
How:	Focus on one step of the procurement cycle at a time. Flow-chart all the steps and eliminate nonvalue-added steps.
Progress:	Have eliminated a large percentage of the 400 steps in the "order" step. This first reduction effort should reduce order time from 180 days to between 110 and 130 days.

These four cases illustrate thousands of examples of changes in work procedures. While the progress to date is encouraging, we are still working to kindle the flame for the cultural revolution. To bring to pass the cultural revolution, at least five challenges must be faced and overcome.

First, we must ensure that Work-Out avoids the trap of becoming a "program." As one employee eloquently stated, "*This is just another 'program.' It comes down from the top like lightning—completely unexpected. I get a coffee mug, paperweight, and pep talk, but nothing else happens when I go back to work*." A primary leadership challenge you face is to make sure that Work-Out is not an off-site program, but an ongoing set of management principles and philosophies that permeate all of our business decisions. "Programs" start, burn brightly, then are extinguished by external pressures. Management philosophies come from convictions that cannot be easily extinguished. Leaders must work to keep focusing on instilling the mind-set of speed, simplicity, and self-confidence rather than attending just another program.

Second, we must manage employee resistance and fear. Many employees resist because they fear what will come as they commit to Work-Out.

Last time we were asked to become more efficient, we worked hard at it and did so. Soon after, three people lost their jobs. If I identify work I can get rid of, what will happen to me?

We must help employees realize that through Work-Out their fear can be replaced by the fire of self-sustaining commitment.

Third, no cultural revolution is completed in a day. Cultural revolutions require enormous amounts of ongoing determination to find small successes. The General Electric culture has taken over 100 years to become what it is today. It will take time to change it. To make this change, we must be persistently feeding the fire with kindling 1000 small successes: to focus on how we can get on base through any means possible. When we originally conceived Work-Out, we thought about hitting a lot of home runs. Since then, we have learned that our challenge is not to hit lots of home runs, but to persistently find ways to get on base. We were going to include "being hit by the pitcher" as an alternative, but thought that this may send the wrong message. Our point here is simple: we must have lots of little successes so that thousands of employees can progress in their work. Once enough kindling is in place, the bigger logs will catch and burn.

Fourth, Work-Out is a means to an end. The ultimate cultural revolution will not just be the extent to which our employees see a new culture of speed, simplicity, and self-confidence, but how much our customers see this culture. We have spent the last year on Phase 1 of Work-Out—getting the concept across and examining work activities. Let me suggest that while this phase is not complete, we need to begin

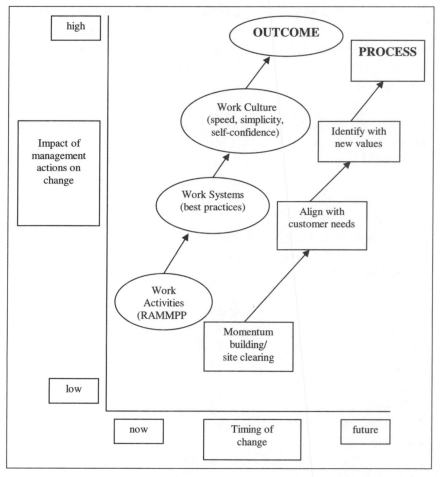

Figure C-I. General Electric: Management Actions for Moving Ahead with Work-Out.

to think about Phase 2 and Phase 3—how to let our fire illuminate those beyond the boundaries of GE.

The figure builds on the figure that Jack, Larry, and Ed have pre-sented and used. [See Figure C-1.] It suggests, along the bottom axis, that time is a critical factor for Work-Out. On the vertical axis, however, it suggests management actions that will be required for Work-Out to be effective. In Phase 1, we have focused on work activities—reports, approvals, meetings, etc. Our jobs as officers and managers have been to build momentum and clear the attic—to assess and get rid of reports, approvals, measures, forms, etc. As we move towards Phase 2, we need to focus on work systems—to identify and implement the best practices of ourselves and other companies. The Continuous Improvement discussion that follows mine holds one source for identifying these best practices. Just as the key to Phase 1 has been to build momentum and do site clearing, the key management action for the next phase is to align all business practices with customer needs. We need to take work out, and put customer value in. The first phase may take one to three years, depending on the business; the second phase may take two to five years. It will require that we systematically assess customer needs and link what we do inside with outside customer requirements. Phase 3 instills the new culture of speed, simplicity, and self-confidence for each employee. This phase will be accomplished when each GE employee, customer, supplier, and major investor identifies with the speed, simplicity, and self-confidence principles.

The key to these three phases is that they do not happen sequentially, but cyclically. We need today to be working with speed, simplicity, and self-confidence while we reassess and revise work activities. The challenge will not be moving through the phases, but making sure that we develop the capability to spiral through them more quickly.

Challenge 5 falls on the backs of leaders of the company. We must learn to exhibit aggressive patience. We spent a long time finding these words. *Aggressive patience* is an oxymoron—two words that don't go together. However, aggressive patience is the management style that must be demonstrated. On the one hand, GE managers discover patience to realize that the Work-Out cultural revolution will take time. On the other hand, we must be more assertive, determined, and aggressive than ever on making sure that Work-Out lasts. We don't want to kill the goose that laid the golden egg in our impatience to see progress. Work-Out will require that we role model the activity, that we lead by spending time and asking questions of participants who do and do not attend workshops that we be champions, and that we share and celebrate successes.

I have laid out five challenges to making sure that the smoldering flame of a cultural revolution ignites. These are not insurmountable challenges, but they are critical to our continued success.

Now let me spend the last few minutes stepping back and offering a confirming outsider's view of the importance of the Work-Out agenda. In its most simple terms, Work-Out must become GE's competitive advantage for the 1990s. Any business competes by adding value to customers in ways that competitors can not easily copy. In the 1990s, all customers will demand more responsiveness, service quality, relationships, and flexibility. Through installing a new work culture, with appropriate work activities and work systems, we will be better able to meet customer needs. Competitors are already trying to learn and copy our Work-Out agenda. They will not be able to catch us if we forge ahead.

General Electric has always been facing and succeeding in managing revolutionary change. For many decades, and continuing today, you have been pioneers of invention, pioneers of diversification, pioneers of financial analysis, pioneers of strategic planning. Now, we must become pioneers of cultural revolution. We have the opportunity to continue to lead the cultural-change agenda facing all industrial firms.

Now, after the first inning, I can confidently state we are in the lead. We are making progress. We have brought enough energy to bear that many employees are beginning to see the light of the new culture. Our greatest challenge lies ahead. We must continue to focus energy, so that the cultural fire we ignite burns not from outside, but within each employee. This is probably the greatest challenge of the Work-Out agenda—to make sure that like aluminum powder and metal oxide, our employees feel for themselves the self-sustaining flame of cultural revolution. This will be our greatest leadership challenge as we enter the next decade, but it will also be our legacy and competitiveness for the twenty-first century.

End Notes

Chapter 2

1. For a fuller description of organizational boundaries and their effect, see Ron Ashkenas, Dave Ulrich, Todd Jick, and Steve Kerr, *The Boundaryless Organization: Breaking the Chains of Organizational Structure*, Second Edition, Jossey-Bass, 2002.

2. The concept of "stretch" has some similarity to what Collins and Porras call a BHAG, a "big hairy audacious goal." James C. Collins and Jerry I. Porras, *Built to Last: Successful Habits of Visionary Companies*, New York: HarperCollins, 1997.

3. See the article, "Managers Can Avoid Wasting Time," by Ronald N. Ashkenas and Robert H. Schaffer, *Harvard Business Review*, (May–June 1982).

4. A more extensive explanation of how Work-Out fosters a new level of organizational dialogue can be found in Ron Ashkenas and Todd Jick, "From Dialogue to Action in GE Work-Out: Developmental Learning in a Change Process," in William A. Pasmore and Richard W. Woodman, eds., *Research in Organizational Change and Development*, Vol. 6, pp 267–287, Greenwich, CT: JAI Press, 1992.

5. See Peter S. Pande, Robert P. Neuman, and Roland R. Cavanagh, *The Six Sigma Way: How GE, Motorola, And Other Top Companies Are Honing Their Performance*. New York: McGraw-Hill, 2000.

Chapter 3

1. For a more complete list of corporate "programs" and the dynamics surrounding them, see Ronald N. Ashkenas, "Beyond the Fads: How Leaders Drive Change With Results," in Craig Eric Schneier, ed., *Managing Strategic and Cultural Change in Organizations*, pp. 33–53. New York: Human Resource Planning Society, 1995.

2. See Robert G. Eccles, Nitin Nohria, and James D. Berkley, *Beyond the Hype: Rediscovering the Essence of Management*. Cambridge, MA: Harvard Business School Press, 1992.

Chapter 7

1. Excerpted from Ron Ashkenas and Todd Jick, "From Dialogue to Action in GE Work-Out," *Research in Organizational Change and Development*, Volume 6, 1992: Greenwich, CT: JAI Press Inc., pg. 280.
2. Much of the material in this section was originally developed by Jeffrey Gandz as part of an internal GE working paper: "The Town Meeting: Transformational Leadership in Action," 1990.

Chapter 9

1. Steven Spear and Kent Bowen, "Decoding the DNA of the Toyota Production System," *Harvard Business Review*, September–October, 1999, pp. 97–106.
2. Todd D. Jick, "Customer-Supplier Partnerships: Human Resources as Bridge Builders," *Human Resource Management*, Volume 29, Number 4, Winter 1990, pp. 439–442.

Chapter 10

1. Material for this account is based on personal interviews as well as several published articles, including "Embedding a Culture for Continuous Change," *The Antidote*, Issue 30, Winchester, U.K.: CSBS Publications, no date,. pp 30–34; Andrew Bolger, "How Eagle Star Was Saved by a High-Flier," *Financial Times*, June 30, 2000, p. 18; and "Making the Difference," *Work-Out Annual Review, 1999*, a publication of Zurich Financial Services, U.K. General Insurance.

Chapter 11

1. Dave Ulrich, Norm Smallwood, and Jack Zenger. (2000). Building Your Leadership Brand. *Leader to Leader, 15*, 40–46.
2. Welch, John F., "Speed, Simplicity, Self-Confidence: Keys to Leading in the '90's," Presented at the General Electric Annual Meeting of Share Owners, Greenville, South Carolina, April 26, 1989.
3. GE 1995 Annual Report, Letter to Our Share Owners, pp. 4–5.

Chapter 12

1. Malcolm Gladwell, *The Tipping Point: How Little Things Can Make a Big Difference*. New York: Little, Brown, 2000.

Chapter 13

1. Malcolm Gladwell, *The Tipping Point: How Little Things Can Make a Big Difference*. New York: Little, Brown, 2000.

Appendix B

1. Source: Robert H. Schaffer & Associates. *Facilitator Training Materials.* Stamford, CT (1998).

Appendix C

1. This metaphor comes from remarks by Richard Scott.

Index

Bold numbers indicate artwork.

About the Authors

Dave Ulrich is a professor of business administration at the University of Michigan School of Business and the author of the best-selling *Human Resource Champions, Results-Based Leadership,* and *The HR Scorecard.* **Steve Kerr** is Chief Learning Officer and a Managing Director of Goldman Sachs. He was previously Vice President–Leadership Development and Chief Learning Officer for General Electric, with responsibility for GE's renowned Leadership Development Center at Crotonville. **Ron Ashkenas** is the managing partner of management consulting firm Robert H. Schaffer & Associates, and senior author (with Ulrich, Kerr, and Todd Jick) of two previous books about GE.